Student Politics in CHILE

STUDENT MOVEMENTS–PAST AND PRESENT
GENERAL EDITOR: SEYMOUR MARTIN LIPSET

STUDENT POLITICS IN
Chile

Frank Bonilla
Myron Glazer

Basic Books Inc., Publishers / New York / London

For Maria J.

For Penina M.

Preface

In 1969 the University of Chile found itself in a deep-rooted crisis. Administrators, professors, and students were once again struggling over the goals and organization of Chilean higher education. Most of the participants were dissatisfied with the quality of national life and posed penetrating questions about the appropriate functions of their own institution.

The student body took a leading role. Left-wing student political leaders were instrumental in precipitating the initial confrontation in 1967, and the FECH, the all-university student organization dominated for the last decade by the Christian Democrats, was most influential in forcing a total re-examination of every aspect of university life. At first, most students had given massive support to reformist leadership; subsequently, they expressed a desire to return to normal classroom activities and refused to condone the excessive politicization of all academic issues.

The two studies reported on in this book analyze student organization and attitudes prior to the most recent events. Part I focuses on the historical development of the FECH and traces its involvement and impact on Chilean national life during the first five decades of this century. Part II explores the attitudes and activities of a representative sample of students during the mid-1960's. Both studies are directly concerned with understanding the role of highly educated youth in national development.

Each of us has found that university students, in spite of their minority, have often demanded and merited national attention for their efforts to expose social injustice. Both of us discovered much to admire and respect about student life. In this book we attempt to describe and analyze student successes and failures, dreams, and compromises.

To achieve this, we have utilized a variety of social science techniques of data collection. Intensive interviews have been supplemented by projective tests, personal observations, and documents. The trust and aid of our Chilean respondents, informants, and friends was, of course, our most crucial resource. We cannot ever fully repay their good will, but we do hope that they will view our work as a sincere effort to understand them, their university, and their society.

Frank Bonilla

Myron Glazer

Rio De Janeiro—Brasil
New Brunswick, New Jersey
November, 1969

Acknowledgments

The study of the Students Federation of Chile reported in this volume was carried out under a Doherty Foundation fellowship. Assistance was also received from the University of Chile through its Institute of Sociology, where all interviews were transcribed and copies of these transcriptions deposited. Copies of the dissertation that resulted from this effort were sent to the Institute of Sociology, to the Student Federation, and to numerous other persons who had been helpful in the course of the field work. The several sections were read in draft by members of the generations concerned before the thesis was submitted. A substantial debt of gratitude is owed to the members of the 1956–1957 FECH executive committee, all of whom cooperated generously during the phase of data collection. Professors Eduardo Hamuy, Hernan Godoy, and Pedro Godoy gave invaluable intellectual support and friendship throughout this effort. Responsibility for every aspect of the execution of the study lies with the author alone.

Frank Bonilla

Beyond the 317 students who answered our lengthy interview schedule, I must specifically acknowledge the assistance, cooperation, and advice of my Chilean friends and colleagues. Luis Alvarado, Daniela Rubens de Foncea, and Carlos Morales aided importantly in the interviewing and the coding of the schedule. Jorge Cauas, Fernán Ibañez, Sergio Bitar, and Roberto Fasani were of great help in contacting student leaders and providing facilities in which to conduct the interviews. Peter Heintz and Edmundo Fuenzalida and the staff of FLACSO welcomed us warmly and provided material support and essential advice. Carlos Tomas, head of data processing at the University of Chile contributed in the analysis of the responses. Beatriz Allende and Renato Julio were important councilors and warm friends throughout our year in Chile. During our recent visit we benefited from the advice and assistance of many university professors. I thank them all for their hospitality and must especially note the contribution of Claudio Foneca, Santiago Friedman, and Roberto Muñoz.

My former teachers at Princeton University were the earliest and most consistent encouragers of the Chilean research. Professor Frederick H. Harbison and the Industrial Relations Section provided time and advice when the prospect of a Latin American journey was but a dim dream. Professor Stanley Stein helped substantially in its realization and has contributed importantly to my understanding of that area. Professor Wilbert E. Moore kindled my interest in social change and I have benefited greatly through my conversations with him. Professor Melvin M. Tumin was my major Princeton liaison during my fifteen months in the field and was a constant adviser in times of difficulty. Professor Harry C. Bredemeier of Rutgers University has been adviser, teacher, and good friend since my first days at graduate school. He has helped me understand the demands of disciplined thought and deep involvement with students and colleagues. I publicly and warmly thank him for his contribution to me and others.

The Henry L. and Grace Doherty Foundation financed a major portion of the field work and I am truly grateful for the opportunity afforded me. The Center for International Studies of Princeton University supported the final months of my residence in Chile and the writing of the preliminary draft of this report.

I would like to thank the *Comparative Education Review* for permission to reprint passages from my article, "Field Work in a Hostile Environment" (June, 1966), pp. 367–376; *Daedalus* for permission to reprint my article, "Student Politics in a Chilean University", (Winter, 1968), pp. 99–115; Frederick A. Praeger for permission to reprint my article "Chile," which appeared in Donald K. Emmerson, ed., *Student Politics in Developing Nations* (New York, 1968); *Revista Latinoamericana de Sociología* for permission to reprint my articles "El proceso de socialización profesionel en cuatro carreras Chilenas" (November, 1966), pp. 333–367, and (with Penina Migdal Glazer) "Los Investigaciones Sociales y el Mundo Real: Los Chileanos y Los Gringos" (July, 1968), pp. 228–249.

My conscience would be far from clear, were I not to publicly express my appreciation to those members of my family who so freely gave of their time and energy. Faye Lichtash, Jordan Rosen, Joel Migdal, and David Lichtash each contributed long hours. My kinsman and dear friend, Mr. Terry Lichtash, holds a special place of esteem for his editorial and moral assistance. My warmest tribute to him is my knowledge that the successful completion of this work is the reward he most desires for his efforts. Penina Migdal Glazer was my co-worker on the Chilean project, and although I cannot here adequately record the importance of her efforts, I can at least once again emphasize that I am aware of them. It is with the deepest affection that I dedicate this book to her. She and Joshua Lester have been the most delightful traveling and research companions.

Myron Glazer

Contents

Contents

Student Politics in CHILE

Introduction

Student Organization: The Changing Generations

In mid-1956 the author of the study reported in Part I of this volume went to Chile with the intent of partially documenting the proposition that the student movement in Latin America was succumbing to the twentieth century trend among youth organization toward bureaucratization, integration with and submission to adult-led groups, and self-serving careerism and a narrow preoccupation with student welfare. A few months later the country was rocked by an explosion of public violence set off by politically motivated student protest that precipitated a major government crisis and brought the capital city under martial law. In the ensuing years a new self-assertiveness among young people throughout the world has kept many other social scientists scurrying both to adequately chronicle new events and to locate and interpret youthful activism within the larger context of ongoing social change.

That context itself has changed and with it the priority interests and theoretical preoccupations of those concerned with the role of youth as an organized force in society. A short decade ago the sparse literature on youth movements still focused on the approach to youth of totalitarian or revolutionary regimes bent on total mobilization (Nazi, Soviet, Chinese, Israeli) or on the response of youth to crises (wars and depressions) in capitalist nations. After the great surge of youthful revolt after World War I, youth organizations by and large had grown and operated under adult tuition. When they were not the self-regulating, self-improvement, and community-service groupings so common in the United States, they were generally the tools of party, church, or state. The lost generation of the early 1930's in the United States, the nation was told in 1956, had been succeeded by a bland, accommodating generation aspiring to nothing more than air-conditioned corporate suites and bright suburban bliss.[1]

S. N. Eisenstadt's *From Generation to Generation* (Glencoe, Ill.: The Free Press), also published in 1956, still contains the most extensive compilation of ethnographic and historical material on age-grade groupings and youth movements. Eisenstadt was in accord with the general view which was then current that saw a declining role for the young in modern society; much of his volume emphasized the progressively limited scope of youth organizations as societies became increasingly specialized. His work did, however, newly center attention on more lasting sociological concerns regarding youth groups. In a wide variety of settings he sought to document the ways in which age-specific groupings served as interlinking spheres between the family and non-kinship-determined adult roles as well as the ways in which such groups contribute to the integration of individual personality at a critical life period.

In the early 1950's, however, the main locus of concentrated interest in student organization in those nations that were just then beginning to be called developing political entities was not among sociologists but among cold-war specialists and the several international youth organizations vying for the favor of national student groups. Ironically, it was probably those organizations that provided a primary impulse and an effective medium for an internationalization of student culture, relevant to both definitions of university life and political roles, that today is being felt as much in the advanced countries as in the nations which the principal cold-war protagonists sought to influence.

More decisive as a stimulus to systematic research on youth in the university has been the more recent shift of emphasis to the cultural and political aspects as against the purely economic dimensions of growth in nations. Even if students had not been stridently calling attention to themselves and the universities, demanding and pre-empting new political roles, and daily making vocational options freighted with consequences for themselves and the nation, the issue would inescapably have moved into the center of attention once both planning and development theory recast growth problems in these new terms.

A recently compiled bibliography, though selective and still incomplete, conveys an idea of the outpouring of new materials in the last ten years.[2] Three in four of the nearly 700 items cited have been published since 1956. About three in five deal with student organization and university problems in Asia, Africa, or Latin America. Although the listing leans heavily to United States materials, it is worth noting that in the case of Latin America, for example, at least half of the sources and authors cited are Latin American.

The new wealth of historical, more recently topical, survey, and other data as well as the beginning efforts at synthesis and theoretical mapping are only beginning to provide encouraging signs of advance.[3] Identifying and defining the key variables and, more particularly, laying out the interconnections among them have been made extraordinarily difficult by the peculiar quality of the phenomenon under scrutiny. Political activism among university youth is both ubiquitous (that is, one finds it almost anywhere that there are students) and rare (it tends to strike only a small number in any student body). Hypothesizing about the motives, correlates, or dynamics of the youthful impulse to political action too readily lapses into a mechanical reeling off of propositions all proving irrefutably that something that rarely occurs is inevitable. The quantum jump in data can hardly be expected to produce an equivalent gain in the refinement of theorizing. Nevertheless the groundwork for well-documented and genuinely comparative analysis is rapidly being laid.

The two studies reported in this volume (Parts I and II), though independently conceived and carried out, complement one another remarkably well. The first (Part I) bears heavily on changing features of organizational structure, on the weight of history and tradition in sustaining student action in a given style, on the relatively unchanging as well as shifting aspects of the context in which students move, and on the small body of leaders that at any given time embody the mood and intent of young people in the university. The second study (Part II) casts a broader net by probing into the perspective on career and politics of students as a body rather than on the minority who act most directly in the student organization. The two studies converge in the shared, deep concern with the basic issue of how young people at a given moment in history resolve the permanent tensions arising from the pressures within the university to arrive at some self-definition, professionally and politically. By viewing this problem from quite different perspectives in what amounts to four quite distinct historical moments in a single nation, the studies convey a strong sense of the basic continuities and the main fronts of change in student orientations.

University student organization in Latin America, and especially the Student Federation of Chile (FECH) on which the first study centers attention, is viewed here as an integral, institutionalized feature of society in the region. The detailed case study of FECH operations is intended to provide an understanding of student organization, not only as a political institution, but also as a distinctive form of age-homogeneous organization operating within a specialized milieu—the university in Latin America. Student organization is not seen primarily as a potential locus of indiscipline or insurrection, but as a long-standing and, in the main, positively valued feature of university life in Chile. The FECH has played a vital role in political events in this century and has provided a context for the political initiation of practically all of the nation's political leadership.

The major research questions flowing from this view concern the *how* of the functioning of the university student organization at particular moments in history. How have students, in fact, defined their roles vis-à-vis the university, the society at large, and the professional and citizen responsibilities for which they were preparing over the more than fifty years of the student federation's existence? What has been the nature of the federation's links and co-functions with the university administration, with political parties, with labor unions, with governments? Whence has the group drawn its leadership, its ideology? What forms has the organization taken? What techniques of political action have students commonly used? To what extent have young people been the instruments of better organized or irresponsible political forces? How lasting have political allegiances formed in university circles really been? What nonpolitical functions has the student organization served for the society at large and for its membership?

The examination of the FECH in Part I goes beyond the conventional case study by conceptualizing the subject of study as (1) an organization of youth, (2) in a university, (3) *in a precise historical period and social milieu.* By selecting three distinctive epochs in the life of the student organization for intensive study, it becomes possible to frame the problem as one of organizational change—to relate changes in the organizational structure over time to other structural changes, conditions, and events in the society at large. This is accomplished by a comparative analysis of the organizational structure of the Student FECH as it was in the mid-1950's (1956–1957) and as it was at two critical periods in its past—the first between 1918 and 1922, and the second between 1936 and 1940. This focus on relating structure in the organization to specific situational elements has the further advantage of suggesting analogies to developments in other countries where similar situations are now or have been present.

Thus, while the focus of attention is on a given organization, the study advances knowledge of student organization in Latin America on several fronts. Chapters 1 to 3 present:

1. A closely documented history of the student movement in a particular country, linking its development to student movements elsewhere in the hemisphere.
2. A systematic analysis of the student organizational structure in three distinctive periods, throwing into relief some of the connections between the structure of organizations and the social systems in which they operate as well as some characteristics of modern youth organizations as such.
3. An exploration of the social backgrounds and certain personality characteristics of student leaders of recent and former periods.

Some background information is required to explain the choice of time periods for intensive study and the derivation of the general hypotheses that guided the work. Actually, there are other critical periods in the life of the FECH that from a historical viewpoint merit intensive study. These particular time periods were selected because they represented distinctive and disparate frameworks for student action and therefore maximized the opportunities to uncover structural variations in the organization.

In them the researcher could examine the organization in an early militant and semi-revolutionary epoch (1918–1922). Subsequently, he could see the organization in a period of ascendancy of the left, when the popular and official temper was extremely favorable to students (1936–1940), and finally, as it seemed to be at the time of the study, a politically moderate force with an accepted role in the university administration.

Since the objective was to trace change, it was necessary to apply an analytical framework that would assure obtaining as complete a picture of the organization as possible at each critical period. It was also imperative to have clearly in mind what was meant by organizational structure and to be able to sort out and isolate to some extent the factors contributing to structural changes. The details of the analytical scheme applied in this organizational analysis are presented in the final pages of this introduction. The intent at this point is to outline the main trend of the changes that were anticipated and to indicate the factors that were regarded as most likely to be connected with stability and change in the student federation during the months the study was being planned. Only some of these relationships were confirmed; these initial assumptions and hypotheses are repeated here to make manifest the point of departure of the research.

In the comparison of different periods in the organization's development that is to be made, the factor of youth was seen as a relative constant, imparting certain enduring characteristics to the organization. Thus at one level it was expected that all three periods would show an idealization and glorification of the idea of youth and an affirmation of the rights of youth to participate in a broad range of decisions seen as affecting the interests of young people. At another level, it was expected to find a certain chronic instability in the organization attributable to the *transience* of membership—to the fact that the membership is defined ascriptively and covers a relatively brief span of years.

The university setting was also a constant in one sense, but the social meaning of identification with the university had changed materially during the thirty-five-year span covered by the research. During those years, the student population of the University of Chile had grown from some 3,000 in 1920 to approximately 13,000. During the same period, eight new faculties operating eleven new schools, and more than a score of research institutes and extension services had been established. A new organic statute in effect since 1931 had broadened the effective autonomy of the university, enlarging the powers of the rector and giving a certain amount of financial independence to the institution.[4]

While this expansion of activities and growth in numbers had inevitably meant a broadening of the social base of the student population as well as the teaching and administrative personnel, it was not this alone that contributed to a fundamental alteration in the relationship of the university to the society at large. Church and conservative circles had viewed with alarm the intellectual independence and liberal spirit of the university from its establishment in 1842. Until 1879 the university had jurisdiction over all levels of education, and until 1931 continued to superintend secondary education; this involved it in a running battle with the church and its supporters over the control of education. In this contest, which was complicated by nonreligious political issues and alliances, it was the church and conservative groups that campaigned for "free" education (that is, sectarian and free from government supervision). In any case, as late as 1920 the university was in the peculiar position of being distrusted to some extent as "radical" by ruling elements and yet having few real links with the mass of the citizenry.

In both these respects, the situation of the university was much more favorable in 1956. Its prestige had grown in the nation and abroad. It was increasingly looked to for nonpartisan technical and scientific guidance on important problems by the government; its concern for educational and social reforms or benefit to popular groups had been demonstrated repeatedly. It was, in short, a different university than it had been in 1920, with a more broadly institutionalized place in the society. Presumably, this broader integration of the university as such in the society had some carry-over for the student organization as well.

These are some ways in which it was believed the fact of youth in the membership and the university setting might lend special characteristics to the organizational structure of the FECH. These structural characteristics had to be related to specific historical conditions as well. What economic, social, and political situations that could be documented in a study of this kind would help to explain the forces behind the changing character of the FECH and other organizations like it in Latin America?

In many ways Chile's basic economic problems had not changed in the thirty-five years spanned by the study. They were also in general terms the fundamental problems of many of her sister nations in the hemisphere. Among them were the dependence on the export of copper and nitrates into a world market controlled by external forces, an anarchronistic system of land tenure and social organization in agriculture, a low capacity for producing capital, a growing but monopolistic and protected industry, and chronic inflation. However, within this framework important economic changes with internal social and political repercussions had occurred. It was hoped that it would be possible to trace differences in each period that could be related to the progressive industrialization of the nation—to changes in the class composition of the student body, to individual and family status tensions connected with changes in the over-all occupational structure, to variations in the economic prospects for youth at given times, to changing attitudes toward jobs and vocations, and to changes in the family (especially with respect to the structure of authority and the place of women) that might be linked to changes in the economy.

Changes in the party structure within the nation (and to some extent abroad as well) were another vital factor that clearly related to changes within the FECH. In 1918–1922 (the earliest period covered), seven political groupings in Chile called themselves parties and were divided into two main coalitions, at least for electoral purposes. The next thirty-five years witnessed the progressive fractioning of these groups and the genesis of new ones, on both the left and right. The new fractions on several occasions represented secessions from traditional parties by youthful splinter groups. In the municipal elections of April, 1956, eleven major parties had polled total votes ranging from 10,563 *(Socialista de Chile)* to 164,677 *(Radicales)*. Six other regional political fractions polled smaller votes.[5]

The worth of this research hinged importantly on how much could be uncovered of the intricate connections between party and FECH. The choice of a comparative approach was especially valuable in providing a chance for analysis in depth of three wholly different situations in precisely this respect.

The final broad area of historically specific factors to be taken into account was that of ideology. The revolutionary cast taken by the FECH in the 1920's reflected the ferment of ideas and aspirations—Marxist, socialist, anarchist—that had been at work for several decades among intellectuals in Chile and elsewhere. The influence of Marx and Communism on student circles, especially in later years, has been great. It was asserted as late as 1950 that no one who was not a Marxist or anarchist could be a leader in student groups on the international level in Latin America.[6]

The Argentine University Reform movement of 1918 provided additional facets of the continental ideology for university youth in recent decades. This called for a rejection of all European models, a search for a new American cultural identity, the glorification of the autochthonous cultures and races, an idealistic nationalism, and a determined resistance of Yankee imperialism. All of these with variations remain important elements of ideology among university students in Latin America. A contending model, emanating from conservative and church sources, reasserted the superiority of the Spanish heritage of blood, culture, and religion and was fairly unrelentingly anti-Communist and intermittently pro-United States. In 1956, there were signs that a growing liberal Catholicism was gaining ground as disillusion with events in the Soviet orbit increased among young people.

The examination of ideological trends was intended to permit an assessment of the impact of various sources of ideas on the organization of the FECH; it would reveal whether the progressive rationalization and shift toward political moderation that was posited had been accompanied by a conscious restructuring of ideas, by a change in intellectual guides that was perceived by student leaders themselves.

In short, it was hypothesized that the cumulative impact on the FECH of the changes mentioned—in size and composition of the student body, in the integration of the university within the society, in the economic, political, and ideological spheres—was in a particular direction. Thus, in the final period, as contrasted with the 1920 era, it was expected to find an increased focus on proximate goals, with a direct interest or gain for students as a group rather than remote, utopian ideals. Along with this, it was expected to find an operational code that assumed the possibility of co-operation and agreement among contending groups—an emphasis on negotiation rather than protest; it was expected to find also increased stability in organizational resources, the acceptance of limitations in the sphere of action, a de-emphasis of party identifications within the FECH, and the emergence of a managerial type in student leadership. These expectations were generally borne out, albeit with some important qualifications.

The choice of periods for the analysis of the qualitative changes in the FECH organizational structure was additionally strategic in that these periods parallel fairly well-established stages in general theories of change in the organization of political movements.[7] The Weberian model of change in organizational forms from the charismatic mass movement toward bureaucratization was only partly congruent with the observed patterns of FECH development. There was obviously more at work than some intrinsic maturational process. The opportunities for the consolidation of power and the cumulation of stable patterns of action proved to be different in some spheres than in others. Thus, while the movement from early charismatic forms to more stable patterns was uneven and marked by frequent regressions, the conceptual ground provided by Weber's organizational types proved a useful point of reference.

A final area in which change was anticipated was in the personalities of the typical leaders of each epoch. Leaders of each generation were expected to differ in their general cognitive and emotional approaches to life, their values, their ways of choosing friends, and their styles of political leadership. It was hypothesized that in an organization that had changed qualitatively, different men would be in the fore, and that the opportunity for such changes to occur smoothly was present to a special degree in youth organizations since the turnover of membership is constant and automatic. Following a number of leads given by T. W. Adorno and his collaborators in their study of the influence of psychological factors on political attitudes, leaders of the early epoch, as contrasted with youth leaders of the 1950's, were expected to display a greater tendency toward the glorification (lack of critical evaluation) of in-groups—family, peer groups, party, nation. They were expected to show a capacity for moral indignation and the exteriorization of aggression less common among student managers of the later period. They were expected also to display fewer tensions regarding social status in conventional terms but a greater dependence on applause—on immediate gratifications from social relationships. A more rigid authority structure—with sharper division of male and female roles and an emphasis on dominance by the male head—was expected to be found in the families of leaders born at the turn of the century. This list of hypothesized differences might have been expanded indefinitely. The basic hope was that it would be possible to provide a detailed characterization of the psychological types in ascendance in each generation.

The principal sources of data on the FECH were intensive interviews with leaders of each period.[8] These interviews cover three broad areas. The first of these, aimed at providing historical detail, consists of a narrative recapitulation of important events in the life of the organization during the respondent's period of participation. These accounts were supplemented and checked by the examination of newspapers, magazines, and other documents.

The second main area of questioning was designed to elicit a detailed picture of organizational structure in each period. Organizational structure was conceived in two complementary ways in order to obtain as full a range of data as possible for purposes of the subsequent comparative analysis. First, organizational structure is regarded as a set of institutionalized value patterns and ideas—a set of images shared by those who make up the organization (and in varying degrees by others outside it) as to what the organization is, who is in it, what its aims are, how they are to be achieved, the meaning of participation, and what the organization's relations with external groups is to be. At this level, the questioning sought to elicit from the leaders of each epoch details regarding the following:

1. *Definition of principal goals* and the relative priority assigned to each, as well as the terms in which it was endeavored to legitimate these goals vis-à-vis external groups.
2. *Operative code*: The principal modes of action considered legitimate and efficacious in the pursuit of the goals estab-

lished, the theoretical structure of leadership, policy-making, elections and representation, definitions of consent and authority within the organization.

3. *Bases of participation*: Criteria of membership, evaluation of participants' contributions, and rewards and sanctions for participation and failure at different levels. How responsible does the organization feel for the individual?

4. *Spheres of competence* claimed for the organization; what limitations, if any, are accepted on the legitimate radius of action of the organization?

5. *Command of resources*: Claims made on membership and external sources for services; other contributions.

6. *Links with key external groups*: Definitions of relationships with the university administration, political parties, organized labor, the government, and the nation.

This dimension of structure is related in each period to a second level which conceives the organization as a collectivity engaged in the concerted pursuit of a set of goals. At this level the organization is analyzed as a network of people at work in a more or less co-ordinated fashion on a set of common problems. Here is determined what people in varying positions within the FECH were doing concretely from day to day to deal with many of the organization problems pointed out at the institutional level that constitute in another sense imperatives for organizational survival. The principal question areas were:

1. *Size and composition of membership*: Total number, age, sex, social class, principal faculties or schools, political affiliation, religion, national origin, regional origin, etc.

2. *Informal organization*: Actual patterns of internal co-ordination and command. How does leadership operate? What individuals or school centers have determinative influence in important decisions? Where are decisions made? What voices or power blocs make their weight felt?

3. *Main activities*: What do individuals at different levels in the organization actually do from day to day?

4. *Mobilization of resources*: What actual resources in money, personal services, etc., does the organization command from within itself or from outside sources? To what extent is the

organization itself a resource for more powerful, organized groups?
5. *Conflicting roles*: How does the role of student leader mesh with other roles competing for time and attention?
   a. As student—work load, hours of study, grades, relations with professors, academic authorities.
   b. As son (daughter)—conflicts with family over political ideas, time allocation, associations, etc.
   c. As party member—is FECH seen simply as an area in which to make party commitment effective and how strong is party discipline within FECH?

This maps out the analytical scheme for describing organizational structures. The final broad area covered by these interviews was a variety of biographical and attitudinal materials that were regarded as essential to an interpretation of the data on organization, and which also provided some clues about the personalities of the leaders of each time period. This attitude and personal backgrounds section covered the following:

1. Attitudes on vocation, religion, and politics
2. Communications: Principal sources of formal philosophical, ideological outlook. Influential books, individuals—intellectual models.
3. Family backgrounds, attitudes toward parents, childhood.
4. Social relationships: Social libido, attitudes toward friendships.

The specific line of questioning followed in each case is indicated in the interview schedule shown in Appendix A.

Since many respondents have occupied key positions in Chilean public life the investigator was often able to obtain information on the organization from multiple perspectives at one time—the former student leader often is now, or has been, a government official, an educator, a political party figure, a diplomat, or several of these at once.

A total of seventy-seven tape-recorded interviews were conducted with present or former leaders and university authorities. These averaged two and one-half to three hours in length, although a few ran as long as eight hours and others were quite brief. The questionnaire schedule was used as a general guide and, except in a few early test interviews, was never followed in its entirety. The biographical and attitude section (in those cases where these data were obtained) were the areas in which the line of questioning adhered most closely to the established plan, in view of the possibility of subsequent quantification of some of this material.

Although these interviews provided the main substance of the data obtained, wherever possible documentary materials have been used to supplement these accounts; newspapers, magazines, pamphlets, manifestos, and personal scrapbooks were consulted for all periods. For the present generation, the interviewing effort was accompanied by five months of personal observation of all meetings, demonstrations, and other organizational functions.

A word should be said here about sampling problems. For the present generation of leaders there was no difficulty in drawing an adequate probability sample. The entire FECH executive council for 1956–1957 and twenty-four out of a probability sample of twenty-five, chosen from among the 127 school delegates and presidents, were interviewed. A report on the twenty-fifth person was obtained from the school social worker. For earlier generations it was impossible to obtain systematic samples of this kind. Inevitably, one had to rely on the memory and good will of informants reached for referrals to other respondents. An effort was made to interview *all* the leaders that could be reached. Fourteen leaders or persons close to the FECH leadership from 1918 to 1922 were interviewed. From only eight of these were full biographical and attitudinal data obtained. For the 1936–1940 period, another fourteen key figures were reached; seven in this case went the full course. All of the current leaders interviewed gave biographical data, since the fact that more of them were interviewed and that their day-to-day activities were under observation meant that some of the questions on organization became unnecessary. The remaining interviews were talks with leaders during the periods not being studied intensively but which serve to provide some historical continuity in the panorama of FECH changes in these three periods.

Since the focus of interest is on the organization rather than individual differences, the problem of statistical reliability is less crucial than would otherwise be the case. The study of the FECH was designed to achieve principally qualitative confirmation of certain hunches and to test an analytical framework that could subsequently be used in a broader comparative effort. This was, to the writer's knowledge, the first systematic effort toward a sociological analysis of the development of a student political organization in Latin America. The effort in planning the study was to strike a balance between the ideal of disciplined observation and the desire not to shut out from this initial research venture the chance to encounter and use the unforeseen.

The years since 1956–1957 have not produced any dramatic changes in FECH organization and action. In 1968 the FECH elected its fourteenth consecutive president of a Christian Democratic persuasion. With the victory of that party nationally, in 1964, the FECH entered again into a new, internally focused "reform" phase. In this new struggle within the university, the Christian Democrat student leadership generally defended existing levels of student participation in university government as adequate for present needs. Opposition groups, calling for a profound restructuring of the university, lost a plebiscite on this issue in 1968. The principal political change internal to the student organization was the decline of Radical party strength and the emergence of new groups on the left. The extension of the crisis in higher education to the Catholic universities was a second new dimension in the picture of student action.

While the new crises of authority and democratization in Chilean universities clearly echoed events abroad, it is well to keep in mind that it is the Chilean experience that most clearly prefigures these modes of student action rather than the reverse. There is some irony in the view of a number of social analysts that events in Nanterre, at Berkeley, or on Amsterdam Avenue reflect a "Latin-Americanization" of student life in developed countries. It is true, as FECH history shows, that the idea of the university as the anchor of a larger and perhaps permanent social revolution are not new. The open university, the fully democratic university, the self-critical university (including student polls and ratings of professors' performance) have been articulate goals backed by efforts of varying intensity at realization on more than one occasion in Chile and elsewhere in Latin America. If the modes of youthful protest in the 1960's begin to take on a common conformation, it is not because United States or European students are being Latin-Americanized. It is rather that, as has been the continuous experience of Latin American youth, the way in which their societies and especially their universities fall short of ideals students have been taught to cherish, has been pressed home in especially dramatic ways in these years. The look back at the FECH's experience is not a simple key to today's events in the university, but it helps in sorting out those elements that are genuinely new or particular to the moment from those that have been enduring factors in youthful activism.

NOTES

1. Maxine Davis, *The Lost Generation* (New York: The Macmillan Company, 1936); and David Riesman, "The Found Generation," *The American Scholar* (Fall, 1956).
2. *Select Bibliography on Students, Politics, and Higher Education,* Comparative National Development Project, S. M. Lipset, Director (Preliminary ed., August, 1966).
3. The June, 1966, issue of the *Comparative Education Review* provides a comprehensive overview of the scope and quality of recent work. David Spencer's compilation for the United States National Student Association *(Student Politics in Latin America)* pulls together in one place much of the relevant materials for the region up to the most recent wave of surveys. Erik H. Eriksen, ed., *The Challenge of Youth* (Garden City: Doubleday & Company, 1965), contains several penetrating treatments of the situation of youth in nations that are well into advanced phases of industrialization (the United States, the Soviet Union, France, and Japan).
4. A history of the university's growth is woven into the subsequent chapters.
5. *El Mercurio* (Santiago), June 7, 1956.
6. Enrique Ibarra, *La Situación Estudiantil en América Latina* (Leyden: COSEC, 1954).
7. Max Weber, *Theory of Social and Economic Organization,* trans. A. M. Henderson and Talcott Parsons (New York: Oxford University Press, 1947).
8. An important source of guidance in the preparation of the interview schedule, especially with respect to the exploration of personality factors, has been T. W. Adorno *et al., The Authoritarian Personality* (New York: Harper & Brothers, 1950). Large parts of the schedule relating to family, childhood, vocation, and friendship have been taken almost intact from that study. The formulation of the scheme for organizational analysis leans heavily on Max Weber, Talcott Parsons, Chester Barnard, and Philip Selznick as well as on some of the suggestive epigrams of Eric Hoffer, *The True Believer* (New York: Harper & Brothers, 1951).

Part I

Frank Bonilla

UNIVERSITY STUDENT ORGANIZATION IN CHILE

Chapter 1

The Agitators (1918–1922)

The First Hundred Years of Independence

Two markedly different interpretative currents may be discerned in Chilean historical writing. The first and more well-established version is perhaps epitomized in the work of Alberto Edwards.[1] Although traditionalist in viewpoint, it is by no means current and popular only among conservatives. The second and more recent interpretation emanates from Marxist, though not exclusively Communist, circles and is best exemplified in the work of Julio César Jobet, Marcelo Segall, and Hernán Ramírez Necochea.[2] Many historical and political analysts in Chile, of course, do not fit neatly into either of these categories. The three last-named Marxist writers, in turn, disagree on points of interpretation and fundamentals of approach to their work. However, a broad summary of these two viewpoints will not only provide a panoramic view of Chilean history, but it will also highlight some of the basic tensions that have afflicted the country from the moment it emerged as an independent nation.

Perhaps the chief strength of the traditionalist view is that it rests upon two of the most hallowed symbols of Chilean patriotic sentiment: order and stability in government and the observance of legal and constitutional forms. Most Chileans feel that these two characteristics distinguish the political history of their nation from that of her sister republics in the hemisphere, and these symbols are paradoxically cherished by many for whom democracy in Chile has never been more than an empty formula.

According to this interpretation, Chile was really launched as a nation in 1831 after a period of anarchy, in which abortive experiments were made with liberal and federalist constitutions, and after the rivalries of the military leaders in the war of independence and the struggles among the factions that grew around them were channeled into more conventional forms of political combat. In 1833 Diego Portales introduced a long period of stable, progressive government under a succession of powerful executives. Portales is exalted as the great architect of the legal dictatorship that early put political power securely in the hands of the landowning oligarchy. This tradition-bound oligarchy addressed itself to the tasks of government with a profound sense of responsibility and austerity; no measure seemed too severe as long as it contributed to maintaining order. The masses of rural workers and urban artisans and the providers of personal services proved docile and submissive under the benevolent tutelage of their masters. The state, symbolizing impersonal law and order, took the place of the king and his viceroy in the popular mind.

Although Portales himself was assassinated, the work of nation-building moved forward. Successful military incursions against Peru served to fortify the growing nationalistic spirit; the occupation of the Straits of Magellan and the opening up to colonization of the south provided further outlets for the energetic young nation. Work on the first railroad was begun. The University of Chile was inaugurated in 1843. The first rector, Andrés Bello, drafted a civil code that remains a model of its kind.

The last of the powerful Conservative executives succeeding Portales was Manuel Montt, who faced determined resistance from Liberal party elements and at least two frustrated revolts during his final term from 1851 to 1861. Although the constitution of 1833 had granted the executive broad powers, Montt was forced to rule with extraordinary powers conceded by a compliant Congress or by declaring states of siege during most of this period. Existing conflict derived in part from accumulated resentment against Portales, whose rise to power had been a crushing defeat for Liberals, in part from rivalry between the wielders of political power in Santiago and resentful provincials (particularly to the south in Concepción), and finally from the clash of interests between an emergent industrial and commercial bourgeoisie and the landed aristocracy that had been ruling unchallenged since Portales.

A new era (1860–1890), during which the Liberal oligarchy gradually moved into ascendancy, was marked by numerous constitutional reforms aimed at curbing the almost unrestricted power of the chief executive. These reforms limited presidents to a single term, placed checks on the use of extraordinary powers, and barred state employees from the legislature. The last measure sought to prevent the packing of the legislature with docile public servants. The struggle for religious tolerance also crystallized in this epoch. A statute allowing private (non-Catholic) worship and education was passed, and finally in 1879 religious instruction in the public schools ceased to be obligatory. For a number of years religious issues dominated the political scene as the Radicals (who had emerged as a splinter group from the Liberal party in the final years of Montt's presidency), along with a wing of the Liberal party, joined the fight against the Conservatives and other Liberals over burial rights, civil marriage, the legal immunity of the clergy, and similar issues.

Some of these triumphs were won after the brief internal political truce forced upon the country by the war against Peru and Bolivia in 1879. In this war Chile wrested from Peru and Bolivia the rich nitrate fields in what are now the northern provinces of Antofagasta and Tarapacá. Despite the great wealth acquired by the nation in this military venture and the industrial growth and the expansion of public works that it made possible, this war is often lamented as the beginning of all of Chile's present troubles even by those who celebrate it most heartily as an example of Chilean military prowess.

According to the traditionalist viewpoint, the corruption of the natural aristocracy, which had held the reins of power up till this time, began with this era of easy money. The austere, frugal, industrious, and Christian ruling class was infiltrated by speculators and adventurers; they left the land to lead indolent lives in Santiago or foreign capitals; they squandered their fortunes on extravagant tastes acquired abroad; they lost contact with the people, leaving the masses to the machinations of demagogues; they became rapacious capitalists ready to sacrifice any principle for a profitable turn; they alienated the growing middle class with their insufferable snobbishness.

At the same time, new life was infused into agriculture with the opening up of the enormous northern market after the war—new lands were put into cultivation, crops were diversified, and some mechanization was introduced. Stock raising supplemented and in part displaced Argentine beef imports. A period of industrial growth began (textiles, food processing, and leather) that was matched in Latin America only by Argentina. Those who captured the major share of the new wealth were relatively free of direct taxes since the government, despite periodic crises, drew enough from the nitrate production to overlook other forms of taxation.[3]

Other problems for the traditional ruling class beyond the fact of its own rapid degeneration arose as a consequence of the war. The concentration of workers in the mineral producing areas of the north (nitrate) and south (coal) and the industrial expansion in the central provinces (especially in Santiago, the capital, and in Valparaiso, the chief port) produced in short order the first organized popular protests. These were savagely repressed, but the harshness of working conditions and the many abuses of the workers in Chilean as well as foreign-operated installations built up discontent and resentment among worker groups. The expansion of industry, the growth of cities, and the increase in government activities, as well as the rapid development of educational facilities, added fresh numbers to the middle class. This middle class, no longer content to take its place in the lower ranks of the military, government, professional, and Church hierarchies, began to challenge the power monopoly of the ruling groups.

The first *caudillo* of the middle class was the ill-fated José Manuel Balmaceda, whose presidential term began in 1886. Balmaceda has been elevated to the rank of folk hero posthumously, and it is only in relatively recent times that he has become a revered figure among leftists. In the rightist catechism Balmaceda figures as a stubborn and ambitious fool who violated constitutional norms and plunged the country into civil war in a vain and unpopular effort to sustain the power of the executive before a rebellious Congress. In the end, abandoned by all, he took his own life, oppressed by the stigma of having brought his country to large-scale civil strife.

With the revolution of 1891, according to this version of Chile's past, began the final era of disintegration of the power of the landed and industrial oligarchies that had by then largely settled their differences and were content to alternate in the seats of power. Five major parties survived the revolution: the Liberals, the Nationals, the Radicals, the Conservatives and a small group of followers of the dead president who called themselves Balmacedists. The Democratic party was already in existence but gained importance only in the early years of the twentieth century.[4]

There followed some thirty years of chaotic parliamentary government during which a succession of executives attempted to bridle an unruly legislature in which no party or coalition of forces seemed capable of providing effective leadership. It was, in effect, an attempt to operate a parliamentary government without parties, or at least without parties that acted on real problems. These were also, for the most part, years of prosperity based on the exploitation of the nitrate wealth won from Peru. Many public works were constructed; new lands were settled; railways, bridges, and public services were expanded. Thus the consequences of the absence of a real national government and a ruinous financial policy passed relatively unperceived, at least among those who were reaping the profits of a long-term inflationary spiral set off by successive paper money issues dating from the first unredeemable paper certificates issued to finance the war against Peru.[5]

The election of Arturo Alessandri in 1920 is conceded by all sides to be a turning point in Chilean history. Although there is some controversy over whether it did in fact represent a crippling loss of power for those who had traditionally held the reins of government, it unquestionably signaled the arrival of a new spirit and a new style of political life in Chile. In the traditionalist version of Chile's past it represents the final defeat of a once vigorous and worthy economic and moral elite and the creation of a political vacuum that has not been filled to this day.

The newer, Marxist rendering of Chilean history seeks to document the role of the masses and popular organizations in the country's development and to demonstrate that much of Chile's traditional democracy and stability in government, as well as the social progress to which she lays claim, are a legal fiction. It attempts to establish the beginnings of class struggle in Chile well back in the last century, challenging the image of the docile, submissive, and inert peon or rural tenant with that of the hardy, astute, and combative *roto,* his urban and industrial counterpart.

This is the same *roto* whose piquant wit, endurance, adventurous spirit, and capacity for work are celebrated on Independence Day and during elections, but who is more commonly represented as improvident, irresponsible, sunken in vice and ignorance, and the prey of demagogues. Sporadic organized protests are recorded from about the middle of the nineteenth century. Some twenty-three strikes are listed before 1879, by which time there existed about sixty mutual aid societies, principally among artisans.[6]

From the Marxist viewpoint, the clash between the landed aristocracy and the emergent mineral and commercial bourgeoisie, beginning around 1850, brought only surface political and juridical changes. Although men like Francisco Bilboa, José Victorino Lastarria, and Santiago Arcos Arlegui propagated liberal and revolutionary ideas and fired the enthusiasm of some youths and a few workers, the exploitative agricultural system remained entrenched in the shadow of liberal reforms and a laissez-faire economic policy. By the turn of the century the interests of the old and new economic elites had fused once and for all. The possibilities of any fundamental changes in the economic structure stemming from this conflict had disappeared.

The exploitation of the nitrate wealth won in the war of 1879 required enormous capitals, which were provided by the most advanced capitalist country of the time, Great Britain. The commercial and money markets formerly centered in Valparaíso, albeit under strong British influence, shifted to London and New York. While capitals were poured into the extraction of nitrate, other industries were neglected, dooming the country to dependence on the fortune of a single product and the semi-colonial status of a nation whose principal source of income was in foreign hands. The concentration of large masses of workers in the nitrate camps under the most primitive conditions made possible at the same time the organization of the first combative and politically oriented labor unions.

Balmaceda figures in this version as a visionary economic, nationalist, self-appointed apostle to an indifferent middle class and a weak and disorganized proletariat. He is seen as the victim of a combination of oligarchs and foreign capitalists who, under the guise of defending the Congress from the arbitrary action of the executive, pushed the country into a civil war to thwart the economic reforms which Balmaceda sought to implant.[7]

At the turn of the century Socialist ideas and the influence of international labor movements began to be felt. A Democratic party and two short-lived Socialist groups appeared. These did not gain firm roots among the workers at once, but the ferment of ideas stirred some to new forms of action. Organized "resistance unions," heavily influenced by anarchist ideas, appeared in Santiago and Valparaíso as well as in the northern nitrate camps. One of the first violent strikes took place in Santiago and Valparaíso in 1905, with hundreds of dead and wounded in pitched street battles. The first two decades of the twentieth century saw repeated violent clashes between workers and police and military forces, in which not only workers were victims, but women and children were shot down. Labor leaders suffered imprisonment, torture, and exile.[8] Labor presses were destroyed, and workers were barred from the polls. When workers succeeded in electing a representative to the legislature despite force and fraud, he was impeded from exercising office by his colleagues.[9] Despite this harsh repression, a confederation of labor unions was formed in 1909, and repeated conventions were held in 1911, 1914, 1919, and 1921. A Socialist Workers party was also formed in 1912, passing in 1921 into the Third International as the Chilean Communist party.

This expanding popular force, allied with an increasingly aggressive middle class, was on the eve of its first victory at the polls as the 1920's approached. This victory, which to some appears as the eclipse of a once powerful oligarchy, is with hindsight regarded by many leftists as an empty triumph that produced no fundamental changes in Chilean social structure. In their view, even today the power of traditional ruling groups, though more subtly exercised, remains in essence intact. The situation of the agricultural worker in the mid-1950's was in substance exactly what it was in the 1850's, and there had been only modest improvement in the lot of workers in a few favored industries. The chief winner in the power shifts and the minor redistribution of the national wealth that had been brought about by economic changes and social legislation in the twentieth century was the middle class.

A major institutional context for that middle-class advance had been the national university. The University of Chile was solemnly inaugurated in the year 1843, just a few years after the

Real Universidad de San Felipe (established by royal charter nearly a century before) ceased to exist.[10] The years of order and prosperity introduced by Portales brought an intellectual flowering stimulated importantly by the presence in Chile of a number of illustrious figures from abroad, notably Sarmiento, Mitre, and Alberdi of Argentina, and Andrés Bello, the Venezuelan. Bello was the framer of the first university statute and the first rector. One of the most brilliant figures in the independence movement of Latin America, he had lived for some time in England, where he was a close friend of Jeremy Bentham and John Stuart Mill. He spent long years in Chile as adviser to the government and strongly influenced the country's early cultural life.

Under its first statute the university was responsible for the supervision of education at all levels. There were five faculties: Philosophy and Humanities, Mathematics and Physical Sciences, Medicine, Law and Political Science, and Theology. The deans and the rector were to be elected by the council of professors of each faculty and the full council of the university, respectively. This election, however, was subject to the approval of the official patron of the university, the president of the Republic. To this day, it is the custom to submit to the president a list of three names, with the understanding that the first name represents the real preference of the council. The will of the council with respect to the designation of rector has almost always been respected, and the few executives who have tried to withhold recognition to a duly elected rector or impose a candidate of their own have seen their hopes dashed.

Initially the university functioned closely with the *Instituto Nacional,* a secondary school dating from the early years of the Republic. The intellectual climate of the university, in accord with the temper of Bello himself, was one of moderate liberalism, of academic freedom within the framework of Catholic doctrine and established custom. Despite obeisances to church and dogma, the university from the beginning inspired apprehension in the minds of conservative circles—fears that sprang in great part from concern over the exclusive control of primary and secondary education granted to the university. The first scandals were not long in coming. In the middle of 1844 the Supreme Court ordered the public burning of *Sociabilidad Chilena,* a book by Francisco Bilboa, a law student and one of the early propagandists of liberal ideas in Chile. José Victorino Lastarria, a young professor who shared Bilboa's advanced ideas, also drew attacks for his works of social criticism. For some years the university, beset by apprehensive conservatives who saw it as a perilous den of Masons and freethinkers, as well as by frustrated liberals who regarded it as a submissive pawn of the church and the government, had to fight for its very life.

Some of the faculties got a slow start, notably Medicine and Mathematics and Physical Sciences. In some cases it was necessary to send students abroad in order to build up a staff since there were no trained persons in numerous specialties in the country. The focus of dissension was the Faculty of Philosophy and Humanities, which was responsible for overseeing primary and secondary schools. The church, with the political backing of the Conservatives, undertook a campaign in favor of "free education" (that is, sectarian and free of state supervision). In 1872, a Decree on the Freedom of Education was finally passed, breaking the university's monopoly on the awarding of secondary school degrees. The furor produced by the many abuses that sprang up, notably the sale of degrees by phantom schools that did not even maintain teaching staffs, brought about the repeal of this decree in the following year.

Women were admitted to the University of Chile in 1877, two years before the dictation of a new organic statute for the university. Under the new statute, primary schools became independent of the university, but control over the secondary school system was strengthened. The autonomy of the rector and his administrative staff over university affairs was also strengthened, although the university remained dependent economically on the government and subject to pressures. Some ten years later, an institute for the training of secondary school teachers was established under the direction of a team of German educators. This soon produced fundamental reforms in the antiquated teaching methods practiced in the secondary schools and a progressively improved level of secondary training in the years since then.

The first two decades of the twentieth century were a period of rapid growth for the university, despite continued tensions with church and conservative circles. The election of Valentín Letelier to the rectorate in 1906 was fought bitterly in the press and in political circles and threatened to produce a cabinet crisis.[11] The Catholic *Diario Ilustrado* expressed horror that the instruction of the nation's youth should be put in the hands of this impious Socialist. Letelier, a prominent member of the Radical party, was a leader of the advanced wing in that party which was beginning to preach the doctrine that social problems were a proper concern of the state. The traditional respect for the will of the University Council prevailed, however, after threats from Liberal and Radical parliamentarians to withdraw from the cabinet and demonstrations from students who were in those very months beginning to organize.

The growth of the university in these years can be inferred in part from the number of degrees it awarded. In 1900, 374 degrees were granted; 693 were awarded in 1909, and 1,354 in 1918. Most of these were secondary school degrees *(bachilleres)* and law degrees. By 1920 there were over 3,000 students in the professional schools alone (Law, Medicine, Architecture, Dentistry, Pharmacy, Engineering, and the Instituto Pedagógico), with another 1,500 or so in Fine Arts and Music. The last two schools provided training for many talented youngsters, who, though technically university students, were at the same time completing their primary or secondary schooling.

Despite this record of growth, the university was beset by numerous problems, which it has faced almost from its inception and which remain in large part unsolved today. Most of these were pointed out by Valentín Letelier himself in his *Filosofía de la Educación* in 1892.[12] According to Letelier, the colonial heritage condemning the independent quest for knowledge had not been overcome. An excessive emphasis on professional training of a narrow utilitarian nature similarly hampered the development of scientific skills or curiosity. The rigid plans of study and the limited programs in most schools, in addition to the low level of teaching as a result of the fact that teaching posts were for all practical purposes honorific and noncompetitive, further contributed to the stifling of independent thought. In short, asserted Letelier, the university did an excellent job of spreading imported ideas but made original investigation impossible within its confines. These problems, coupled with the university's chronic poverty of means, have perennially agitated students from the

moment they emerged as an organized force in the life of the
university and the nation.

The Student Federation of Chile, characteristically, sprang to
life on a wave of youthful indignation and enthusiasm. The
scandal rocked staid Santiago society of 1906. An enraged crowd
of medical students had shouted, jeered, and cascaded torn paper
from the galleries of the Municipal Theater upon the president of
the Republic, the entire diplomatic corps, and the most aristocratic families in the city, forcing these dignitaries to retire in
confusion from a ceremony that had been intended to honor the
very students who had staged this demonstration.[13] The students
had been called to the theater to be decorated for their help in
quelling an epidemic of smallpox in Valparaíso (Chile's main
port) during the previous year. Their indignation sprang from
the fact that, although the ceremony was in their honor, they and
their families had been relegated to the upper galleries of the
theater, while the better localities were reserved for local and
diplomatic officials and for the "best families" of the city.

The next day some five hundred students gathered on the
Alameda in front of the university and heard José Ducci,
President of the Medical School student group, propose the
formation of a federation of all students in Chile. The cheering
crowd marched off to the home of Valentín Letelier, who, though
not yet officially elected rector, was looked to as a spiritual and
intellectual guide by many students. Letelier received the student
delegation cordially and addressed the group briefly, wishing
them good luck on their new enterprise. That same afternoon a
delegation of students visited the president of the Republic,
Germán Riesco, who also received them well but with firmness.
Although the president conceded that the affair had not been
handled in the best way, he maintained that the dignitaries who
had been invited to honor the students had to be given preferen-
tial seating. The next day the students declared in the press that
although they did not blame the president for the insult to their
families, they were not entirely satisfied with this explanation.

There was a second cordial exchange of views with Valentín
Letelier, who by then had assumed the rectorate despite the bitter
opposition of the Conservatives. The new federation assured the
rector that he could count on the loyalty and co-operation of

students. Letelier replied that no educational reforms were possible without the full confidence of students, and that he hoped to be able to serve them well. Thus the first years in the life of the Student Federation of Chile (FECH),[14] except for minor difficulties over local problems in certain schools, are not marked by any serious conflicts between students and university authorities. The FECH received a great deal of material aid from the rector, and when he was forced to resign in 1911 by what appears to have been a political stratagem of his enemies, students were among the first to protest.

Early activities of the FECH centered around the cultural improvement of members—lectures, discussions, and reading groups. This was soon extended to the education of workers, who had independently started small programs of self-improvement around the time the FECH was born. There had been sporadic contacts between some workers and students with educational problems; notably the high rate of illiteracy among workers led some of the schools to establish night instruction courses where the rudiments of reading and writing were taught to workers. The first FECH night school was established in 1910, although in the schools of Law and Medicine courses had been operating for some time before. By 1916 the FECH and affiliated schools were running eleven study centers for workers, as well as medical, dental, and legal service centers for students and the needy public. That same year the FECH offered seven hundred volunteers to the government to undertake a census of the school-age population in Santiago. The FECH was by then firmly committed to a program of social and cultural improvement for workers as well as students.[15] However, while there was a climate of vigorous social protest, the revolutionary spirit that was to be manifested later was not yet present.

These early years saw the celebration of a number of international student conclaves. The first of these was held in Montevideo in 1908, the second in Buenos Aires in 1910, and the third in Lima in 1912. The Lima meeting was notable in that the "Hymn of the American Student," for many years the battle song of students in Latin America, was written there. These early conferences were not very political in nature, except insofar as they were dedicated to forging a new cultural and political solidarity among the Latin American states. The delegates spoke tentatively about university reforms and the important role to be played by youth in the direction of the university and in shaping the future of their countries; however, the meetings served chiefly to cement friendships among students from the several countries. The friendly ties established between Chilean and Peruvian students, whose governments had been involved in drawn-out litigation over the final disposition of the northern nitrate provinces that were ceded to Chile after the War of 1879, were later to have important repercussions in the life of the FECH.

Such, then, was the FECH in the early years of the century. Its initial concern was primarily for the moral and intellectual improvement of its members, inspired by an idealistic nationalism which led to a preoccupation with all problems affecting the country. The first stirring of organized popular protest by workers thrust social problems into the foreground of political concern, and through educational efforts among workers and early contacts with unions the social conscience of the students began to be awakened. Coming largely from modest middle-class families, they felt themselves to be partially victims of a system that condemned the mass of their fellows to grinding poverty. However, these vague aspirations for social justice had taken no political form. Few students were active militants in political groups, and the FECH was in no sense the instrument of any party. Along with other popular elements, the FECH was moving toward forthcoming events of national importance. It was soon to appear in the vanguard of the forces clamoring for change.

Chile: Post-World War I

In 1920, Chile had a population of close to four million, nearly half of whom were living in places with a thousand or more inhabitants. The major urban concentrations were the mining towns in the north, a coal-mining and industrial complex beginning to take form around Concepción in the south, and above all Valparaíso, the chief port, and the capital, Santiago, with half a million residents. The central provinces, with these two great cities and their large rural population, occupied one-quarter of the national territory and contained four-fifths of its people.[16] It was a young population; nearly 50 per cent were twenty-four or younger. The birth rate was high, but deaths (especially among infants) decimated the nation. Life expectancy at birth was approximately thirty-one years, reflecting the hard conditions under which the urban and rural masses lived.

Racially, it was a relatively homogeneous population. The Negroes who were introduced in small numbers during the colonial period had been completely absorbed. The Araucanian Indians, who fiercely resisted the white man's penetration even into the nineteenth century, had been reduced to small enclaves in the extreme south of the country. The remaining masses represented various degrees of racial mixtures, with Spanish and European types predominating at the top of the social scale and Indian characteristics more readily visible among the lower classes. Immigration had been more important economically than racially in republican times. In 1920, there were only slightly over 100,000 foreign-born persons in Chile—chiefly Spaniards, Bolivians, Peruvians, Italians, Germans, and English. However, one-half of the country's industrial establishments and about one-third of the commercial firms were foreign-owned. In mining, British and German interests were still dominant in the nitrate field, while the United States was establishing its hold on copper.[17] Immigration was selective; no mass of unwanted poor descended on Chile. The new arrivals came to fortify the growing middle class and leaven the aristocracy.

The country was by faith and by law Roman Catholic, although liberal interpretations of constitutional provisions permitted non-Catholic worship. There were only about 50,000 Protestants in Chile in 1920 and some 2,000 Jews. Ninety-six thousand reported no religion, and seventy-two persons declared themselves Positivists to the 1920 census takers.

Educational statistics are notoriously unreliable in Chile, as in many other countries, but even the most optimistic of them leave no doubt that the country had serious educational problems. The 1920 census gives an illiteracy figure of 50 per cent for the country and 33 per cent for Santiago, based on the total population. The first four years of primary school were made obligatory in August of 1920. Enrollment in all primary schools in that year totaled well under half of the school-age population (ages six to fourteen), according to the census. Secondary schools, special training establishments, and the universities were serving a total of some 75,000 students; this was about 10 per cent of the population between fifteen and twenty-four years of age. Low enrollment, coupled with poor assistance, large drop-out rates, understaffing, ramshackle school buildings, and overcrowding, are problems that continue to plague Chilean education despite many advances since then.[18] However, the country had in 1920 (as today) a good number of first-rate secondary schools. The growth of the *lyceé* is rated as a prime factor in the development of the middle class in Chile, and it should be noted that as far back as 1920 there were almost as many girls as young men in these schools. This was not the case in the university, but professional degrees had been granted to women in Chile well before 1900.

Chile, like several other countries where industrial progress has been fitful, has on occasion been described as an "economic museum." Carlos Keller writes:

> In Chile there are economic forms that correspond to the paleolithic. Others have been conserved at the level of primitive people (widely extensive, for example, in agriculture); the social organization of our agriculture is perfectly medieval (the feudal system has been preserved almost in pure form); there are elements belonging to primitive capitalism (most industires and the small mining enterprises); others have the characteristics of modern capitalism (the larger industries favored by the state); finally we have the super firms with the typical characteristics of the economy of the future (the North American companies).[19]

Keller's concise appraisal speaks volumes. His observation is appropriate for 1920 and even has some applicability today.

Chile in 1920 was still essentially a rural and agricultural country. Nearly 500,000 of the 1,300,000 economically active were working the land. Probably not more than 50,000 of the 326,000 who are classified by the census as engaged in industry were employed in industrial establishments of any size. The vast majority of these were craftsmen and artisans who worked independently. Although mining gave employment to a relatively small number, it was the most vital activity for the national economy and especially for the government. Copper had begun to gain in importance, but nitrate was still king.

Although the war years had been prosperous for Chile, nitrate exports fluctuated wildly beginning from about 1913.[20] The value of nitrate exports dropped vertiginously with the peace, and the country was plunged into depression. As mine after mine in the north closed down, hordes of hungry and unemployed moved south, concentrating in Santiago, where they were put up in makeshift shelters and fed from improvised soup kitchens. The deplorable situation of the thousands of unemployed was aggravated by the rise in the prices of foodstuffs and other essentials. Labor agitation increased in intensity, strike followed strike, and the turbulent atmosphere that reigned in Santiago was accentuated by the excitement over the presidential campaign for the election of 1920.

Arturo Alessandri

The forces of discontent and unrest that had been smoldering in Chile for more than twenty years found a champion and idol in the figure of Alessandri. His defiance of the corrupt political machine in Tarapacá in the senatorial election of 1915 had won him popular favor, especially among young Radicals in Santiago and the northern nitrate workers. In the last days of the Sanfuentes regime (1915–1920), Alessandri was head of the cabinet and succeeded in consolidating his position as presidential candidate. The *Alianza Liberal,* including Radicals and Democrats as well as some Liberals and Independents, acclaimed Alessandri as its candidate on the second ballot in convention.[21] The *Unión Nacional,* which was in effect the ancient coalition (Liberals, Nationals, Conservatives, and Balmacedists), raised the name of Luis Barros Borgoño in opposition.

Alessandri's free-wheeling, demagogic style brought a new kind of political excitement to Santiago. He promised a "government of love," and the idle rabble in Santiago formed a constant retinue that waited attendance on him at all hours. His fulminations against the privileged and corrupt in high places delighted the populace and struck fear among unionist ranks. The campaign was bitter and hard fought. When the tallies were counted, the vote was so close that a special tribunal had to be set up to settle the dispute. The spirit of turbulence and the threat of mob action persisted throughout the long months of haggling and arbitration. The tribunal finally decided in favor of Alessandri by a bare majority, and the Congress ratified his election.

The new president was soon in trouble both with his friends and with his enemies. His high-handed and arbitrary methods alienated supporters as well as opponents. His programs of social reform in behalf of workers were sidetracked by an unco-operative legislature; the government floundered from one cabinet crisis to another; unemployment continued high; labor groups were restive; some of his friends proved inefficient and dishonest in office; the parties that had supported his candidacy became enmeshed in petty intrigues; he lost the favor of students; his efforts to negotiate the border question with Peru to Chile's advantage were misunderstood at home and abroad. In short, he met with all the frustrations and disappointments calculated to infuriate a man of his temperament. By the time the 1924 legislative elections came around, he was evidently determined to go to any lengths to obtain a favorable majority in both houses. In an election which was noteworthy even in Chile for the abuses committed in behalf of official candidates, he achieved this end. A few months later, when this legislature sought to vote itself remuneration, ignoring other urgent financial problems and a constitutional provision expressly forbidding this, the army stepped in. Alessandri resigned and quit the country, but he was to be heard from again before long. His hard-won legislature was dissolved, and a military junta assumed control of the government.

The generalized discontent and disposition for protest that Alessandri capitalized on for political ends was not entirely a reaction to deprivation experienced or observed. The frank misery of large numbers and the meager subsistence eked out by others was certainly at the roots of the sudden clamor for change; however, especially among students, there was an intellectual impulse as well. Perhaps the most exciting single event was the revolution in Russia, which seemed to herald a new era of freedom and an end to the economic exploitation of the many by the few. Chile had remained neutral throughout World War I, and though the sympathy of her young people was probably almost unanimously with the Allies, the war was seen by many as the death dance of capitalism. Neither the work of Marx nor that of his commentators was very well known in Chile, but news of the revolution and the exploits of Lenin and Trotsky was closely followed in the student and labor press. The Communist party, established in Chile in 1921, did not achieve firm doctrinal footing until several years later.

The writings of early socialists and anarchists were much more widely disseminated and commented upon. Jaurès, Reclus, Proudhon, Saint Simon, Sorel, Kropotkin, Bakunin, and Tolstoi were among the most influential of the time. The works of these authors, as well as those of the Russian novelists Gogol, Dostoevski, and Gorki, circulated among students in cheap translations published by a Spanish press, *Sempere*. The Argentine Ingenieros and the works of the Spanish, Italian, and Argentine syndicalists also attracted a great deal of attention. The student organ, *Claridad* (it called itself "a magazine of sociology, art, and criticism"), filled its pages with excerpts and commentary on all these works, as well as those of Unamuno, Barbusse, Anatole France, and Le Bon. Anything that smacked of protest or attacked existing institutions was eagerly snapped up.

The very catholicity of interests made this a period of confusion and speculation. The accent on individualism in many of these writings and the disparate viewpoints encompassed made concerted action difficult. Each one sought his own synthesis, and the result was an ideological babel. These were, nevertheless, the raw materials that constituted the bases of the FECH faith and action.

As has been seen, even before the four-year period, ranging from about mid-1918 to mid-1922, the FECH had been in contact with groups of workers, principally in the study centers maintained by student and labor organizations. These early joint activities had occasioned little alarm; this was, after all, no more than what a number of prominent society women of the day were doing in behalf of Santiago's underprivileged.[22] The first sensation of threat from this new alliance and the correspondingly angry reaction came early in 1919 with the constitution of the awkwardly named Workers' Assembly for National Nutrition *(Asamblea Obrera de Alimentación Nacional).*[23]

This assembly brought together a heterogeneous group of organizations in the new FECH headquarters, where the group began to meet shortly after its inception. Delegates from the Workers' Federation of Chile (FOCH), the Industrial Workers of the World (IWW), the Socialist party, and the Association of

Educators met to discuss the grave situation created by an increasing cost of living in the face of mass unemployment. One of the first decisions to be made was whether the assembly should present any formal petitions to the government for the solution of the economic hardships that were being suffered by workers and others with modest incomes. The combative resistance unions and anarchist elements in the FOCH and IWW finally agreed to do so, considering that this would provide an object lesson for the workers, demonstrating that the proletariat can expect nothing from politicians in a capitalist system.

Although the assembly as an organization did not survive long (in part because of internal dissension), very close contacts were maintained between the FECH and worker groups, particularly the IWW, during the next few years. Some of the most outstanding FECH leaders of the time were closely identified with the IWW and its revolutionary doctrine and methods. In its first convention in 1919 the IWW declared itself the enemy of capital, the state, and the clergy, and declared its preferred methods to be sabotage, the strike, boycott, and labeling. This last was a system of identifying goods produced in shops that were resisting the organization. In Santiago worker neighborhoods, this often led to the overturning of delivery trucks and carts "labeled" as coming from strike-bound or hostile plants. The scaffolding on construction jobs was another common target.

The climate of violence in Santiago and other parts of the country grew with the combativeness of worker elements and the increasingly repressive measures of the government. A roundup of IWW leaders in Valparaíso and Santiago in 1920 netted, among others, Domingo Gómez Rojas, a young poet and student, who, it appears, had only token membership in that organization. His death as a result of ill treatment in prison, which he entered in delicate health, roused public indignation as had few other such tragedies. A silent procession of some 70,000 escorted his red-draped coffin past the presidential palace to the cemetery, where some twenty orators denounced the government's complicity in police and military brutality against the people. Previous months had seen the bloody repression of a strike in Puerto Natales, as well as the burning of a FOCH meeting hall in Magallanes. A press that published a number of anarchist news sheets had been destroyed in Santiago, and the quarters of the FECH itself had been sacked by an angry mob of "patriotic" youths in July, 1920.

This attack on the FECH had been provoked in part by its more aggressive support of worker demands but was closely related to two other events. One of these was the first convention celebrated by the FECH in June, 1920. The principal purpose of this convention was to make a pronouncement regarding the ideals and principles of action guiding the FECH. Although the convention declared that the FECH "would try to realize its aspirations independent of all external influence and through rational and evolutionary means," some of its announced goals did not sit well with the government, large sectors of the public, and even a good number of students. The establishment of a scale of values (the individual, the family, the nation, humanity), in which the interests of the nation were subordinated to those of justice and fraternity among peoples, offended nationalist sentiment. The declaration also asserted that only the socialization of productive forces could lead to the solution of the social inequities disturbing the nation, and that until this socialization was achieved it was unlikely that peace among nations or effective international cooperation could exist. The FECH also officially assumed an attitude of permanent criticism of all social institutions, based on the belief that the constant evolution and renovation of human values precluded the definitive solution of social problems.

The strongly pacificist position taken by the FECH was particularly disturbing because of the growing tensions between Chile and Peru and Bolivia, her long-time rivals. The precedent established by the Treaty of Versailles had led Peru (who had figured in the war as an Allied nation) to hope that she could bring international pressure to bear toward a favorable solution of her controversy with Chile over the provinces of Tacna and Arica. These had been ceded to Chile in 1883, supposedly for a ten-year period, after which a plebiscite was to determine future ownership. This plebiscite had never been held because the two countries could never reach agreement about the conditions under which it was to be celebrated. In the meantime, Chile had proceeded to colonize the area, and there were continuous protests from Peru over abuses committed on her citizens still resident in these provinces.

Things came to a climax in July, 1920, when the Chilean government announced the mobilization of a number of regiments to go north where, it was rumored, Peruvian and Bolivian forces were gathering on the frontier. A military coup in Bolivia, it was said, had just unseated President José Gutiérrez Guerra, with the connivance of Peru, as a preliminary maneuver in a war to be undertaken jointly against Chile. Patriotic sentiment was stirred to a fever pitch. Great crowds in Santiago cheered and wept as the gallant soldiers marched bravely off to face the enemy in the arid pampa.

In the midst of the patriotic fervor that swept the city, a lone, discordant voice was heard. After heated debate in open assembly, the FECH passed a vote asking the nation to maintain a serene attitude and calling on the government to give the public more details of the situation which made the mobilization necessary. Secret diplomacy, they asserted, was outmoded, and the public was entitled to some concrete evidence that the mobilization was more than an internal political maneuver that could bring the nation a serious loss of prestige abroad as well as the other tragic consequences of a precipitate belligerent action.

This was enough to loose the fury of the frustrated rear-echelon patriots and the conservative press on the FECH and its more prominent leaders. On July 21, 1920, after seeing off a group of reservists at one of Santiago's two railroad stations, a crowd of the city's "gilded" youth paused to pay their respects to the president. From the balcony of the presidential palace they were harangued by a senator, who pointed out to them that the enemy was here in their very midst, just a few blocks away in the FECH quarters. It was midday, and although the FECH had been guarded through the night in anticipation of just such an assault, only a handful were on hand to defend it at that hour. The enraged mob swept through the FECH, completely destroying furnishings, files, statuary, and paintings. The raid was climaxed with the public burning of the books and magazines of the FECH library, under the complacent eyes of the police, who proceeded to arrest the small group of FECH members who tried to turn back the marauders.[24]

The FECH was deprived by the government of its corporate status, which had been granted in 1918. An effort was also made to oust from his university post one of the few public figures that came to the defense of the FECH, Dr. José Ducci, the first FECH president. Those FECH leaders who were not already imprisoned or fugitives as a consequence of their links with the IWW, or who had not been picked up during the assault on the FECH, struggled to get the organization back on its feet. This difficult situation lasted until the end of the year, when, upon the final designation of Arturo Alessandri as president of the Republic, FECH leaders were released and students began to make their voices heard anew. To this day, the anniversary of the attack on the student club, as well as that of the death of Gómez Rojas, are recalled as symbolic dates in the life of the FECH.

Although no armed conflict materialized, the situation between Chile and Peru continued to be tense, especially after Alessandri embarked on the tortuous negotiations that would finally lead to arbitration of the dispute. The FECH's pacifist and internationalist position and her friendly ties with Peruvian students were to bring still more trouble to the organization. A note sent by the FECH to Peruvian students on the occasion of the anniversary of the battle of Ayacucho (in which Peru won its independence) gave rise to a new furor in Chile, even though the lofty senti-ments it expressed won high praise internationally. The results were doubly painful to students, for in addition to the virulent attacks at home, they received a cold rebuff from Peruvian students, who were at the time divided into two rival organizations.

At the same time, in a new debate on the Declaration of Principles, which had come out of the first FECH convention, Carlos Vicuña, a professor and honorary member of the FECH directorate, declared that the Peru-Chile dispute should be settled with the return of the provinces of Tacna and Arica to Peru and the granting to Bolivia of a corridor to the sea. His almost immediate dismissal as a professor for expressing views on public issues not in line with government policy gave rise to a great debate on the freedom of opinion.[25] Vicuña, a brilliant orator with a keen, analytical mind and mordant wit, defended himself ably but was abandoned successively by the rector of the univer-sity and other highly placed political friends, including President Alessandri. The FECH, which demonstrated in Vicuña's behalf, was again accused of harboring traitors bought by Peruvian gold.

Throughout these hectic years, the FECH had sustained its educational efforts among workers. Since 1918 a popular univer-sity *(Universidad Popular Lastarria)* had been in operation under the direction of a former FECH president and philosophy professor, Pedro León Loyola. The university was not organized with any specifically utilitarian end in mind; its purpose was merely to broaden the intellectual horizons of the workers and stimulate them to think more intelligently about their problems. There was initially no organized study plan; students, writers, artists, professionals, and other interested or interesting persons were invited to give nightly talks on a wide variety of topics—physics, astronomy, philosophy, literature, and so on. Although efforts were made to use it as a political sounding board (in part because of the presence in strong numbers of anarchists who resisted the influence of political parties), it never became the pawn of any political group or an indoctrination center for any particular ideology.

The repercussions of the University Reform movement, started in Argentina in 1918, were much more profound in other countries in the hemisphere than in Chile.[26] Although the FECH soon incorporated into its demands on the university during its recurrent conflicts some of the outstanding reforms propounded by the Córdoba movement (for example, free attendance, freedom of teaching, no permanent tenure for professors, voice and vote for students and alumni in running the university, and so on), there was no formal and studied program of reforms prepared or presented during this period by the students. Nevertheless, the combative spirit displayed by students in support of their worker allies and in behalf of their own principles was equally evident in their encounters with university authorities and in the defense of their professional prerogatives. There were repeated clashes over decisions of the Council of Public Education *(Consejo de Instrucción Pública)*. These gradually deteriorated into outright provocations by the more radical students, but this signaled, not a high pitch of enthusiasm, but a beginning decline of the FECH.

During the years from 1918 to 1922 the FECH had been headed by a series of forceful and relatively experienced individuals, most of whom had completed their university careers, and some of whom had established professional reputations before they assumed FECH posts. After 1922 this was no longer true. Moreover, a rival National Student Federation, reputedly sponsored by President Alessandri and his sympathizers, had been set up. Only the School of Engineering joined the "fiscal federation" as a body, although a fair number of members were recruited on an individual basis. Anarchist groups, which had formed into little societies in various schools (notably the *Grupo Lux* in the Medical School), began to preach the doctrine that the FECH was just another bourgeois and decadent organization that sapped the spirit and deformed the personality. *Claridad,* which began publication as official organ of the FECH in 1920 but had always been controlled by anarchists and those with the most radical views, also began to attack the FECH, urging workers to have nothing to do with the few who were still trying to pump some life into the organization. Some efforts were made in 1924 to revive the organization and to fuse with the rival federation, which had also quickly come upon hard times. However, little came of these efforts, and in 1925 a small group of students came to power with the express purpose of liquidating the FECH as an organization until it regained its strength at the roots.[27] Not until five years later was the FECH to reappear on the national scene as the ebullient, dynamic force that it constituted from 1918 to 1922.

The Institutionalization of Protest

No one knows who first spoke in Chile about "the generation of 1920" or just when it happened. However, from the first, those who are numbered among that now-famous generation were a self-conscious, thoughtful, and introspective group—at pains to understand themselves, or at least to explain themselves to others. This is at once a help and a hindrance in the work of reconstructing an objective picture of the organization which they infused with their spirit and which gave form and substance to their action. The researcher is faced not only with the rationalization and idealization of youthful acts by men advancing in age and sharing in the multiple experiences that have led their successors to place conflicting interpretations on those acts. He is faced also with ancient error and inattention compounded by time and forgetfulness.

Still, few groups have sought so determinedly to record and confront explicitly the ends and the meaning of actions undertaken and the organization through which they set out to bring life to cherished principles. The Declaration of Principles of the

FECH convention, held in June, 1920, constituted perhaps the most complete expression of the new spirit that swept through the organization in the months after the first great war.[28] After four days of impassioned debate among about 1,200 delegates, representing not only university students but various secondary and specialized training establishments, as well as professors and other sympathizers, the convention approved the statement of aims that was to provoke such controversy. Nearly two years before, in the fall of 1918 (on the occasion of its incorporation as a legal entity), the FECH had passed a set of bylaws prefaced by a statement of aims.[29] The difference between the objectives outlined in this earlier constitution and the goals embraced in the convention two years later indicates dramatically the change in the students' vision of the character of their own organization and its place in the society in which it functioned.

The 1918 FECH proposed as its first aim to study and co-operate in the solution of national problems. This was closely linked to its then-current preoccupation with educational problems, particularly a long-time campaign in favor of the establishment of free, obligatory, and secular primary education (a law that was not passed until 1920). In addition, four general purposes were listed in the first article of the bylaws: (1) the moral and physical betterment of members; (2) the progress of public education; (3) the cultural and material improvement of the lot of workers; and (4) the provision of club facilities for members. These, as has been seen, were the kinds of goals and activities that had typified the FECH from its inception up to this period.

The convention manifesto of 1920 was a much more pretentious and exhaustive document. It opened with a declaration of fundamental principles. Although these included a scale of values in which individual interest was subordinated to the collectivity (family, fatherland, humanity), the free expression of the individual and total freedom for the development of individual personality were also exalted as guiding values. This opening paragraph, with its dedication to individual self-perfection, the tranquillity and welfare of the collectivity, and the fight against all immorality (all this by "rational and evolutionary means"), was not the most alarming or novel part of the declaration.

It was the articles dealing with social problems and international affairs that represented innovations. The first of these was based on the premise that human values are in a process of constant change. This, according to the youthful ideologues, meant that all solutions to problems of social organization are transitory and, therefore, an attitude of permanent criticism should be maintained regarding all aspects of social life. It proposed that the principle of co-operation replace that of competition among men; it urged the socialization of the productive apparatus and a more equitable distribution of what is produced in common; and it reaffirmed a belief in the right of every individual to a full and independent moral and intellectual life. It endorsed the organized action of the proletariat but not through political parties. A final clause observed that all social progress implies the moral and cultural perfection of individuals.

After stating that patriotism is a noble sentiment involving the sacrifice of individual interest to a collective need, the declaration went on to say, in its article on international affairs, that in international questions it would always subordinate the interests of individuals, the family, and the nation to the supreme ideals of justice and fraternity among men. It condemned all wars and asserted that the capitalist form of social organization gives birth to armed conflicts between nations and that true peace would not likely be achieved until the elements of economic production were socialized internationally. It wound up with a call for disarmament and the abolition of all armies, along with the application of the rules of civil law in international litigation.

The youthful convention also declared that the educational system should be geared to the formation of free men, bowing only to reason and duty—idealists, able to live a better life themselves and bring the nation to a more pure, just, and fraternal way of life. Education was defined as a responsibility of the state. It was to be gratuitous, secular, and, for the primary grades, obligatory. The primary and secondary cycles of school training were to aim toward the rounded development of the individual rather than any immediate utilitarian purpose. It called for the formation of advanced centers for scientific, literary, and philosophical study in the university in addition to the professional schools, the formal training of professors, and economic independence for the university. To help achieve these goals, the FECH would fight for representation in the directive bodies of the educational system.

The hodgepodge of libertarian and socialistic principles embodied in this declaration reflected the multiple ideological currents at play within the FECH at this time. *Juventud* and *Claridad,* the principal FECH organs of the period, also revealed the turmoil of ideas that characterized these years—the agitated search for new impressions, the eagerness to know and emulate the work of others engaged in the great battle for freedom that was felt to be going on all over the world. The convention declaration was important because it was, in effect, a synthesis of many ideas; it represented a compromise measure that satisfied the more radical anarchist leaders as well as the larger body of moderates within the organization.

There was unanimity regarding the rank injustices of the existing social system and the need for students to strive to bring about a new and more equitable system. There was unanimity regarding the need for continuous protest and criticism of existing institutions, a passion for change, and a willingness to fight in the defense of the right of students and workers to make their voices heard. However, the very idealism and inchoate mixture of generosity, the spirit of sacrifice and patriotism that moved these young people, led them in part to believe that a system based on the selfishness and rapacity of a few would collapse under the weight of its own corruption. Moreover, the anarchists (followers of Kropotkin and Tolstoi), who were influential in injecting the high moral tone and the plea for self-perfection into the FECH declaration of principles, were actively preaching against the idea of revolution. They condemned very early the dictatorship of the proletariat as just another intolerable form of totalitarianism. The work of Marx was still relatively unknown among students. The convention declarations of the period are notably nondialectical.

Thus, although the intent and meaning of FECH action in this period was to overturn and destroy the old, its action was only marginally revolutionary. Youth was idealized as the only pure and disinterested critic of society; the FECH provided a forum for the competing voices crying the doom of capitalism. The new note was in the scope and aggressiveness of the attack, in the refusal to be silenced, in the close identification with the other protest groups, and, perhaps most notably, in the attempt to give broad theoretical and philosophical justification to FECH action and belief. It is not to their discredit that this generation failed to produce a coherent vision of the good society or how it was to be achieved. Their time was brief and embattled, and their ultimate frustration and disillusion loomed early on the horizon.

The change in the temper of the FECH—the elucidation of new and more radical objectives—was thus not accompanied by the institutionalization of violent or terroristic action. Although the aspirations and values of the FECH changed during these years and individuals or small groups within the FECH undertook action in keeping with the new revolutionary postulates, the main forms of the organization remained the same, and there was no radical innovation in the pattern of activities at most levels.

The 1918 constitution provided for a central association in Santiago (all schools of the University of Chile plus any secondary or special schools that wished to join) and a number of provincial associations. Although the provincial associations never achieved great importance, in 1918 and 1919 there were six such associations in Atacama, Coquimbo, Valparaíso, Santiago, Nuble, and Concepción.[30] A *junta general* (general assembly) of all members and a *directorio* (assembly of delegates) were the two deliberative bodies of the organization. An executive council, including a president, two vice-presidents, one secretary, a pro-secretary, one secretary of committees, a treasurer, and a pro-treasurer, was to orient the action of the two larger bodies and carry out their decisions. The president could be any active member, but the remaining officers had to be chosen from within the directorate and were elected by that body and not by a direct vote of all members. The directorate was made up of one delegate per course (year of study) in member establishments and by the presidents of the different school centers and recognized associations. Any change in the bylaws required study in committee, a three-fourths vote of the directorate, two-thirds of the *junta,* and the approval of the national government.[31]

The 1921 constitution varied only details of this formal setup, although it expressly provided that the FECH would never again petition the government for incorporation as a legal entity in view of the fact that recent experience (that is, the looting of FECH quarters in 1920) demonstrated that the rights and property of legal and private persons were violated with impunity in Chile. Particular school centers were allowed to form legal corporations, and the FECH, in fact, carried on its business and legal affairs under the corporate identity of the Medical School organization.

While the 1920 declaration of principles seems to represent a deliberated and hard-fought distillation of the conflicting sentiments of active participants, the formal mechanics of the organization were given much less thought. Few informants recalled more than the barest outlines of these provisions, although all of them had outstanding roles in events during this period. None remembered with certainty whether the FECH had ever been a legal corporation. The organizational setup of the epoch, they affirm, was characterized by elasticity and fluidity. This does not mean that the FECH action of the time was wholly without structure or regularity. It is simply that in this case the declaration and other documents provided a less reliable map of patterned behaviors than they did with regard to the ultimate values and goals discussed previously.

A great part of the student activity of the time was focused in the various university schools, which were dispersed throughout Santiago. It was common that those who achieved high office in the FECH had once been school delegates to the FECH and presidents of their school centers beforehand. The most important schools and the ones which gave most presidents and outstanding leaders to the FECH in this period were the schools of Medicine, Law, and Engineering. The Pedagogical Institute, the center for training secondary school teachers, also contributed some notable talent.

The qualities that were demanded and prized in higher-echelon FECH leaders are a good indication of the types of activities that took up most of the organization's time. The big names were made and the glory won in the directorate. Speaking ability was the prime requisite—the impassioned orator and the skilled debater were the men of the hour. The man who could present his viewpoint most forcefully and parry his opponents' thrusts most deftly had the best chance of building a personal following. The leader had to appear fearless and unswerving in principle, untouched by political venality or personal ambition. Although individual leaders were known sympathizers with given political currents, there were no *party* candidates, and identification as a disciplined party man would have been the kiss of death to a candidacy in most cases. The campaigns were run by close friends of the candidate, who, of course, shared his views, but the quality of the man, the weight of his ideas, and his moral stature were moving considerations. In these years of strife it was also a practical advantage for the candidate to have already completed his university training, for this put him beyond the reach of possible reprisals.

In each member school the FECH associates in each course chose their delegate to the directorate; the course also chose delegates to the school center. Theoretically, only those who had paid the nominal dues to the FECH and the center were eligible to vote; however, this was no serious impediment to voting, and anyone could speak his mind in any session whether he was a student or not. The delegates presided over the open meetings of their courses; they collected dues and kept a roster of members in good standing for their courses. They also kept the courses informed of events and decisions in the directorate and presented petitions or motions from their courses to the directorate. As course representative, a delegate was expected to be bound by the decisions of his constituents insofar as these were made clear to him; however, actual practice in this regard seems to have varied widely, as is to be expected.

The delegates to the school center and the school executives were the heart of the local organization. Here were met the day-to-day problems of student relations with school authorities, study programs, and examination schedules. Cultural and sports programs were maintained along with the traditional literacy training centers for workers and the professional services to needy students and workers offered by each center according to its field of specialization. The centers had almost complete local autonomy, although they were theoretically bound by the majority agreements of the FECH directorate. Relations between the FECH directorate and particular centers were occasionally strained, but crises such as the assault on the FECH usually brought a closing of ranks.

At the FECH level the main activity was that of agitation and propaganda. In the endless debates within the *directorio,* in the conferences sponsored by the protest groups of all ideological hues, in the meeting rooms of unions and political parties, from the improvised tribunes on the Alameda, wherever a few souls could be gathered and made to listen—student leaders could be found adding to the torrent of words that roared across the ears of the nation during these years. Several thousand copies of *Claridad,* the combative FECH organ published by a small group of anarchists, circulated weekly in Santiago and the provinces. Street demonstrations were frequent, and, by all accounts, easily set in motion. The concentration in Santiago of large numbers of unemployed provided a mass of curiosity seekers ready to tag along on any venture that promised excitement. It was enough for a few medical students to run shouting down Independencia from Plaza Chacabuco (near their school) toward the river Mapocho and downtown Santiago. A crowd of several hundred, shouting just as loudly, would gather behind them before they had gone more than a few blocks. A clash with the police was inevitable and regarded, in part, as a sportive event. When the FECH was urged to reconstitute itself explicitly and exclusively as a propaganda organization, no radical change in FECH function was implied. The critic, a confirmed positivist, was merely calling for a recognition of the realities of FECH action and urging that it be put on an efficient basis.[32]

From the beginning the FECH officially defined its membership broadly; it sought to embrace all university students as well as those in secondary schools and specialized-training establishments. Despite these liberal definitions of membership, the FECH was regarded to be, and was in fact, the organization of the students of the University of Chile in Santiago. Valparaíso law students had their own federation, affiliated to the FECH, and there were also university students in Concepción. Students from the Catholic University in Santiago also occasionally participated in FECH-sponsored organisms or campaigns. But the FECH belonged to the University of Chile and to Santiago, the cultural and political nerve center of the country.

Another significant aspect of membership practice was the custom of electing honorary or extraordinary members to the directorate from among former FECH presidents or outstanding alumni. This, coupled with the fact that the FECH presidents during these years were almost all young men who had already completed their university careers, assured the FECH throughout this period leadership of a high caliber and lent the organization a prestige and dignity it would not have enjoyed with less mature men at its head.

The claims of the organization on its members were only vaguely defined—what a particular student contributed rested largely upon his own disposition, the effects of circumstances, or the enthusiasm that particular leaders could stimulate. The only permanent levy on members was a small amount paid as dues. However, this was never thought of as a real source of income; even if it had been paid by all, the total collected would have covered only minor organizational expenses. The big sources of money income were the spring festivals, which were especially successful in 1918 and 1919. The years that followed saw a gradual decline of public interest as well as competition from the rival student federation created in 1921. In truth, from the time of the assault on the FECH club in the middle of 1920 until the end of the period covered here, the FECH was in continual financial straits.

On the other hand, the organization during these four years from 1918 to 1922 did not seem to suffer any shortage of manpower. That is to say, while there was not 100 per cent participation by all students, the level of commitment and spirit of participation was strong enough so that no FECH activity languished because of the lack of enthusiasm of members. Enough eager participants were about so that the leadership was occasionally hard put to think up outlets for the energy of the rank and file.

Though the spirit of dedication and sacrifice was high, not many members were called on to run serious personal risk. The most dangerous activities were the sorties into the Alameda where encounters with the police were inevitable, but even in those days no one was expected to defy the armed policemen. It was perfectly respectable to run when the police charged, although the impulsive and the reckless few who stood their ground grew in the estimation of their companions. The police in Santiago did not carry firearms at that time, so that the main danger was from police clubs, the lances of mounted contingents, and sabers. Students seldom faced the prospect of more than a few hours or a night in jail for participation in any demonstration; the ringleaders of particular campaigns against university authorities were sometimes expelled, but could always look forward to reinstatement after things had blown over. The point here is that for the great mass of students, FECH participation did not mean commitment to unusual self-sacrifice or extreme personal risk. Students were able to serve to some extent as shields for workers because the student *did* enjoy certain immunity. The same policeman who could club a worker mercilessly to the ground would normally be more gentle with the student.

Just as there was little that was regularized or well defined about what the FECH had the authority to command or could expect from its members, so was there little stability in the resources it obtained from outside groups. The university provided help on particular projects, such as the operation of the Popular University, student welfare, and social and cultural activities generally. However, this was always at the discretion of the pertinent authority, and each petition had to be negotiated individually. There were also no permanent channels for the exchange of organizational resources either with unions or with political parties. There was a continuous interchange of information, a frequent sharing of publicity channels, and often joint undertakings—but these exchanges were not coordinated or regulated in any formal way. They depended entirely on circumstantial contacts and the urgencies of the moment.

The FECH leaders of this period, looking back, pride themselves on the independent spirit of the organization. One of the chief charges they make against today's students is that they are servile to party interests. The Convention Declaration of Principles of 1920, of course, declared that the FECH would carry on its work "independent of all external influence." However, no live organization is devoid of all external influence; it is a matter of uncovering what kind of relations the FECH sought and managed to maintain with key outside groups in these years.

As has been remarked, from its earliest days the FECH enjoyed an informal voice in university affairs. This was particularly the case of student organization at the school level; that is, it was normal for the director of a school to discuss problems affecting the school with the local student executive, and for student representatives to bring their problems to school authorities. The principal clashes with the university administration were not strictly related to university problems. It was when the rector, as a member of the Council of Public Education (the body which directed all education in Chile), participated in decisions which students felt were made under government pressure that protest was most vociferous.

Thus, the news of the revolutionary Córdoba University Reform of 1918 stirred less excitement in Chile than in countries like Peru and Mexico. Although the University of Chile was still far from being the "republic of learning peopled by the builders of the spirit and the creators of truth and beauty" envisioned by the Argentine reformers, neither was it the stronghold of reaction and clericalism that the students in other countries were struggling to rouse to twentieth-century realities.[33] The extension of learning to workers via the university and her students was an established tradition in Chile well before 1918; that same year the Lastarria Popular University had been established. Moreover, the more radical leaders, who dominated the FECH during most of this period, considered that the isolated reform of the university was a chimerical goal. According to them, as long as the university depended on the government and the government rested on a system of semi-feudal and capitalistic exploitation, all such reforms were bound to be frustrated. Since the real revolution was more or less imminent, there was no point in distracting attention and resources to the secondary task of democratizing the university. Not until near the end of this period, when the FECH was at a low point in organizational strength, did the Chilean students incorporate into their demands on the university the basic points of the Córdoba program.[34] The question of university reform faded into the background until the 1930's.

Relations with the university administration, then, were much like those between any two independent power blocs. With regard to political parties, the matter became more complex. Although relatively few students or leaders were militant members of political parties, many were known sympathizers of one or the other of the leftist parties of the time. The principal division was less by party than by those who believed in the efficacy of political action via parties and those who condemned all parties as venal and corrupt interest groups. In the former group were Radicals, a small wing of the Liberal party, some Democrats, and partisans of the Workers' Socialist party, later to become the Communist party of Chile. The fact seems to be that lines between these two main groups and among the parties mentioned here were never sharply drawn. The things that separated the youthful partisans of one group or another were fine points of doctrine or belief that interfered little with day-to-day collaboration and friendship. There was a continuous crossing of ideological lines, and there were no disciplined party units within the university.

The political organization with which the FECH had most direct relations was perhaps the *Centro de Propaganda Radical*. This center was the organization of Radical party youth. Theoretically it was meant for young men between the ages of fifteen and twenty-one, but many stayed on long beyond this. The Centro was important as a sounding board for the socialistic ideas which Radical youths and their leftist friends and tutors wished to see the Radical party embrace more wholeheartedly.

It is this outgoing, propagandizing action that is most characteristic of FECH contacts with organized political groups at this time. Even those who most bitterly opposed the Radicals in the FECH as politicians of the same unsavory stripe as their elders, now admit that they were not simply party tools. Actually, the Radical party had always been known as a stronghold of Freemasonry, and some of the young Radicals in the FECH were known to be initiates of the secret order. In the hard-fought FECH election of 1921, the anarchists launched a campaign charging that Radicals and Masons had no right to occupy FECH posts since they were subject to the discipline of a secret authority. *"Ni masones, ni radicales!"* was the battle cry. However, this campaign seems to have been inspired as much by passing tactical considerations as by the general opposition of anarchists to all forms of authority, particularly authority operating under the cloak of secrecy. There is little evidence of any widespread feeling at the time that the Masons were, in fact, trying to manipulate the FECH for their own secret advantage, although when a few months later the rival student federation appeared on the scene, it was suspected that the Masonic lodges had had a hand in the affair. Be that as it may, it can be said that in these years it was not the FECH that was infiltrated and manipulated by external political forces, but FECH youth who penetrated the established leftist parties with the call to abandon narrow, partisan bickering and join the great crusade for freedom and social justice.

Despite the close bonds of friendship and the unity of sentiment of students and workers in these years, there were similarly
no organic or formalized ties with labor unions. The principal
contribution of the FECH was made via the Popular University
and the speakers and lecturers it sent at the request of the unions
to the meeting places of workers. There was a continuous
exchange of invitations to send representatives to meetings and
demonstrations planned on both sides, but no permanent co-
ordinating body existed. The group of students in direct contact
with workers was relatively small, but the general attitude was
one of solidarity on both sides.

There were two major labor organizations in Chile in the early
1920's. The Workers' Federation of Chile (FOCH) brought together a large number of trade unions, mutual benefit societies,
and a few syndicalist and "resistance" groups which gave the
federation a combative cast after 1919. Through its great leader,
Luis Emilio Recabarren, it was closely tied to the Workers'
Socialist party. The FOCH has been compared to the United
States' AFL, which it resembled insofar as the main lines of
organization were on the basis of trades or crafts. The FOCH
believed in the political action of workers through popular
parties, and Recabarren, who led the FOCH into the Third
International in 1921 and transformed the Socialist party into the
Communist party of Chile, occupied a parliamentary seat during
these years. The domination by Moscow of national Communist
parties that came in the Stalinist era had not yet been implanted,
although Recabarren did visit the Russian capital in 1922 for the
Fourth Congress of the Communist International.[35]

The International Workers of the World (IWW), with its
program of direct action, disdained participation in the parody of
democratic government which, according to their views, party
organization and elections constituted.[36] They opposed the formation of workers' parties, urged workers to refrain from voting,
and, in later years, resisted organization as legalized unions when
a labor code was finally dictated in Chile. They also fought for
the organization of unions on an industry basis rather than a
trade basis. The IWW had a strong influence on the FECH. Some of
the most notable FECH leaders of this period were very closely
identified with IWW activity. It won many adepts, particularly
among medical students, and the fact that the official FECH organ,

Claridad, was owned and operated by anarchist sympathizers gave it a powerful propaganda medium that was identified with student opinion.

The collaboration between workers and students in these years has on occasion been described in a way that would lead one to believe that students took on the role of tutors to their unlettered compatriots, providing them with cadres of organizers and programs of action. This is true only to a very small extent—throughout this period the workers were a much stronger and better organized force than the students. The students taught the rudiments of reading and writing, broadened the cultural horizon of many workers, attended to their medical needs, and, perhaps most importantly, demonstrated on a sizeable scale for the first time in Chile that true friendships across class lines were possible. Many of the friendships born in those days subsist to this day, and their significance in later political developments and for the individuals concerned is not to be underestimated. Moreover, there were among the workers a number of notable figures who, because of the purity of their idealism, their wide-ranging curiosity and knowledge, and their abnegation and disinterest, proved inspiring models for students. The students taught and learned, gave help and were helped in return. The FECH did not lack dissenters who preferred that it keep more distance from worker groups, but the keynotes of the period were sustained protest and solidarity with the workers.

In the Ranks of the Intransigents

There were in 1920 approximately 5,800 students in establishments dependent on the University of Chile.[37] Of these, some 3,500 were in the major professional schools such as Medicine, Law, the Pedagogical Institute, Chemistry and Pharmacy, Engineering, Dentistry, and Architecture. The first three schools alone accounted for over 2,500 of the above figure, and these highly rated schools dominated the life of the FECH. Students in these schools normally ranged in ages from seventeen to twenty-five years, although not infrequently individuals stayed on for longer periods. It was also not uncommon for students to combine more than one course of study (particularly law with the course in philosophy in the Pedagogical Institute). Ideological reasons also led some in these years to abandon halfway the study of "parasitic professions," such as law, to dedicate themselves to more humanitarian pursuits, such as medicine or dentistry. All of this contributed to keeping a fairly mature group active in FECH affairs, especially since graduation in itself did not cut off the alumnus from participation. In the years from 1918 to 1922 the FECH was an organization of youth, but (especially in its leadership) it was not in the hands of juveniles.

Although the university had opened its doors to women in 1877, there were still relatively few women among the students. Not more than a handful of these were involved in FECH activities at any time during these early years.

The majority of students came from modest middle-class homes. They were the sons of small businessmen, school teachers, and white-collar workers in government and commercial establishments, with a sprinkling from among the more successful artisans and skilled workers. Professionals were not very numerous in the country and could not replace themselves from their own ranks. The most proper and desirable careers for aristocratic youths were politics, diplomacy or other high government employment, and the management of estates or industries. The only worthy profession for them was that of law, although engineering also attracted some upper-class youths. As a general rule, however, the situation of the student, especially in pedagogy, was modest and often marked by privation.

Large numbers of students came to the University of Chile in Santiago from the provinces, especially from the area of Concepción in the south, from nearby Valparaíso and other cities in the central provinces, and from the *Norte Chico*—the mixed farming and mineral region lying between the nitrate wastes to the north and the fertile central valley. Regional origin does not seem to have had any importance in itself; that is, there is no evidence of any organized defense of *regional interests or viewpoints*. However, it is known that provincials tended to gather in pensions according to region of origin. They are also reputed to have been among the most active and the most extremist elements in the FECH. A healthy proportion of the best known leaders of this period came from outside Santiago. While the extreme north and the Concepción area have traditionally been focal points of leftist agitation in Chile, few students came from the mining regions or had direct contacts with workers before coming to Santiago. Their militancy does not seem to have been a transfer to Santiago of a regional viewpoint. It may be explained in part, without doubt, by the new freedom that big-city anonymity gave to these small-town youths and by their liberation from the restraints of close family supervision.

Foreign students as a group also did not figure importantly in the FECH in these years, but the incidence of foreign names among outstanding leaders of the time should be remarked. It is not possible to muster any statistical evidence to show that immigrants or the sons of immigrants were playing a bigger part in directing FECH affairs than their total number in the university would call for. However, it is certain that men who were themselves immigrants or the sons of immigrants unmistakably left their stamp on the organization during these years and came to personify the FECH in the public mind. It is no less certain that those who attacked the FECH fastened on the fact that these spokesmen for the FECH did have foreign names, thereby insinuating that the organization was in the hands of subversives, imported agitators, and Jews. Within the FECH, on the other hand, foreign birth or Jewishness could prove a positive advantage in that the elevation of such individuals to office was one way in which students sought to certify their lack of prejudice.

The overwhelming majority of students in this period were by all accounts politically independent. The consensus among informants is that a broad plebiscite, with the participation of all students, would have produced a majority of moderate leaning to the right. However, as we have seen, the most active students and the most important leaders were declared enemies of everything that smacked of tradition in Chile. They were early labeled indiscriminately "Bolshevists" or "maximalists," although these names really referred to the activist wings of two different parties in Russia, neither of which had any connection with the FECH.[38] These extremist groups, who were growing dissatisfied with the slow tempo of FECH action by the end of 1921, formed a number of societies modeled on student anarchist clubs in Argentina. The best known of these, *Lux,* functioned in the Medical School. Together with others of its kind, such as *Spartacus* and *Insurrexit,* a Soviet of Students was formed in 1921.[39] *Lux* was for some months very powerful and probably represents the only disciplined political group to function within the FECH in this period. When the group despaired of giving a truly revolutionary cast to the FECH's action, it began to attack the "bourgeois collaboration-ism" of the student organization and to call for its dissolution.

Who then *was* the FECH in these years? Like most organizations it had a number of identities. In moments of crisis or jubilee (the spring festivals) it was nearly all students as well as their many sympathizers. On a day-to-day basis it was, first of all, those who paid their dues and voted in local elections in each school—perhaps 2,500 to 3,000 students. Of these, perhaps a third became involved in organizational activities at the school level. Business of the federation itself and meetings of the directorate, except in times of unusual excitement, received sustained attention from no more than 150 to 200 members (a generous guess). The heart of the organization was in the directorate—in the forty-five or fifty school delegates who regularly attended meetings. Most of all, and especially in the public view, the FECH was the handful of leaders that were the voice of the organization.

Such crude statistics provide a vision of the *working bodies* available to the organization at different levels under ordinary circumstances as well as a few of the major characteristics of the membership. They are not in themselves an index of organiza-tional strength or debility, the efficiency of manpower for the tasks undertaken, the responsiveness of members at different levels to the organization's demands, the vision and acumen of command and co-ordinating elites. However, criteria such as these are almost impossible to apply in this context. Except for those routinized tasks that the FECH inherited from its more peaceable predecessors and that were carried on beneath the turmoil and agitation of this period, the prevailing climate was one of instability and vagueness, of great passion but little order. The community of agitators sought to create for itself a state of mind and to communicate it to others. Precise definition of rights and obligations was antithetical to the spirit of the enterprise; administrative success brought little in prestige or celebrity. The main arena of action was the FECH directorate, the assembly of delegates and presidents from the schools. Here the spokesmen for the several points of view represented within the FECH made their most impassioned appeals—each leader with his small circle of sympathizers sought by every device of exhortation and parliamentary stratagem to swing the sentiment of the directorate in favor of the proposal or candidacy espoused by his group.

Debate was often on an elevated plane, but elections were not always without an element of force or fraud. Some did not find it easy to accept defeat, and others were always prepared to embark on mischief of any kind, especially if some political advantage could be derived therefrom. By the middle of 1921, groups like *Lux* were functioning as disciplined claques in the directorate and in school assemblies. While the *Lux* group had won respect for its idealism and for the integrity of many of its members, their action was resented by more moderate elements who found themselves stampeded by the *Lux* phalanxes. In May, 1921, *Claridad* carried a small item that suggests the gradual change taking place in the etiquette of political combat during these years:

> One of our readers, a subtle observer, writes us: "In all the school centers the electoral battle for Presidents and delegates to the Student Federation has taken a different turn than in previous years. In general, violent means have prevailed, contrary to the Federation's Declaration of Principles which recommends that "rational and evolutionary" means be used as far as possible.
>
> "In the course of these disturbances the roll of members has been stolen in 4 schools; the lights have gone out in the course of sessions in 6; in 3 the partisans of opposing contingents have exchanged blows; revolvers have been drawn to cow adversaries in 2; a shot was fired in 1; 3 students have been injured and 7 have suffered contusions; and finally, students have insulted each other to such an extent in 15 schools that if these insults were placed side by side a chain extending from Santiago to Puerto Montt [a town in the extreme south of Chile] would be formed.[40]

The element of sheer mischief—of mocking authority and tradition, the elaborate practical joke, the sharp, sardonic thrust in debate—is an integral part of Chilean political life. This is a native talent, carefully cultivated by its more successful exponents; more than one political or journalistic career has been built on little more than quick wit and the ability to produce at the right moment the precise, caricaturing phrase.

There were other opportunities to give these qualities play in the FECH besides floor debate, parliamentary strategy, and election campaigns. However, the great mass of students was not involved in the elaborate pranks or the behind-the-scenes skull sessions and caucusing that went into promoting a candidacy or squeezing a "declaration" or *voto* through the directorate. They were, in fact, seldom called on to do anything for the FECH beyond paying the small amount in dues and voting in the election of class delegates.

The chief recurrent events that required large-scale mobilization of attention and participation were elections and the spring festivals. The indirect system of voting for top FECH posts kept elections focused on the local scene. Although candidates to high FECH offices made stumping tours of the schools to help insure the election of school delegates which were favorable to them, the election for the all-important offices of FECH president and secretary was of vital concern only to those students whose interests ranged beyond the school organization as such.

Between the top leaders and the great mass were the school delegates and presidents, as well as those who ran some of the relatively stable FECH and school activities. The numerous study centers run by the schools and the Popular University may be included here. The various clinics which offered, among other primary services, treatment for venereal infections for workers and unlucky students, as well as other professional services to members and the needy public, should also be counted among them. The publication of the magazine, *Juventud,* was carried on over a number of years, as was *Claridad.* There was, in a sense, a built-in proto-bureaucracy with some continuity at the lower levels of the organization. Here were accommodated many of the less extremist and flamboyant leaders, the second echelon who gave some permanence to FECH action. Side by side with those who called for the destruction of the capitalist society or heralded its imminent collapse, many continued to work whose chief concern was to service some of the victims of the system.

The Person of the Agitator

The generation of 1920 is the "great man" era of the FECH. There have been many outstanding leaders before and since then, but it was in these years that individual personalities stamped FECH action most indelibly. An entire folklore has grown up around these magic names. In times of crisis, the glorious days of this generation are recalled and held up as the noble tradition to be sustained. Down through the years, since the legend was launched, FECH leaders have measured their own performance and worth against the yardstick of the real or imagined achievements of that generation.

The paragraphs that follow probe into the early family lives of a few of these men, trace their professional and political careers, try to reconstruct some of their ideological development, and report on their present attitudes toward political and economic problems in Chile. No claim can be made that these are the most representative men of the period in any statistical sense. Extensive biographical material was obtained for only eight of these major figures. Several of the most colorful leaders of the time have died prematurely—a number of them by their own hand. A few others were out of the country on diplomatic missions during the year of field work. These men have been labeled "agitators," without wishing to imply that they constitute today a single political or personality type. Nor has any attempt been made to reconstruct in full the personality organization of these individuals as it was thirty-five years ago. They have played different roles within the FECH leadership and have followed disparate paths politically since leaving the university.

Nevertheless, these men were in the forefront of FECH action at a time when the organization was predominantly an instrument of agitation. Their behavior as youthful leaders, though responding to a variety of motives which are perhaps impossible to unearth at this distance, can be presumed to have had some links with early childhood experiences and family relationships. There are also presumably some enduring facets of personality and cognitive organization that may be revealed in the interviews.[41] The approach taken in this study assumes, moreover, that these men did not rise in the FECH by sheer accident, but that they had some qualities individually or as a group *before* they moved into leadership that allowed them to perform successfully as FECH leaders at that particular time. Given the limitations of the data, nothing that is genuinely conclusive can be reported on any of these points. Still, it is of interest to know something about the backgrounds of some notable leaders of the 1920 generation and to follow their political careers beyond the university.

The eight leaders who were interviewed came from middle-class families—their fathers were farmers, school teachers, small businessmen, a building contractor, and an army officer. Most of them were born and raised in provincial cities far from the capital, Santiago. Four of the eight men were the sons of immigrants—a Sardinian, a German, a Rumanian Jew, and a French Swiss Calvinist. However, nearly all of them had Chilean mothers.

Neither the fathers nor the mothers (with minor exceptions) had received much formal education. Although, by and large, the fathers were Masons and anti-clerical by inclination, in general these agitators did not come from intellectual households. These were solid bourgeois families, ranging from fairly well-to-do landowners to modest, but respectable, small-town school teachers. As a group, they were set apart from the Chilean middle-class norm principally by their moderate nonconformism as well as the foreign origin of the fathers.

These leaders of the 1920's were in 1956 between sixty and sixty-five years of age. They were all professionals—lawyers, engineers, a dentist, physicians. Some combined professional with political or academic careers; they included a university rector, a well-known penologist, and more than one former cabinet minister and diplomat. Four of these eight leaders of the 1920 generation might be considered professional politicians. They had held high office in political parties (the Radical and Socialist parties), sat in the legislature, and occupied ministerial and diplomatic posts. They remained public figures, although all four were on the sidelines politically at the time of interview. Two more might be considered party regulars—they were Radicals and had never belonged to any other party, but they had never held important political office. The remaining two had never found party life congenial. They had held to their principled individualism, and, except for episodic flirtations, had remained aloof from political organizations.

It is with regard to the nature of the self-image that it becomes most difficult to generalize about this small group. Within a general framework of realism and objectivity about the self, one encountered varying degrees of capacity for introspection, insight, and frankness. The two doctrinaire individualists provided perhaps the most detached self-appraisals, with a calm cataloguing of shortcomings and a critical perspective on achievements. Both men were idealistic, full of humanitarian impulses, who had had little success in dealing with people. Both had withdrawn into the laboratory. One, an engineer, confessed that he has had no success as a teacher—students did not learn from him in the classroom, although he felt able to demonstrate things in a practical way in the laboratory. The other, a physician, had abandoned private practice for laboratory work. As a student, he evaded surgical duties because he was unable to stand inflicting pain or the sight of blood. Later, he found himself unable to practice the small deceptions that physicians use to calm the hypochondriac or neuropath; he rejected the element of quackery that remains an intrinsic part of the therapeutic process. He sought subsequently to establish himself as a family physician—the friendly counselor in time of crisis—but found himself being exploited and passed up for more fashionable practitioners behind his back. These are presumably minor infidelities encountered by all but a few doctors. They produced not anger or bitterness in this man but chagrin and disappointment. For him, the pettiness and inconstancy of patients meant, not only that they were withholding love, but also that it was impossible for him to love them. At any rate, both men faced squarely their own inadequacies and were not overwhelmed by them. They continued to pursue an ideal of self-perfection—an internal and individual harmony that must build on the inner resources of the person alone.

The two party regulars had followed rather conventional paths in their professions as well. They lacked the intellectual passion of the two men just discussed and showed no signs of the almost morbid self-criticism to which the others seem to be given. They showed flashes of vanity, but their prestige claims were couched in symbols of middle-class success—discipline and regularity in work and the approval and esteeem of superiors and colleagues that they enjoy. They were the only two subjects who took some pains to document the comfortable economic situations of their families in childhood and whose interviews showed no references to personal fallibility or weakness.

Two of the four professional politicians that are still to be discussed were founding members of the Socialist party in Chile. This party was formed in 1932, although, as we have seen, there were socialistic movements in Chile well before that year. Both men were frustrated physicians: one almost completed his medical studies after repeated interruptions of his university career because of political problems of one sort or another; the second had been unable to study medicine because of economic difficulties. Both seemed to be suffering from extreme political exhaustion. Without entering into a history of the party here, it may be said that there has been enough tragedy, failure, deceit, and shortsightedness in its past to give pause to any man. Both of these men continued to believe (albeit half-heartedly) in the possibility of building a Socialist party with strong popular roots and a realistic program of reform in Chile. Experience told them that party organization is indispensable, but they no longer had much stomach for mass politics. Since they were beyond self-deception, their disillusion bordered on cynicism.

The remaining two subjects are almost prototypes of a particular kind of agitator. Both were FECH presidents between 1918 and 1922 and were reputed to have been among the most fiery orators of the time. In the years since then, they had never been far from the public eye. They remained colorful and controversial figures. They have been called professional politicians here mostly because they have been close to political events throughout most of their lives—they have been closest to the Radical party although they have always been political mavericks.

They displayed perhaps the most frankly narcissistic streaks of all these leaders, revealed in part by a readiness to celebrate at length their own achievements. However, this tendency toward self-glorification was offset by a capacity for self-deprecation and mockery. It fell short of the immodest because their candid enjoyment of the telling made these accounts appear like boyish bids for applause.

Frank enjoyment of their own superiority and the power they had to move others was also readily perceivable in the words of these men. Of the leaders of this period who were interviewed, these two alone radiated self-confidence, an assurance of self-potency. They alone were still involved in the struggle to impose their will, to have their way, to establish their ascendancy. They seemed cut off from the conventional supports of family, friendship, party, and religion. Their struggle with the world now appeared to be a personal one, devoid of political content or direction.

The present political attitudes of these men probably ran the full gamut of non-Communist leftist thought in Chile today, with considerable overlap into ideas held by groups considered to be right of center. The generation of 1920 has never won much praise from Chilean Communists, who have generally viewed with contempt the intellectual and organizational indiscipline and the lack of a truly revolutionary perspective of this anarchic and anarchistic group. The prominence of leaders of the 1920 period in the Radical and Socialist parties has served to exacerbate these tensions since the three parties have been battling for control of the voting Chilean left for nearly a quarter of a century.

The kinds of varying political positions that these men took at midstream in the 1950's has been suggested in the discussion of self-images. It will be useful to retain the informal grouping into political types which was suggested in that discussion: the withdrawn individualists, the party regulars, the party builders, and the political virtuosos. The two nonpolitical men defined the present crisis as a moral and individual problem. According to the first, there is not enough attention given to the intellectual and moral training of leaders. The left is suffering from activism without principles. Young people are caught up into political parties too early and have no chance to study independently. The ignorance of youth about non-Marxist socialist writers is abysmal. Personal spiritual independence must be won in order to seek solutions that go beyond narrow party interest. The second nonpolitical man defined the problem as economic but handled it in a similar way: Chile's basic difficulty is one of production—people all earn more than they produce. Chile must look to education as a way of changing these habits in her people. People must acquire the *mystique* of work.

Only one of the party regulars gave details of his present views. He celebrated a then-recent and substantial gain in votes by the traditional parties at the expense of personalistic fractions as symbolic of the great civic culture of Chileans. He applauded a governmental program aimed at curbing inflation, calling his own party's opposition to the plan demagogic. Although his party's official position is socialistic, he said that the government should orient, but not dominate, the economy and that he is against stringent government controls himself. He remarked that the masses are better off today than ever before in Chile, noting that in recent demonstrations against high prices almost all those marching wore shoes and neckties.

Chile's main problem, according to the first of the Socialist subjects, is the reorganization of the industrialization process. The aspiration level of consumption among all sectors is beyond the capacity of the country to produce. Political leaders are as much to blame as businessmen for the present crisis. An independent socialist force that is not so strongly influenced by Communists is needed in order to use to best advantage the opportunities for foreign aid which are indispensable to Chilean recovery.

The second Socialist asserted that socialism must lift itself out of its narrow class orientation. It must help *man*—not only the worker, but the other classes who suffer the effects of capitalism, the mechanization of life, the tensions of competition in a profit-oriented economy. The conflict of party and individual interests clouds the issue and makes an early solution improbable. The left is weak and without clear aims. It must regain its moral ascendancy by forgetting the old clichés and producing a program which closely reflects popular needs and is possible to realize. He also warned that the Communists must be isolated, or at least not allowed to dominate in any leftist combination.

Full civil liberties, the decentralization of government, and a controlled economy are the cardinal points of a national reconstitution, according to one of the two political "virtuosos" in this group. The masses in Chile are prone to Caesarism because the parties tear each other down. The leftist parties were unused to governing and went to pieces in power. Therefore, personalistic leaders are able to appear on the political scene as national saviors. The parties are engaged, as always, in a mad scramble for power, but political stability can only be built on parties. The country has hit bottom. He saw the establishment of several free ports as symbolic of the political and economic disintegration afflicting the nation. He assigned great importance to the factor of "chance" in history, ascribing momentous events and changes in the course of Chilean history to the unpredictable conjunction of chance factors, looking on much of his life as similarly determined by luck or random, unforeseeable events.

The prevailing tone in this political material, as in other biographical information, was one of realism and objectivity. Even though a clear relation exists between the political history of the individual and his proposed solutions for present problems in Chile, there was little evidence of stereotyped or "ticket-thinking" in the discussions. It is true that the nonparty men emphasized individual regeneration or education as a solution, that the party regular expressed the "middle-of-the-road" optimism of his own party, that the builders of socialism continued to hope for the achievement of the millennium, and that the "virtuoso" showed especial preoccupation about the place of the great man and the chance factor in political developments. However, emphasis on one factor did not lead to gross oversimplification or deterministic thinking. The attitude of these men was by and large analytical. They singled out no group or individual to load with guilt for the nation's difficulties; they raised no heroes and sought no scapegoats to pillory.

This is probably one of the most remarkable revelations of the interviews. Through most of their adult lives all of these men have been engaged intellectually, if not actively, in the political battleground of the struggle to achieve social reforms in Chile. Yet the interviews betrayed almost no sign of lurking political animus, of any deep-lying hatreds or resentments that act as the affective impulses behind political views and actions. There was aggression in these interviews but not blind rebellion against the powerful or diffuse rage directed at the weak. Attacks on others were focal and personal, intellectualized, and occur usually in response to rejection from a loved person. This control of aggressive impulses may, of course, be related to the relative maturity of these individuals. If it could be shown to constitute a general characteristic of Chilean political attitudes, it would go a long way toward explaining certain distinctive phenomena of Chilean political history—namely, the talent for the bloodless coup and the almost total absence of real revolutions despite internal tensions that are no less severe than those of neighboring countries where revolutions are the order of the day.

Linking present political perspectives to early childhood experiences and attitudes toward parents is complicated by the remoteness of childhood for these respondents as well as by the fact that conflicts that may have been potent motivating forces at earlier periods may have been resolved in the intervening years. These men have matured and mellowed; none of them are the firebrands they were thirty-five years ago.

Three characteristic threads linked the early family histories of these men; all three contradicted the conventional stereotype of the patriarchal Latin family. There was a certain amount of idealization of both parents on all sides, but it was the *mother* who emerged from almost all of these accounts as the strong character—the driving, stabilizing force within the family. The status aspirations of the family seemed to flow from and were channeled by the mother. She was the one most concerned about the education and career choices of the young ones; she dispensed discipline or dictated the sentence to be meted out by the father. The image of the father being punished by being forced to punish the children was evoked repeatedly.

At the same time there was little evidence of close childhood identification with the father. The main theme was one of distance—the male parent spent a great deal of time away from home, had died young, was a severe pedant or an ineffectual dreamer. The tyrant father appeared in only one case (a Calvinist fanatic on *punctilio*). Minimization of the father constituted a second very characteristic note in the interviews. Fathers were described as good at heart, well intentioned, but *mild* in character—timid, noncombative, and unrealistic (especially in business or financial affairs). There was a patronizing tone to many of the comments about fathers.

Early separation from the family and independence from parents was the third biographical data that tied these men together. Those who came from the provinces to study in the capital made their lives in Santiago and never returned to the parental home for more than brief visits. Their own households were not extensions of the patriarchal circle; once separated from the parents, communication seemed to have been sporadic and superficial, except in times of family crisis.

The description of parents by these men had the ring of

objective appraisals. There was little vindictiveness or adulation in their accounts. Both positive and negative qualities were mentioned for both parents in almost every case. Nevertheless, even the perspective of the years did not seem to have brought about a complete resolution of some childhood and adolescent tensions vis-à-vis parents and other intimate, affective figures. Without embarking on speculations about the precise mechanisms by which these tensions may have found expression in political attitudes and behavior in 1920, the interviews pointed to some conflict over problems of dominance and submission, masculinity and femininity, in almost every one of these cases. These conflicts may be thought of as especially laden with meaning in a culture in which male dominance is made almost a fetish. While the Chilean woman is among the most emancipated in Latin America, and the cult of virility and male superiority finds somewhat less crude expression there than in other Latin American countries, the dominant value pattern still assigns unquestioned ascendancy to the male. This he may temper with indulgence but only as long as his rightful predominance goes unchallenged.

Similar preoccupations cropped up in the discussions of friendship. These subjects claimed to have few true friends at present, and several said they had no one that completely meets their criteria of friendship. There was surprising unanimity about the quality most sought after in friends—unquestioned loyalty, sincerity, and disinterest. None of the men complained about duplicity on the part of ostensible friends; their experience with others seemed more disappointing than embittering. They gave an impression of disconnection, of short-circuited social libido. They demanded too much or had too little to give. Almost all recognized personal limitations that block more friendships of a conventional nature and that made the kind of friendships they really wanted almost impossible. An incapacity for the easy barroom camaraderie that is the basis of many male friendships in Chile, ideological incompatibilities, the vicissitudes of political party life—all have limited the maintenance of intimate, enduring friendships. The only subject who revealed a manipulative attitude toward friendship—focusing on the material advantages to be derived from having well-placed friends—was at the same time the one who took the most conventionalized view of the meaning of friendship. The prevailing note was one of love seeking, of an unfulfilled longing for unconditional acceptance and nurturance. The easy flattery and adulation of the political circle had never attracted some and had failed to satisfy others.

The group manifested heterogeneous religious roots, although the present attitude of its members toward religion and the existence of God was at best one of tolerant skepticism. The general pattern for Catholic, Protestant, and Jew was one of early religious training and some religiosity up to adolescence, and then a turning away from religion at that time, with only token opposition (usually from the mother). This was accompanied by the tacit approval of the fathers (most of whom were indifferent to religion or actively anti-clerical). Present views ranged from a vague deism, through indifference and agnosticism, to a principled atheism. The adolescent transition seemed to have been effected with little internal or overt conflict. None of these men were rabid anti-Catholics, although politically they had all attacked the church as an institution. Religion did not seem to be an area of personal tension for these subjects.

Practically none of the tentative hypotheses formulated about the personality organization of these 1920 leaders seems borne out in the interviews.[42] This may be attributable in part to the fact that we are looking at "agitators" thirty-five years after the fact, so to speak. Some conflict over dominance and submission, stemming from rigid patterns of authority within the family, was hypothesized. It was further predicted that this first generation of student leaders would show a lack of critical perspective toward the self and in-groups, a high capacity for diffuse moral indignation, and the exteriorization of aggression. Lastly, these subjects were expected to show few status tensions in conventional terms but a dependence on applause and immediate gratification in social relationships. Of course, none of these propositions has been submitted to rigorous tests in this study (the exploratory nature of this section in particular has been stressed previously).

Some evidence of childhood and adolescent conflict over problems of dominance and submission has been found, with the reversal that it is the passivity of the father, rather than the rigid enforcement of parental authority, that seemed the focus of tension. Realism and objectivity are high among these subjects on all topics discussed; they showed, in general, a well-balanced perspective on the self and in-groups. Externally directed aggression seemed controlled and not excessively affect-laden. In a highly status-conscious culture, these former leaders made few appeals to conventional prestige symbols in order to certify their standing. However, the early autonomy from the family and sustained independence of these men were coupled with a pattern of unfulfilled love-seeking and frustrated social libido.[43]

It is probably fruitless to speculate about the significance of these personality patterns for the political behavior of more than four decades ago. The general serenity of outlook displayed may be the fruit of experience and the prize of advancing years; the underlying concern about friendships may reflect the loneliness and isolation that may also come with age. On the other hand, the reversal of expectations is so complete that a fundamental error in approach may be involved. It seems quite probable that these hypotheses about the psychological concomitants of political radicalism are to some extent culture-bound. Gabriel Almond's study of Italian and French Communists suggests that psychological maladjustment plays a much smaller role in bringing recruits into the party in those countries than in the United States.[44] The findings of this and later chapters support the conclusion that Chilean radicals may be much like their fellows in France and Italy in this regard.

Summary

The foregoing discussion has presented various perspectives on university-student organization of a particular epoch in Chile. Attention has been focused on broad historical trends, on events in which the student federation itself was a main actor, on the institutional framework that the student organization took from and gave its action, on the people acting within the organizational fold, and on the personalities of some major figures of the time. The usefulness of this multi-faceted approach to organizational analysis lies primarily in the detailed generational comparisons that it makes possible. Nevertheless, some indication should be given here of how the material from these different levels for this base-line period can be seen to work into a coherent whole.

The final years of the nineteenth century and the first decades of the twentieth century were years of expansion for the middle class in Chile and of incipient organization of the workers—artisans, miners, and those in the gradually growing industries. The economic crisis that followed World War I threatened to wipe out hard-won gains for the middle class and for the combative organized fraction of the workers. The instability and irresponsibility in government that had characterized the years of parliamentary rule became intolerable in the face of economic ruin. Abroad, the success of the Russian Revolution gave reality to the hope that the past could be erased, and that a new era of economic and political equality was within reach. The prophecies and exhortations of the anarchist and socialist ideologues, whose writings had been circulating in advanced middle-class and labor circles for twenty years, suddenly took on fresh meaning. When a presidential candidate (Alessandri) appeared promising just these things in ringing and persuasive terms, many were ready to believe that salvation was at hand.

It was in this setting that, almost overnight, the FECH began to take on the classic stigmata of the charismatic mass movement. The keynotes were a complete repudiation of the past, an attitude of permanent criticism and intransigence, a claim to omni-competence, all of which were validated in terms of broad humanitarian principles thought to override all claims to legitimacy of the old order. It was a time of personalism in the leadership, of unstable and vague organizational lines, of similarly vague definitions of membership and their obligations, of relative indifference to economic and administrative problems. Although the organization was not totally absorbed into the agitational and propagandistic effort, the main function of the group became one of sustained protest.

But the passion and zeal for change fell short of the revolutionary—terror and violence never became established modes of action. The quantum of animus that revolution requires seemed to be absent, the pressures dissipated in rhetoric. Some of those who were thought of as the most radical leaders of the time certainly are not angry men today. However, even back in 1920 they seem to have accepted the limits of their role as propagandistic. The incidents of property destruction were sporadic and isolated; there is no record of organized student aggression against persons other than minor scuffles with police. The students were more often the victims than the attackers. Most students were moderates throughout the period. They were at heart placid, respectable, middle-class individuals. It was the leadership that swept the mass along into the forefront of the clamor for change. It is around the leaders that the legend has grown, and it is they who in many ways have contributed to keeping it alive to this day.

NOTES

1. Alberto Edwards Vives, *Bosquejo Histórico de los Partidos Políticos Chilenos* (Santiago: Editorial Ercilla, 1936). See also, by the same author, *La Organización Política de Chile* (Santiago: Editorial de Pacífico, 1943); and *La Fronda Aristocrática*, 4th ed. (Santiago: Editorial del Pacífico, 1952).

2. Julio César Jobet, *Ensayo Crítico del Desarrollo Económico-Social de Chile* (Santiago: Editorial Universitaria, 1955); and *Los Precursores del Pensamiento Social de Chile,* 2 vols. (Santiago: Editorial Universitaria, 1955–1956). Hernán Ramírez Necochea, *Historia del Movimiento Obrero en Chile* (Santiago: Editorial Austral, 1956). Marcelo Segall, *Desarrollo del Capitalismo en Chile: Cinco Ensayos Dialécticos* (Santiago: Editorial del Pacífico, 1953).

3. Oscar Fabres Villaroel, *Consecuencias Socio-Económicas de la Guerra del Pacífico* (Memoria del Instituto Pedagógico, Universidad de Chile, 1937). This thesis is not sympathetic to the traditionalist viewpoint being described here, but provides a full discussion of the social and economic consequences of the War of the Pacific.

4. Edwards Vives, *Bosquejo Histórico de los Partidos Políticos Chilenos.*

5. A survey of Chilean monetary policy going back to the last century is provided in Frank Whitson Fetter, *La Inflación Monetaria en Chile* (Santiago: Universidad de Chile, 1937).

6. Ramírez Necochea, *op. cit.,* chap. 4.

7. *Ibid,* chap. 5. See also Jobet, *Ensayo Crítico del Desarrollo Económico-Social de Chile,* chap. 2.

8. Carlos Vicuña Fuentes, *La Tiranía en Chile* (Santiago: Imprenta y Encuadernación O'Higgins, 1945), Vol. I, gives a graphic account of the persecution of "subversives" in Chile in the first two decades of the century. Other essays covering the period include: Guillermo Feliú Cruz, *Chile Visto a Través de Agustín Ross (1891–1924)* (Santiago: Imprenta y Encuadernación Pino, 1950); Tulio Lagos Valenzuela, *Bosquejo Histórico del Movimiento Obrero en Chile* (Santiago: Imprenta el Esfuerzo, 1941); and Aristódemo Escobar Zenteno,

Compendio de la Legislación Social y Desarrollo del Movimiento Obrero en Chile (Santiago, 1940).

9. For a biography of a heroic figure in Chile's early labor movement, see Fernando Alegría, *Recabarren* (Santiago: Editorial Antares, 1938).

10. The writer has leaned heavily for the material in this section on Luis Galdames, *La Universidad de Chile (1843-1934)* (Santiago: Universidad de Chile, 1934).

11. A running commentary on the controversy appeared in the Santiago daily, *El Ferrocarril*, throughout most of the month of August, 1906.

12. Valentín Letelier, *Filosofía de la Educación* (Santiago: Imprenta Cervantes, 1892).

13. *El Ferrocarril* (Santiago), August 6, 1906. In the following weeks and months periodic reports on developments concerning the new student organization appeared in this daily. Additional details were obtained in personal interviews with student leaders of the time.

14. The abbreviated designation of the Student Federation, FECH, did not come into popular usage until the 1930's. A student paper called *FECH* was first published in May, 1937. The term FECH is nevertheless used throughout this study as a shorthand term for the Student Federation of Chile.

15. *El Universitario*, Organo Oficial de la Federación de Estudiantes de Chile. Nine numbers appeared between July, 1916, and August, 1917.

16. *Censo de Población de la República de Chile: levantado el 15 de diciembre de 1920* (Santiago: Imprenta y Litografía Universo, 1925).

17. Alfonso Lastarria Cavero, *Chile, Geografía Económica* (Santiago: Imprenta Cervantes, 1923).

18. Amanda Labarca, *Realidades y Problemas de Nuestra Enseñanza* (Santiago: Universidad de Chile, 1953). See also, Eduardo Hamuy, *El Problema Educacional del Pueblo de Chile* (Santiago: Editorial del Pacífico, 1961).

19. Carlos Keller, *Un País al garete; Contribución a la Seismografía Social de Chile* (Santiago: Editorial Nascimiento, 1952), p. 64.

20. *Ibid.*, chap. 1.

21. Arturo Alessandri, *Recuerdos de Gobierno (1920-1925);* (Santiago: Editorial Universitaria, 1952), Vol. 1. Refer also to Armando Donoso, *Conversaciones con don Arturo Alessandri* (Santiago: Biblioteca Ercilla, 1934); and Ricardo Donoso, *Alessandri, 50 Años de Historia Política* (México: Fondo de Cultura Económica, 1952). The last volume covers this period in the life of the controversial president in considerable detail. Vicuña Fuentes' biting commentary on these same events *(op. cit.)* provides additional intriguing sidelights. The student organ, *Claridad*, published regularly throughout this period, reveals the shifting attitudes toward Alessandri among students.

22. *Zig-Zag*, XV, No. 758 (1919).

23. This account of FECH events has been pieced together and cross-checked through personal interviews, magazines, newspapers, and other published and unpublished sources.

24. A full issue of *Juventud*, II, No. 11-12 (1921), the official FECH magazine of the time, was given over to a report of the events leading up to the assault, the attack itself, and the aftermath of the rioting. *Zig-Zag*, XVI, No. 805 (1920),

carried several pages of photographs of the participants on both sides and the damage done to the student club.

25. Carlos Vicuña Fuentes, *La Libertad de Opinar* (Santiago: Imprenta Selecta, 1921).

26. Gabriel del Mazo, *Estudiantes y Gobierno Universitario* (Buenos Aires: Editorial el Ateneo, 1946).

27. *La Nación* (Santiago), June 2, 1925.

28. This Declaration of Principles is reproduced in its entirety in *Juventud*, II, No. 11–12 (1921).

29. *Juventud*, I, No. 3 (1919).

30. *Juventud*, I, No. 3 (1919).

31. The FECH was legally incorporated by Decree 1726, dated November 20, 1918.

32. Carlos Vicuña Fuentes, La Cuestión Social...., p. 73.

33. Del Mazo, *op. cit.*

34. *Claridad*, II, No. 59 (1922).

35. Julio César Jobet, *Recabarren* (Santiago: Prensa Latinoamericana, S.A., 1955), p. 55.

36. *Acción Directa*, Organo de los Trabajadores Industriales del Mundo. Thirty-five issues were published in Santiago between June, 1920, and May, 1926.

37. Lastarria Cavero, *op. cit.*

38. As explained in *Claridad*, I, No. 27 (1921), the Bolsheviks were the activist wing of the Social Democratic party, and the maximalists were their counterpart among the non-Marxist social revolutionaries.

39. *Claridad* carried reports on the activities of these groups throughout 1921.

40. *Claridad*, I, No. 17 (1921).

41. As was noted in the Introduction, the interview guide and method of analysis for the data on social backgrounds and personality of student leaders were modeled closely on the qualitative interviews in T. W. Adorno *et al.*, *The Authoritarian Personality* (New York: Harper & Brothers, 1950). Although the fact of ethnocentrism was not at issue here, the syndrome of the "high" scorer and the "low" scorer seemed to provide a sound framework within which to explore the links between attitudes toward authority, political ideology, and certain aspects of childhood experience and social background. (Refer to Part II of the above volume, "Personality as Revealed through Clinical Interviews," by Else Frenkel-Brunswik.

42. These hypotheses predicted that the 1920 agitators would approach the high scorers, the authoritarians of the Adorno study, in a number of respects. The predictions were based on existing analyses of the personalities of charismatic leaders and professional agitators. See, for example, Max Weber, "The Types of Authority and Imperative Coordination," *Theory of Social and Economic Organization*, trans. A. M. Henderson and Talcott Parsons (New York: Oxford University Press, 1947). See also: Harold Lasswell, *Psychopathology and Politics* (Chicago, Ill.: University of Chicago Press, 1930); and Eric Hoffer, *The True Believer* (New York: Harper & Brothers, 1951). The literature on mass movements and radicalism (political and religious) in the United States has generally emphasized the pathological and neurotic aspects.

43. This pattern checks out in almost every respect with the low scorers on

authoritarianism. "... unprejudiced individuals often manifest an unrealistic search for love in an attempt to restore the type of early relations they enjoyed within their family." Adorno *et al., op. cit.,* p. 388.

44. Gabriel Almond, *The Appeals of Communism* (Princeton, N.J.: Princeton University Press, 1954), pp. 380, 394.

Chapter 2

The Party Militants (1936–1940)

Dictatorship and Depression

The gradual decline of the FECH and its formal dissolution in 1925 brought to an inglorious close the burst of student activism sparked by the 1920 generation. For all practical purposes, students ceased to function as an organized force until about 1930, except for local school problems. There were, of course, politically minded youths who were active in the coups and counter-coups, both realized and thwarted, that succeeded one another until General Ibáñez finally consolidated his hold on political power in 1927. Also, throughout these years there were periodic efforts by leaders from different schools to reconstitute a university-wide student organization. Students as a group, however, remained on the sidelines.

A strongly biased but detailed account of President Alessandri's ouster by military coup in the fall of 1924, his triumphal return on the wave of a second bloodless coup early in 1925, his success in re-establishing the power of the executive via constitutional reform in that same year, and his final defeat at the hands of General Carlos Ibáñez is given in Carlos Vicuña's *La Tiranía en Chile.* Another perspective on these events is provided by Alessandri's own volume of memoirs, *Recuerdos de Gobierno.*[1] By and large, students remained aloof, playing only a peripheral role in these events. The open assumption of political power by the military had caught students in a state of disorganization from which they did not recover for several years.

Several reforms of the statute governing the university were decreed by the Ibáñez government beginning in 1927. These

79

reforms tended to strengthen the university, granting it some financial independence, expanding its facilities, and providing special status in the state bureaucracy for university professors. In December, 1928, students were given representation on faculty councils at the government's request, and formal provision for a university-wide student organization was made in the university statute.[2] However, as the Ibáñez regime took on an increasingly dictatorial cast, there was stronger student repudiation of the university authorities, who were seen as the agents of the military strong man. A new, official student organization was rejected, much like its predecessor in Alessandri's time.

The mounting sentiment in favor of revitalizing the FECH had no particular political intention. In fact, students sought to disassociate themselves from others who were against the Ibáñez regime for political, partisan motives. This included almost all the traditional parties, which had been reduced to almost complete impotence,[3] and also supporters of former President Alessandri, who continued to conspire against Ibáñez from exile in Paris and Buenos Aires as well as within Chile. As the foreign credits on which General Ibáñez had maintained a large-scale program of public works and expanded his government services began to dwindle, the effects of the economic crash of 1929 began to be felt in Chile. A vicious cycle of discontent, protest, and repression went into accelerated play.[4]

By 1931, the full effects of the collapse of the world money markets in 1929 were being felt in Chile. Copper and nitrate exports had fallen off 89 per cent in those two years, probably as terrible a foreign trade disaster as any country had to face at that time.[5] The heavy payments required to service the large foreign loans that had gone to finance the public works and other government operations during General Ibáñez's regime proved a heavy drain on the gold reserves of the Central Bank of Chile, an institution established upon the recommendation of an American economic mission in 1925.[6] In June, 1931, the government finally suspended payments on foreign obligations. The government budget had been shaved to a fraction of its former size; the salaries of government employees were cut and their number drastically reduced. The curtailment of mining operations in the north loosed a tragic caravan of hungry and jobless that roamed the countryside, creating alarm. Santiago became the stage for the public display of the despair and misery of thousands who came from other parts of the country to add to the numbers of unemployed already in the capital.[7]

Like many another head of state of the time, the Chilean dictator found public anger and resentment focusing on his person. His frantic efforts to smash any attempt to give this diffuse, popular discontent political form and direction served only to exacerbate public sentiment against him. Meanwhile, his political enemies sought to fan the general anxiety for their own ends.

It was in this tense setting that a mass meeting called by students to map details of the reconstitution of the FECH declared a strike in protest over the dismissal by Ibáñez of a cabinet minister, Juan Esteban Montero, a university professor. The dismissal of Montero was interpreted as an indication that Ibáñez was determined to proceed without regard to individual rights or legal norms, and the students decided to occupy the university, announcing that they would abandon it only upon the restoration of civil rights in Chile.[8] The heroic gesture of the students was hailed by the public. Some small arms found their way into the university, and shots were exchanged between the students who were barricaded behind its massive walls and the police and soldiers surrounding it. However, no serious attempt was made to dislodge the students by force; instead, representatives of the government came to parley with student spokesmen.[9] The students were finally persuaded to abandon the university by a ruse, but the government was already tottering. By then, a wave of strikes was sweeping the country, principally among white-collar workers, professionals, and small businessmen.[10] The government collapsed when medical personnel joined the passive-resistance movement after the shooting of a physician just as he emerged from a meeting in which doctors had agreed *not* to strike. Ibáñez resigned and fled the country. In the public jubilee that followed, students were hailed as the heroes of the day. Their leaders were called upon to help pacify the crowds that now turned their animosity on the police, who were seen as one of the chief instruments of Ibáñez's regime of violence. Montero, the minister whose ouster by Ibáñez had led the students to strike, took over as provisional head of state. A new slate of university authorities acceptable to the students was named, and the first moves toward the re-establishment of a civil and constitutional government were taken.

The united effort to form anew the student federation and to give civil liberties meaning once more in Chile had masked a beginning and definitive cleavage in student ranks. The Communist party had dwindled into a small, select, underground group during the Ibáñez regime. Early in 1931 there appeared in the university the group *Avance*. It brought together a carefully chosen number of Communists, variegated Marxists, Socialists, and independent leftists. Whether or not the Communists themselves began it, they are generally acknowledged to have been in control almost from the beginning. For the next few years, *Avance* was, in effect, the arm of the Communist party in the university. Parallel to the formation of *Avance* and partly as a reaction to it, a group of progressive Catholics shaped a second organization, *Renovación*. Politically, *Renovación* was identified with the Conservative party, although within the party it represented a youthful reformist current, imbued with the spirit of the social reforms embodied in papal encyclicals and the program of the Catholic Action. Between these two groups there functioned a number of independents, outstanding leaders with personal followings, representing diverse ideological currents. An influx of Peruvian students who were fleeing dictatorship in their own country brought the influence of the *Alianza Popular Revolucionaria Americana* (APRA) to Chile in new force in 1932.[11] The first election for the new FECH in 1931, just after the overthrow of Ibáñez, ended inconclusively with charges of fraud on all sides and the withdrawal of one of the candidates. A provisional executive committee was set up, but the lack of unity and the inexperience of leaders meant that the students won far less by way of reforms in the university than they might have obtained at this favorable juncture. *Avance* came forward with an intransigent program of reforms that was a Marxist adaptation of the postulates of the Córdoba Reform movement.[12] They demanded equal participation for students in running the university, the elimination of all fees and entrance requirements, and complete liberty of teaching and expression (that is, anyone who could muster an audience should be allowed to teach, and professors and students should enjoy immunity for any ideas expressed within the university). In response to these demands, a mixed commission of professors, students, and alumni was formed to study the complete reorganization of the university. During the first months of 1932 this commission worked out a plan for a wholly autonomous Central University of Chile. The university was to be governed at all levels by committees formed of professors, students, and alumni in the proportion of 4:2:1, respectively. The rector was to be elected by a *consejo superior* whose decisions were not subject to review. Students were to enjoy immunity for all expressions of opinions and ideas pronounced within the university, whether or not these were considered incitations to criminal acts. A long-range program to build up a financial endowment that would make the university independent of yearly appropriations by the government was included. A draft of this law was transmitted for study to the national legislature in March of 1932.[13] Agitation for its immediate acceptance filled the following months. In June, the *Avance* candidate to the FECH presidency beat the candidate of the *Renovación* group by a small margin, and the FECH had its first legally elected president since 1925.

On the same day that the new FECH president took office, still another bloodless coup unseated President Montero and declared the establishment of the Socialist Republic of Chile. This short-lived Socialist experiment was the bizarre product of the political disorganization that engulfed the country upon the fall of Ibáñez. At least a half-dozen socialistic factions mushroomed during these months. Divisions within the Communist party had arisen over internal local problems, and these were in competition for recognition by the Third International. The labor movement was reborn divided, just as it had passed away under the dictator.[14] The older parties, weakened and discredited, maneuvered feverishly to arrive at some coalition of forces around which a stable government could take form. Partisans of Ibáñez, Alessandri, and new aspirants to power sought by every means to turn the confusion to the advantage of their man. The military clubs, the ships, the garrisons of the armed forces were besieged by politicians seeking armed support for projected uprisings. There was no dearth of conspirators among the officers of the several services.[15]

Circumstance drew together a strange triumvirate from this turmoil of competing forces—Colonel Marmaduke Grove, Eugenio Matte Hurtado, and Carlos Dávila. Colonel Grove had been reinstated as commander of the Air Force in order to thwart any attempt by General Ibáñez to enlist support from airmen for a counter-coup. Matte, a prominent lawyer with socialistic ideas and a high position in the Masonic hierarchy, was prepared with the armed support of Grove to seek a socialist solution to Chile's desperate situation. Dávila, a former diplomat and newpaper-man, had evolved a plan of his own for a state-controlled economy and had the support of the commander of the School of Infantry, Colonel Pedro Lagos. Although the elected president, Juan Esteban Montero, was unable to muster any armed force against Grove and Matte when their intentions became clear, Colonel Lagos with his infantry was able to impose Dávila and a General Puga as additional members of the new socialist junta. The junta dissolved the legislature, declared a thirty-day morato-rium on commercial debts, and returned to the public all the unredeemed personal property held by a *Caja de Crédito Popular* (a sort of national pawnshop). There was talk of making a small gift in money to every man, woman, and child in the Republic.

These measures were naturally hailed with enthusiasm by the impoverished masses in the capital but were denounced as demagogic by more conservative elements. The Communists did not support the new Socialist state. Moreover, the indecision of Grove and Matte permitted Dávila to consolidate his position. Twelve days after the three had taken power together, Grove and Matte were on their way to exile on Easter Island, and Dávila assumed full control.

Although students were probably inclined to favor the new Socialist state, and efforts were made from the beginning to obtain their support, the FECH remained aloof for the most part from Grove and Matte. Leaders of *Renovación* were asked by the revolutionary junta to reassure the Catholic hierarchy that the church had nothing to fear from the new government, but the group maintained a reserved and watchful attitude nevertheless. When the Communist leadership of the FECH through *Avance* dictated the taking of the university as a "precautionary" measure, the new government made a conciliatory gesture, sending a representative to assure the students that they also had nothing to fear. All students who had been suspended or expelled, or who faced prosecution on political counts, were reinstated. In addition, the junta passed, by fiat, the project for reforming the university that had been presented by the committee of professors and students shortly before. For a few days students and professors together ran the university.

Despite these efforts to court the students, a Communist-controlled Revolutionary Council of Workers and Farm Laborers (CROC) began to meet within the university with the avowed purpose of building the people's soviets that were to move into power upon the disintegration of the infant Socialist Republic. Dávila showed no forbearance to students. After students refused to accept the conditions under which he offered to maintain the new university statute, he simply closed the university, arrested most of the student leaders, and shipped them to various points of the Republic. He also closed the FECH headquarters and confiscated their files, library, and other materials. An attempt by a handful of student supporters of Grove and Matte to occupy the university was smashed without compunction. A cannon was rolled up to the main entrance and the gate blown open with one round. Troops marched in and dragged out the youths, who were brought before a military tribunal and threatened with the death sentence.

The harsh regime of Dávila, which ironically retained the designation of Socialist Republic, lasted about one hundred days. His arbitrary procedures and the inefficacy of the measures taken to deal with the still desperate economic crisis soon lost him support in all quarters. Early in September he was forced to resign, and a few weeks later his successor, General Blanco, faced still another military rebellion. However, the pressure for a return to a legally constituted civil regime was strong, and the elections that Dávila had promised for October, 1932, were held.

Arturo Alessandri, now the candidate of moderate middle-class forces calling for constitutionality and order, won a resounding victory at the polls.[16] Once again the Lion of Tarapacá had sensed accurately the mood of the electorate. The next six years would see him shed the role that had been his a decade before—that of prophet and saint to the oppressed. He was to govern with the support of the traditional parties of the right (Conservatives and Liberals), protected, in the first uncertain years, by a civilian militia of middle- and upper-class patriots.[17]

The new president stepped into a chaotic situation. He faced an overwhelming foreign and domestic debt, mass unemployment, a threat of epidemic as a result of the deteriorated sanitary conditions in the country, a restlessness in the armed forces that in the face of recent events was not reassuring to the new government. Taking full advantage of the constitutional reforms he had himself imposed in 1925, Alessandri took over with a firm hand. The broad constitutional powers held by the executive were further reinforced by extraordinary faculties granted to the new president in April and December of 1933. An end was put to the merry-go-round of cabinet ministers that had persisted throughout the years of parliamentary government and beyond that. A Republican militia, which at one time had 50,000 men under arms throughout the country but whose existence was officially disclaimed, served to neutralize any thought of unseating the government by force. An upturn in the sales of nitrates and copper brought new money into the national coffers and new activity in the mines. Under the able manipulations of Gustavo Ross, Alessandri's controversial Minister of Finance, national credit was restored, the foreign debt was again serviced, the marketing of nitrates was centralized under government supervision, construction was stimulated, commerce and industry took an upswing, and, by 1936, unemployment had almost disappeared. However, much of this recovery had been financed through paper money issues by the Central Bank. The inflationary effects of this policy fell most heavily on the workers, whose wages failed to keep pace with the increasing cost of living. But Alessandri would tolerate no opposition and had the legal means to stifle all protest in the extraordinary faculties granted him by the legislature and a later Law of Internal Security. The opposition parties, divided and persecuted, put up little effective resistance. It was not until the "popular front" began to take shape as a coalition in 1936 that the real struggle was declared between Alessandri and his beloved masses of the twenties.

Dávila had struck a hard blow to the already faltering FECH. Although there were sporadic strikes by students during 1933 and 1934, all hope was lost of achieving the kind of over-all reform that had been projected by the commission of professors, students, and alumni in 1932. The mass of students was disillusioned and apathetic. The FECH presidential election in 1934 was close enough so that both the leftist group and the *Renovación* candidate claimed victory. No compromise was reached, and a schism was produced. For a year the two groups pretended to function as the official representatives of students, who, by and large, were indifferent to both. Efforts were made to revive the student festivals of earlier years and to found a new Popular University, with only limited success. It was in this weak and divided state that the FECH entered upon the second period that is to be studied intensively, the rise to power of the "popular front."

The Chilean Popular Front

The ancient enemy—the persistent evil of harsh economic and social inequality coupled with political repression—remained at the roots of student and popular discontent. By the end of the 1930's, Chile's population had shot to nearly five million (from approximately four million in 1920). It remained a youthful population; more than half were in the reproductive ages between fifteen and fifty-four.[18] The movement into urban places continued; the population of the capital, Santiago, had almost doubled and now approached nearly a million. Still, a crushing infant death rate kept the average life expectancy down to 41.8 years. Although this represented an increment of about ten years over the average life span in 1920, as late as 1937 it was estimated that half of the infants born alive died before reaching the age of nine, most of them before reaching age one.[19]

There had been a substantial degree of economic recovery after 1933, under the astute direction of the financier Gustavo Ross. Ross figures as the silent hero or the chief villain of the epoch, depending on the source consulted, but he is generally acknowledged to have been something of a financial wizard. However, despite Ross's fiscal legerdemain, in 1939 mineral production still lagged below the 1927–1929 peaks.[20] Copper had displaced nitrate as chief export and source of foreign credit. Industrial production had increased substantially, but remained in an incipient, protected stage of high costs and low productivity. Small enterprises were still the rule—there was one employer for every fifty industrial workers in Chile (compared to 1 for every 770 workers in the United States). Eighty-six per cent of the commercial establishments in Chile were operated by their owners (compared with 31 per cent in the United States).[21] A minimum-wage law, scaled to living costs and passed in 1937, benefited only white-collar workers. A balanced budget, new public works, the re-establishment of foreign credit, and the limited industrial growth had done little to change the hard conditions of life for most Chileans.

The small gains in national productivity were more than offset by population growth and by the loss in value of the national currency as inflationary pressures mounted. By 1939, the cost-of-living index had soared to 186.7, taking 1928 as the base year. As a matter of fact, per capita consumption was not to reach pre-depression levels in Chile until 1952.[22] The large agricultural population had almost no buying power, and in no line of activity was the wage scale adequate to take care of an average worker's family. In 1940, only about one-third of the population were among the economically active. Poor pay and the large number of dependents per employed person kept the standard of living down to the subsistence level. Illiteracy continued to be high; only one in five of the children who enrolled in elementary schools succeeded in reaching the sixth grade. In short, as the country approached the final years of the decade of the thirties, grinding poverty, disease, alcoholism, and early death were commonplaces of Chilean life.

It was at once a time of despair and of great hopes. If the students of the 1920's saw in the Russian Revolution and in World War I signs of the imminent collapse of capitalism, those of this period saw about them what appeared to be the final wreckage of a society based on greed. The question was what to build on the ruins. Events at home and abroad were to cloud the basic issues and confuse the struggle to achieve a more humane social and political balance in Chile. The political battle to be joined in the country and within the university was to be in many ways but a shadow-play of the world-wide ideological and armed skirmishes leading up to World War II.

While there was little progress to point to in the economic sphere and little change in the material conditions of life for most Chileans between 1920 and 1936, politically there had certainly been great changes. The chief new situational element in this second period is, in fact, the presence of several new parties and the direct action of political groups within the university. The chief actors within the university in the drama that unfolded in these years between 1936 and 1940 were the Communist party, the Socialist party, and the National Socialist movement. The Radical party, although it served nationally as the middle-class anchorage of the popular front that was soon to give an illusion of victory once more to the voting left in Chile, had only secondary importance within the university. The Liberals and Conservatives, the governing parties from 1933 to 1938, similarly had few supporters in the state university. A Social Christian current, stemming from the early Renovación group of young Conservatives, was to come into its own politically as the Falangist party, but only toward the end of this period.

The Socialist party was established in Chile in April, 1933. It was a fusion of nearly a half-dozen Socialist splinter groups that had appeared in the months after the fall of Ibáñez and during the year of the abortive proclamation of a Socialist Republic in Chile. The new party declared itself Marxist in doctrine and revolutionary in intent. It was attacked bitterly by the Communists and systematically persecuted by the Alessandri government. Nevertheless, it mushroomed into a powerful voting force; in 1937, the Socialists obtained 46,050 votes (11.2 per cent of the total), electing nineteen legislators. The Socialists at first resisted Communist overtures for a popular front in Chile. They tried to maintain a leftist bloc of their own but were out-maneuvered by the Communists. In the end, they joined in the popular front and contributed importantly to its victory at the polls in 1938. Unlike the Communists, they participated directly in the new front government.

The Socialists came upon hard times almost as soon as they got into power. Their running battle with the Communists was intensified, especially after the Nazi-Soviet pact in late 1939. Personal rivalries among party leaders, revelations of corruption among party men in office, and ideological differences among the heterogeneous elements represented in the party weakened its action. Late in 1940, the uneasy collaboration of the Socialist and Communist parties within the popular front was broken definitively. Despite the withdrawal from the Socialist party of a dissident fraction which insisted on an exclusive working-class front *(Partido Socialista de Trabajadores),* the Socialists in 1941 polled 17.9 per cent of the national vote. During the period with which we are concerned here, the Socialist party was the leftist group with the broadest popular base.[23]

The National Socialist movement *(Movimiento Nacional Socialista)* was formally organized in Chile in April, 1932. The movement called itself "Nazi" from the beginning, and although disclaiming any direct links with German or Italian fascism, it adopted the paramilitary organization and other outward symbols of European fascism. The movement was not conceived as a political party but as a direct-action organization. The Nazis never became a threat electorally, but the unaccustomed violence that they introduced into political life in Chile gave reality to the anti-Fascist slogans of the popular-front era. The failure of the movement to take hold in Chile has been explained by its chief, Jorge Gonzáles von Marees, as reflecting public disillusion with strong men (the country had just shed Ibáñez), the failure of the public to recognize the weakness of the party form of organization, and national blindness to the threat of communism.[24] In their earliest statement of aims, the Chilean Nazis declared, ". . . the highest mission of the State must be to control and regulate private activities in order to impel every individual to render a maximum of efficiency for the benefit of the collectivity. Its intervention in all national activities is therefore licit and necessary." This early manifesto also declared that the parliamentary form of government was anachronistic, and that a select and disciplined hierarchy, fully empowered and responsible, must occupy the highest positions.[25] The ruling coalition of Liberals and Conservatives was attacked as a decadent and corrupt vestige of the moral elite that had led Chile to greatness in the nineteenth century. The Chilean Nazi movement was shattered in a bloody massacre following an attempted coup by a small group of Nazi youths just before the 1938 presidential election. Ironically, the death of these creole storm troopers (they were designated within the party as *Tropas de Asalto*), some of them university students, assured the electoral victory of the popular front.

In the early 1930's, Chilean Communists, like their fellows in other countries, maintained an aggressive and intransigent attitude toward all other leftist groups. Although they suffered equally with other Marxist and non-Marxist revolutionaries through the early years of Alessandri's second term, they continued to denounce all non-Communists as bourgeois deviationists and class traitors. The Seventh Congress of the Third International in July, 1935, heralded an epoch of intense activity for the Chilean Communist party. That meeting announced the new policy of united peoples fronts against fascism, and Chile was designated as the proving ground in Latin America for the popular front. A delegation of Moscow-trained party notables was dispatched to Chile, under the leadership of the Peruvian Eudocio Ravines, to assume direction of the enterprise.[26] Their success in revitalizing the party and in launching the Chilean popular front made Chile for a time the focus of attention of the party in the hemisphere and aroused widespread admiration and sympathy from leftists throughout the world. The party tripled its votes in parliamentary elections between 1937 and 1941. In 1937 the Communists elected six deputies and one senator; in 1941 they seated fifteen deputies and three senators.[27]

The possibilities of success for the popular front rested almost entirely on the chances of winning over the Radical party for the new leftist coalition. According to Ravines himself, the apathy and timidity of the established local Communist leaders were the greatest obstacles to his work in Chile. It was the young men in the Communist party, non-Communist intellectuals, and sympathetic Radicals who laid the groundwork for the new front. The party opened its arms to all who could serve the new cause.

The Communists found some of their most ardent supporters for the popular front among left-wing Radicals who opposed the collaboration of their party with the ruling Liberal-Conservative coalition. The death of one of the most prominent leftist Radicals, Pedro León Ugalde (numbered among the famous student leaders of the 1920 generation), was taken by Communists as an opportunity to extend a hand in friendship to the Radicals. The funerals of popular public figures in Chile often turn into mass demonstrations of public affection, and León Ugalde's burial seems to have been one of the most spectacular of all time. Communists turned out en masse to honor the Radical leader, and one of the party's most able orators, Marcos Chamudez, called on all Chileans to unite in the fight for liberty and against fascism.[28] Communist support for Radical candidates was given freely in the following months. As the Communist party demonstrated its growing vigor and apparent disposition to collaborate unstintingly in behalf of its allies, the resistance among old-guard Radicals and Socialists and Trotskyites gradually gave way. The insistence of the Communists that the next president of Chile must be a Radical helped to seal the new Communist-Radical friendship.

In February, 1936, Justiniano Sotomayor, a Radical deputy, officially proposed to his party that it join the popular front.[29] The Radical Assembly of Santiago approved his proposal in March of that year. Soon thereafter, representatives of all the leftist parties met, and the popular front in Chile became a reality. To all outward appearances, the Radicals were the chief architects of the new unity of the left, and a Radical was named to the presidency of the new people's front.

The emergence of the popular front in Chile is not simply a testimonial to the resourcefulness, patience, and daring of international communism. Certainly Communists were able to exploit the cupidity and ambition of a few politicians and to turn to their own advantage the cynicism and idealism of others, including many in their own ranks. But the popular front had meaning and captured the popular imagination in Chile because it fulfilled an existing need. The harshness of the economic and social situation for workers and the lower middle class has already been described. The presence of a native Nazi movement, still small but increasingly aggressive, gave actuality to the announced menace of international fascism. The mounting antagonism against President Alessandri and his minister Ross Santa María was another powerful impetus for the unification of the popular parties. It was clear that a divided left had no hope of dislodging the Liberal-Conservative government in the upcoming presidential election. There were manipulators and dupes among Communists, Radicals, and Socialists—the popular front was an uneasy entente from the start.[30] Few of the men who served to forge it—whatever their political loyalty—can look back on the time entirely without remorse. Still, as did Alessandri in 1920, the popular front seemed to promise a new day in Chile.[31]

One of the immediate side effects of the front was a unification of labor unions. There had been repeated gestures between 1931 and 1936 to unite the various craft and industrial organizations of workers in Chile. The passage of social legislation and a basic labor code by military edict in 1924 had divided Chilean unionism into "free" and "legal" wings. One camp (chiefly the anarchists and Communists) rejected the tutelage of the state over labor and repudiated social legislation as a reformist sop to bourgeois consciences. This split in workers' ranks made their organizations easy prey for the dictator Ibáñez. Still, the end of the Ibáñez regime in 1931 saw Chilean unionism rise again, just as divided as when it had gone under a few years earlier. The political fragmentation of the left in the years immediately following compounded the effects of the older cleavage and frustrated all moves toward unity.

The year 1936 opened with a drawn-out violent strike of railway workers that touched off a wave of labor disputes in other fields. The government responded with the declaration of a state of siege and by calling up military reservists. Alessandri also sought extraordinary faculties from the legislature to deal, not only with the labor unrest, but also with the threat to public order represented by the newly constituted popular front. He failed to get these because of a stalemate in the senate. However, armed with an earlier Law of Internal Security, he was in a position to harass labor leaders and the political opposition with arbitrary arrests and relegations.

The new unity of the leftist parties was soon reflected in more cordial relations among the myriad organized labor groups. Labor leaders from all corners of the Republic met in a mammoth convention in Santiago during the last days of December, 1936 and created the Workers' Confederation of Chile (CTCH). The CTCH accepted the Marxist thesis of the class struggle to build a socialist state in Chile. It also proposed to work for the improvement of existing social legislation, in this way accepting the basic principle of state collaboration in solving the problems of labor. Although it was originally felt that the confederation should remain aloof from all political ties, in the middle of 1937 it entered officially into the popular front.

Some idea of the work of the confederation can be drawn from statistics on the number of disputes in which it became involved.[32] In 1937, the CTCH figured in the resolution of 204 labor conflicts affecting 38,358 workers; in 1938, it took part in 188 conflicts affecting 48,394 workers. In the first six months of popular-front rule in 1939, 267 labor conflicts were resolved favorably in benefit of 32,354 workers. By the end of 1940, there were some 1,888 unions in Chile, with 171,297 members. Not all of these were in the CTCH—an important group of anarcho-syndicalist shoemakers, bakers, and construction workers were united in a General Confederation of Workers (CGT). Some white-collar and state employees had made stabs at organizing themselves, but sporadic campaigns to stir farm workers and small farmers to organize had borne almost no fruit. In any case, as the popular front approached the decisive electoral test of its strength, it had the backing of the most powerful national confederation of workers that has existed before or since that time in Chile.

Gustavo Ross Santa María, right-hand man to Alessandri, was chosen by Liberals and Conservatives as the presidential candidate to succeed Alessandri. The choice of Ross, who was seen by the opposition as the personification of everything evil in the landholding and capitalist classes in Chile, was widely interpreted as a provocation and a defiance of popular sentiment. That choice cemented the unity of the left, and some of the Radicals who had been wavering, reluctant to embrace their new-found Communist allies, accepted the inevitability of the popular front.[33] Still, a few of the Radical old guard, many of them landowners and industrialists of some account, continued to resist the collaborationist current in the party. They warned that the Radicals would be unable to control the Communists once the popular front reached power. They insinuated that the party did not need a Radical president of Chile in order to run the country, as the frontist Radicals insisted. In the end, a number of the dissidents were expelled from the Radical Assembly in Santiago, and presumably in other Radical strongholds as well, while others, no doubt, went along without great enthusiasm.[34]

In April, 1938, the Chilean left met in full convention to select the candidate who would oppose Ross. Early votes produced a deadlock between Pedro Aguirre Cerda, an old-line Radical with many years of political experience, and Marmaduke Grove, the colorful air force officer who had proclaimed the Socialist Republic of Chile in 1932. The withdrawal of the Socialist favorite made possible the unanimous acclamation of Aguirre Cerda as candidate of the Chilean popular front. Ironically, Aguirre Cerda was known to be in opposition to his party's alliance with the Communists. It was his reputation for scrupulous honesty and fair play that made him acceptable to the heterogeneous elements making up the front. Although he was a relatively wealthy man, he was a school teacher, active in university administration, and led a modest life of study and hard work. His was not the patrician bearing of the traditional Chilean president. In the figure of this short, stocky, affable man, the great mass of Chileans could see its own face, its own person, being draped for the first time with the presidential sash.

Yet a third candidacy was in preparation. An Alliance for Liberation *(Alianza Libertadora),* made up of a hodgepodge of splinter groups and personal supporters of Carlos Ibáñez del Campo, was backing the former dictator for the presidency.[35] Ibáñez had returned from Argentine exile in May of 1937. The *Alianza* made a strong bid in its propaganda to present Ibáñez as the logical man to lead the popular front to victory. Ross and fascism must be defeated at all costs, they declared, and Ibáñez was the only man in Chile who could do it. Ibáñez pronounced himself to be anti-Fascist, anti-imperialist, and pro-popular front. According to his supporters, this made him a more sincere and appropriate front candidate than Aguirre Cerda, who was known to have strong reservations about working with the Communists.

The proclamation of Aguirre Cerda by the popular front doomed Ibáñez's chances of reaching power legally. As the Nazi chief Gonzáles von Marees was to declare some time later, Chile was gripped by two mystiques—*Rossismo* and *Frentismo.*[36] But the Nazis, who were the most determined force behind Ibáñez, proposed to force on the country their own brand of realism and their own candidate as an antidote to this popular intoxication.

The first major violent clash came on May 21, 1938. On that day, traditionally the presidents of Chile appear before a joint session of both legislative houses to report on the state of the Republic and the plans of the executive. There was especial tension on this occasion because it was anticipated that there might be some demonstration of hostility against the president by representatives of opposition parties. As the president began his speech, a small bomb exploded in a palm tree outside the legislative chambers. While the president droned on impassively, disorder broke out in some corners of the chamber and the corridors of the legislature. Gabriel Gonzáles Videla, a Radical deputy, rose to announce that the front representatives would not hear out the president. As the legislators began to leave the chamber, a scuffle with police ensued and a shot was fired into the air by Gonzáles von Marees, who was also a deputy at this time. In the melee that followed, a number of legislators were clubbed and dragged unceremoniously off to jail through the crowds that had gathered in the streets. All were subsequently freed, but bad feelings on both sides grew more intense.

As the day of balloting approached, the Nazi leadership became increasingly impatient with Ibáñez's irresolution. Apparently counting on forcing his hand by a show of strength, Gonzáles von Marees and a small group of his elite shock troops carried out an assault on the university, a government building giving a commanding vantage point over the presidential palace, and a few other strategic points within the capital. When it became clear that no military support was forthcoming for the revolutionaries (Ibáñez himself took refuge in the Infantry School), the police proceeded to rout out those holding the university and marched them to the building in which their companions were barricaded. Fifty-eight young men, most of them middle-class youths and fourteen of them university students, were brutally slaughtered by the police on the upper floors of this building after they had surrendered.[37]

The massacre of the young Nazis, which according to the rumor circulated at the time, had been carried out at the indication of President Alessandri, solidified resistance against the candidacy of Ross. More importantly, it swung the Ibáñez and Nazi votes to the popular front. Aguirre Cerda's victory over Ross was thus claimed by the Nazis as the vindication of their revolution. The crushed National Socialist movement was reborn almost at once as the Popular Socialist Vanguard *(Vanguardia Popular Socialista),* which sought to enter the popular front government but was rejected by Radicals and Communists.[38]

There was great public rejoicing upon the victory of Aguirre Cerda in much the same spirit as the jubilation over the triumph of Arturo Alessandri eighteen years before. The fears of frontists that the Liberals and Conservatives would not accept defeat and would try to challenge the election with the backing of the army proved as unfounded as the fears of rightists that the rabble now in power would loose a bloody persecution of church and property-owners on the country. The fervent optimism of the supporters of the front, as it turned out, had almost as little basis in reality as the exaggerated fears of its opponents. Symbolically, the raised fist with which Aguirre Cerda acknowledged the ovation of the crowds at his inauguration was gloved in white.

In line with its Socialist orientation, the new government sought to reorganize and diversify the national economy in such a manner that the worker would be assured a decent share of the national product.[39] No attempt was made at expropriation or toward the nationalization of major industries; governmental intervention in the affairs of private enterprise was moderate. The statistics given previously on the growth of unions and the number of labor conflicts resolved in favor of workers suggest that the government, by and large, threw its weight in support of workers, as might be expected. Notable gains were made in education, especially at the primary level—not only in school construction and teacher salaries, but in providing clothing and lunches for children. The government enlisted the aid of students of physical training to attack alcoholism and gambling among workers through sports and recreation programs.

Aguirre Cerda's program for improving the condition of workers and revamping the national economy was frustrated, not only by the determined opposition of the right, but also by the internal schisms within the front. When the rightist parties finally lost control over the parliament in 1941, the popular front had already collapsed. The Communists, who had remained outside the government presumably in order not to embarrass Chile internationally, were unrelenting critics of Aguirre's moderate approach. Radicals and Socialists were in constant rivalry for posts within the government, and the Radicals themselves were split internally between those who supported Aguirre's line and others who demanded a more aggressive and revolutionary vindication of the rights of workers. The Nazi-Soviet pact in late 1939 and the subsequent partition of Poland also hastened the repudiation by many non-Communist leftists of further collaboration in a front including Communists.

The pressures of internal divisions, an adept opposition, and events abroad finally brought the popular front to an abrupt end. The death knell was sounded by Oscar Schnacke, a top Socialist leader and a minister in Aguirre's cabinet. After the Havana Conference of Foreign Ministers in 1940, Schnacke visited the United States, where he undertook preliminary negotiations toward obtaining credits vital for Chile. The close links of the front government with Chilean Communists was clearly no recommendation for Minister Schnacke's pleas in Washington. Schnacke himself had from the beginning been among the strongest opponents to Socialist collaboration with Communists in the popular front. In any case, upon his return to Chile, he made a devastating attack on the Communist party in a major speech in Santiago's Caupolican Theatre.

The sudden death of Aguirre Cerda in November, 1940, spiked a new trend toward leftist unity that followed upon the German attack on Russia. New loose coalitions of the left would succeed the popular front in Chile, but Schnacke's speech heralded a fresh fractioning and disintegration of Chile's popular parties.

Although the impact of ideological differences on practical politics was manifestly profound, no one has claimed that this was an especially studious or meditative generation. The new ideologies were capsuled in slogans, leaflets, and posters; they were hammered home by tireless repetition, only hastily, if at all, digested. The new converts were out in the street trading blows or insults with their adversaries long before they had absorbed or thought out the refinements of party doctrine. There was a sense of urgency, an impulse to action that did not require or permit deep thought.

Marx and Lenin were the ideological deities of the day—not just for the Communists, but for Socialists and many independent leftists as well. One of the strongest and most unifying sentiments on the left was the repudiation of fascism, feelings that were brought into sharp focus by the war in Spain. The gutting of the Spanish popular front by the combined forces of Franco, Hitler, and Mussolini profoundly stirred Chileans who saw it as perhaps presaging events at home should their own popular front win a victory at the polls. The presence of the small but vocal and aggressive Nazi movement in Chile gave body and immediacy to the larger struggle in Europe.

Anti-imperialism was a second unifying formula. Imperialism and nationalism were then defined in the Communist lexicon as the mainstays of capitalism. There were variants on the classical interpretation of imperialism, but real events rather than the doctrinal controversy lent visceral impact to this theme. The Puerto Rican Nationalist movement had won great sympathy throughout the hemisphere; the repeated interventions in Cuba and the landing of United States Marines in Nicaragua were events fresh in the public mind. The Chaco War between Bolivia and Paraguay was being widely denounced as inspired and prolonged by United States and European oil and munitions interests.[40] In Chile, American interests had consolidated their hold on the copper and nitrate resources of the country. Although this process had not been accompanied by the violence and scandal that were common in other areas, this did not keep the Chilean operators from being identified with their compatriots who were seen as systematically looting the continent. Sandino, the Nicaraguan general who had organized fierce guerrilla resistance against United States Marines in his country, had received a stirring poetic tribute from Gabriela Mistral, one of Chile's most beloved public figures.

The isolated voices raised in the United States deploring diplomacy by economic blackmail and force were taken more as confirmations and fresh evidence of the predatory practices of the United States than as signs that any respectable body of opinion at home was seeking to curb the rapacity of a few. The announcement of Roosevelt's "good neighbor" policy and the accompanying self-denunciation of past mistakes by administration spokesmen did something to assuage these injured feelings. With the final unification for the war effort against the Axis, this battle within the hemisphere was postponed, but it was only a truce. It was the Communists who were most prepared to let bygones be bygones for the time being; other groups, such as the Socialists and the APRA, who were closely linked in Chile, insisted on maintaining the struggle against United States imperialism even while supporting the Allied cause in the war.

Anti-United States feeling united not only leftist groups. It was at once an ideological prop and a diffuse resentment growing out of feelings of patriotism and solidarity with other Latin American countries, with whom a certain racial and cultural affinity was felt. It was a sentiment and a symbol that might be mobilized as readily by a Marxist as by an industrialist pleading for protectionism or a Nazi reaffirming the sacred rights of the Chilean race.

The Chilean National Socialist movement borrowed most of the ideological as well as the external trappings of European fascism. The Nazis rejected democratic equalitarianism and the parliamentary system, which they saw as democracy's most corrupt and impotent institution. They glorified youth and struggle, direct action, and sanctity of property, and Christian morality. They raised the specter of communism and asserted the right of the enlightened minority of "responsible elements" under a strong leader to thwart the implanting of mob rule in Chile.[41]

The last of the new ideological currents importantly influencing university youth in these years was a resurgence of liberal Catholicism that had been incubating among a small group of young Conservatives since the early 1930's. Its beginnings went back to the 1920 period, but its first important manifestation in the University of Chile had been the appearance of the group *Renovación,* already noted. Although *Renovación* faded from sight within the university, its old leaders continued to act politically within the Conservative party. They rebelled after the party endorsed the candidacy of Gustavo Ross Santa María in 1938, and some months later they formally cut themselves off from the Conservatives. The new group took the name of *Falange* and adopted the red arrow as its symbol, although it did not take on the violent, fascistic characteristics of its Spanish counterpart. It was, in effect, a new affirmation of the possibility of achieving political and economic democracy through the application of Christian principles and Catholic doctrine. The *Falange* did not emerge as an important force in the university until very near the end of the popular front period.

Within the student federation, where the doctrinal cleavages and factional disputes among the several leftist groups in Chile were perhaps most sharply crystallized, the popular front produced no lasting political combination. The temporary unity of Communists and Socialists at the national level only served to intensify the struggle by both groups for control of the student organization. Nevertheless, some of the early feelers in the Communist move to seek collaboration from other leftist and from "democratic bourgeois" elements were made within the student federation.

The counterpart of the popular front on the university level was the United Anti-Fascist Group *(Grupo Unico Antifascista)* or GUA, as it became known. The Communist-dominated *Avance* group, early in 1936, approached the Radicals in the university with an invitation to participate in a broad anti-fascist front.[42] The GUA sought to win the adherence of independent leftists in the university by disavowing the narrow political identifications that had come to characterize the various groups active among students. The GUA declared that the political parties had sought to impose on students a revolutionary mission that was not really theirs, that political factions and personal cliques dominated the FECH without a prior "socialist transformation." The chief goals, other than student welfare and university reform, were to fight fascism and imperialism at home and abroad; around these objectives leftist youth, regardless of doctrinal or party inclination, could unite.[43] The immediate enemy was the Nazi element within the university, which had grown strong, especially in the School of Engineering. Violent encounters between Nazis and leftists in the university were becoming increasingly frequent.[44]

In the election of 1937, GUA won by a small margin over the Socialist-dominated Leftist Front *(Frente de Izquierda)*.[45] Under the energetic direction of the young Communist president, the FECH had one of its most active years. Taking stock of the year's accomplishments in the middle of 1938, a GUA spokesman enumerated an impressive roster of achievements.[46] By that time, GUA claimed control of nine of the seventeen school centers represented in the FECH, including such important schools as Law, Medicine, Engineering, the Pedagogical Institute, and Architecture. For the first time in several years the FECH published an official organ, the newspaper *FECH*. The first national convention of students held in Chile since 1920 was celebrated during this year. A second convention of students from some sixteen Latin American countries, most of them represented in the student body of the University of Chile, was also held.

At both of these meetings the principal topics of discussion were the fight against imperialism and the need for university reform. The Communists made every effort to create an identification between these two objectives, arguing that the fight for democracy within the university was simply one facet of the struggle to free the nations of the world from imperialist oppression.[47] The cause of Puerto Rican nationalists, who in those months faced trial in Boston, was taken up with great fervor. The war in Spain and especially the death of the poet García Lorca provided occasions for additional mass meetings, poetic readings, street demonstrations, and press protest.

A semblance of unity between Communists and Socialists within the university was won briefly when both endorsed the program of the Anti-Imperialistic Students Confederation of America (CEADA) born in a 1936 Guadalajara conference during the presidency of Lázaro Cárdenas. The FECH also linked itself to the *Rassemblement Mondial des Etudiants* with headquarters in Paris. A national committee of sponsors was organized for the Second World Youth Congress to be held at Vassar College in August of 1938. The committee included most of the better-known writers and intellectuals in Chile, as well as three university rectors, including the rector of the Catholic University. Chile sent to this mammoth peace meeting a large delegation of young people, ranging over the entire spectrum of political, labor, and religious organizations in the country.[48]

On the home front, a number of minor school strikes over local grievances were fought successfully. The perennial protests over rises in bus fares and the demands for student rates led to sporadic incidents with the police. However, the most spectacular innovation was the holding of a student plebiscite during May, 1938. Along with a number of ingenuously leading questions—Do you think the present registration fee is too high? Do you think the FECH should get financial support from the university and the state? Do you think the annual state appropriation for the university should be larger?—the poll asked students to name the good and bad professors in their schools. The publication of the results, understandably, led to much controversy and recrimination; there were threatened resignations, demands for ousters, charges of ill-will and fraud. Still, no changes of any consequence were made in the university.

As time for FECH elections rolled around again, the GUA was calling directly for student support of the popular front and the candidacy of Aguirre Cerda to the national presidency. Although the FECH for the first time officially endorsed a particular candidate to national office, within the university the parties of the popular front remained divided. It was a collapse of Radical-Communist unity in the GUA that brought a Socialist into the presidency of the FECH in August, 1938. Thus the three major parties of the popular front were most divided within the university in the very year of the front's triumph on the national level.

Nevertheless, the FECH gave decided support to the popular front candidate. Student leaders were at the head of the national and regional *comandos* of youth formed to support Aguirre Cerda. They paraded, distributed handbills, made speeches, voted (sometimes more than once and even if under age), and got out the vote. They also worked on the electoral boards and stood guard over ballot boxes. When there seemed to be some danger that Aguirre's victory by a small margin might be challenged by the rightist parties, the students hastened to acclaim him as president-elect, making clear that they would resist any attempt to prevent Aguirre Cerda from occupying *La Moneda,* Chile's presidential residence.

The FECH also protested vigorously the police slaughter of Nazi youths in the Social Security Building. Manifestations honoring the dead were carried out at considerable personal risk by the same young men who shortly before had been engaged themselves in pitched battles with the Nazis. For some this may have been perhaps no more than an opportunity to make political use of the massacre against Alessandri, but the event was unusual enough in Chilean politics to shock even the most cynical.

In summing up FECH activities from 1938 to 1939, the Socialists emphasized heavily their achievements in winning concessions of direct benefit to students.[49] A large grant was obtained to pay registration fees for needy students, especially those from the areas devastated by the January, 1939 earthquake. Examination requirements were eased, special rates on railroads and buses as well as to theaters, were obtained for students. A symphonic concert was held as well as a competition for university theatrical groups in which ten faculties participated. Efforts were made to put the FECH on a more secure financial and organizational footing, and the reform aspirations of the several schools were catalogued and presented jointly to the rector as an over-all program for change within the university. In line with the new emphasis on student problems and the search for a program of unity rising above political factionalism, the Socialists chose as their candidate a young poet, who was more an intellectual than a political figure within the university. The Socialist front won easily; their candidate received one of the largest votes ever registered in a FECH election.

By mid-1940, the war in Europe, the Nazi-Soviet pact, and the obviously imminent collapse of the popular front at home had further divided, discredited, and weakened the parties of the left and their leaders in the university. The Catholic *Falange* moved in decisively with a Revolutionary Anti-Communist Front *(Frente Revolucionario Anti-Comunista)*[50] On this occasion the former Nazis threw their weight with the *Falange*. A close race resulted in which both the *Falange* and the Communists claimed victory. This time a real schism was produced. Neither group ever got off the ground. Once again the FECH entered into a period of eclipse. It was to remain inactive until nearly 1943.

Factionalism Entrenched

The generation that was in the university during the gestation and brief lifespan of the popular front in Chile, unlike its counterpart of the 1920 period, gave birth to no great legends. The youngsters in the university today can, by and large, recite the main outlines of the FECH saga of the 1920's and name a few of the student heroes who fought off the assault on the federation headquarters in July, 1920. By contrast, the events within the university that have just been recounted, as well as the names of the men who lived them, have, for the most part, passed into a historical void. This is true despite the fact that many of the student leaders of the years between 1936 and 1940 figure prominently in present-day political party life or have established reputations as professionals or intellectuals. The difference is not simply one of the caliber of the individuals or the human raw materials at work in each period.

As has been seen, the generation that approached maturity in the years of the popular front had lived in adolescence through dictatorship and economic crisis; it had seen civil resistance, touched off by the agitation of students, topple a dictator. It had seen how ineffectual was the protection afforded workers by the entire apparatus of social legislation passed in 1924. These young men had watched the birth and proliferation of leftist parties in

Chile during their early years in the university; they had seen the near anarchy of the depression years succeeded by vigilantism and arbitrary police controls under Alessandri after 1933. They had been witnesses and actors in the first great battles among political factions for control of the student organization. It is this factionalism, the extension of the political struggle at the national level into the ranks of students, that gave the FECH organization of the time its most characteristic institutional stamp. This was the heyday of the political cabal, the artful tactician, of plot and counter-plot.

There was no formal synthesis of student aspirations and ideology such as *The Declaration of Principles of 1920* for the years between 1936 and 1940. This does not mean that there was not a great deal of discussion and much written about the proper aims and methods of action for student organization during those years. There were, in fact, two major conventions of Chilean students in this period, both with ambitious agenda and long hours of earnest cerebration and disquisition on such themes as war and peace, imperialism, social problems (poverty, illiteracy, crime, and alcoholism), university reform, and student organization.

The first of these student conventions became a pitched battle between Communists and Socialists and their sympathizers. The second meeting, the *Jornadas del Estudiante,* held in 1939, sought to bring about a confrontation, a sort of intellectual joust, between the students of the time and student leaders of earlier generations. The Communists had only marginal participation in this convention since they had, in effect, seceded from the student federation during that school term. It was in these *Jornadas* that the liberal Catholic viewpoint of the new *Falange* for the first time was put before students at large in a forceful way.

However, neither of these conventions produced a pronouncement of student goals of any resonance—the mass of students and the general public apparently remained unmoved. Each orator was seen as seeking to use the convention platform as a sounding board for his own party; each vote or resolution was seen as a test of strength among the numerous blocs vying for position. The discussions were carried on in an atmosphere of mutual disbelief and mistrust. Thus, although each convention took preliminary steps toward setting up a national student organization encompassing all the universities, the project was stillborn in both cases. [51]

Early in 1936 a call to unity from the United Anti-Fascist Group, whose beginnings were described in the last section, began with these words:

> At present there is no group that is capable by itself of mobilizing the entire student body. The division of the Left into diverse groups does not really stem from any differences in viewpoint regarding university problems but is rather an expression of the struggle among the political parties of the Left on the national level. [52]

In 1939, in a campaign leaflet, one of the candidates to the FECH presidency remarked:

> The election victory of October meant for Chile the recovery and continuity of her ascending political and social progress that for a time seemed irretrievably lost. [53] The students of Chile have nothing to match the brilliant example which the populace has given us by their edifying victory; we have not even made an intellectual contribution to an event that, in fact, has taken us by surprise, disorganized and without orientation.

The FECH had become, even for its own leadership, more a simple tool than a value-laden institution—thus, the readiness to cripple it by secession or schism when this served partisan ends.

Yet even the political machinators faced the need to appeal to some unifying symbols that could override the underlying political cleavages. There were areas in which a degree of consensus existed. The propaganda appeals and exhortations of candidates to FECH offices during these years provide some clues to the generalized values that moved students to action or were thought of by student leaders as potent enough to mobilize student support.

Not untypically, the Communists reacted first in an organized way to the growing disillusion of the mass of students with the petty political bickering, the demagoguery and ineptitude of student leaders identified with the political parties. The United Anti-Fascist Group did most to revive the almost forgotten program of the University Reform movement. The Côrdoba

University Reform movement of 1918 in Argentina had had some repercussions in Chile in the 1920's, and the idea of university reform had been agitated again in Chile in the early 1930's. At that time, it had been charged that the extreme position taken by Communists had defeated the chances of achieving any reforms, despite the strong position of students and the willingness of the shaky national government and university administration to make concessions. Many Marxists had attacked the University Reform movement as an empty and outdated bourgeois delusion that must be put aside by students; the fight for an autonomous university, they asserted, imperiled the success of the true revolution.

The generally softer attitude adopted by the Communist party in the popular front days was accompanied by a shift in their view of the university. According to this new position, the university was to be considered an institution with its own lines of development. Students were a particular stratum of society with special needs that were distinct from those of workers, professionals, and other elements of the middle class. The student was not called on to be a leader of the proletariat in the great socialist transformation; his duty was to work for the democratization of the university and to prepare it to become a free institution (governed by students, professors, and alumni), providing cultural services to the whole people rather than to a narrow intellectual or professional elite. An early leaflet from the United Anti-Fascist Group stated the problem thus:

> It is evident that an integral transformation of the system of public education presupposes a profound and radical transformation of society; but the University Reform encompassing those well known postulates for which we are again ready to fight, requires no other change than the establishment of a true democracy on the basis of the abolition of the *latifundio* and the liberation of the country from the imperialist oppressor.

In this way the objective of reform within the university, presumably revived in an effort to concentrate student energies on their own needs, remained linked to the class struggle and the fight against imperialism.

Although there was some initial resistance from the Socialist camp to this shift in the Communist position, from 1937 until the end of this period, each party within the university outdid itself to stand out as the champion of student interests. In every election from 1937 through 1940, the chief claims of past accomplishments and the key promises of campaign platforms centered on issues of student welfare and university organization.

The chief point of attack by students was on registration fees and entrance requirements, which were held to be discriminatory and restrictive. Most of the professional schools required the baccalaureate degree for admission. In Chile, this degree is officially conferred by the university, although it is granted upon completion of six years of secondary school study in a lycée, which may be a private or public establishment. Educators have disagreed for a long time about the merits of this system. Many feel it is unfair to make a youngster's entire professional career rest on the outcome of one set of intensive examinations frequently taken under difficult and unfamiliar circumstances. The system, however, is still in force. Students, then and later, have had some success in having the baccalaureate requirement waived in some schools. These schools admit students provisionally so that they can advance their university careers while waiting to retake the baccalaureate examination. However, in some cases this has proved an empty victory because the relaxation of entrance requirements has often meant that the elimination process is simply postponed until the end of the first university year, when large numbers fail the stiff examinations.

The improvised and haphazard nature of the reforms and benefits sought by students, or demanded in their behalf by the various political groups active in the student federation during these years, reflected the basic indifference to long-range objectives and the purely manipulative interests of those who agitated the banner of University Reform. Student energies were dissipated in pursuing such limited objectives as postponement or rescheduling of examinations—in gaining extensions of the period within which certain examinations might be retaken. The accomplishments of the Socialist FECH president from 1938 to 1939 are catalogued in a campaign leaflet in the following order:

1. A reprieve was obtained for all those who had been suspended during 1938 for failure to meet academic requirements.

2. Persons with conditional grades in two subjects were allowed to go on to the next year's work.
3. Examinations were postponed in almost all faculties.
4. A considerable number of students were exempted from paying matriculation fees.
5. The students from the Concepción area (devastated by earthquake) were exempted from matriculation fees.
6. About a thousand students received grants distributed by the FECH from monies obtained through the rector for payment of matriculation fees.
7. A 50 per cent reduction in train fares for students was obtained. The list continues at some length.

Interestingly, it is almost devoid of references to any political activity, other than a statement that enthusiastic support was given to the candidacy of Pedro Aguirre Cerda. Similar documents for the years 1937 to 1938 and 1939 to 1940 show the same emphasis on nonpolitical objectives of immediate interest to students. The latter year (1940) witnessed an intensive effort in the direction of expanding cultural and artistic activities within the university.

A second unifying current was a vague sense of tradition, growing out of the exploits of the 1920 generation. There was a definite ambivalence and a certain defensiveness in the attitudes toward this tradition, particularly among student leaders, who tended to measure their own stature as captains of the student body in terms of an idealized image of early student heroes. Early in 1936 a spokesman for the United Anti-Fascist Group, writing in *La Opinión,* a leftist Santiago daily, said:

> We university youths do not look back; we do not see in the achievements of 1920 just an example to imitate, but rather a path to follow and a stage of development to be surpassed.[54]

A few months later, the student newspaper *FECH* referred to the 1920 Declaration of Principles as "confused and disoriented, at times supporting principles that are frankly reactionary."[55] In August, 1939, the *Revista Universitaria,* another FECH organ, declared, "The survivors of the 20's have shamefully compromised their ideals—we are more loyal to the masses."[56]

Some of this criticism was indicative of no more than partisan spleen since the 1920 men were much more closely identified with the Socialist and Radical parties than with the Communists. In part, it seems to reflect a true difference in the prevailing political outlook of the two generations—an impatience and contempt in the disciplined party man of the 1930's for the romanticism and lack of organization attributed to the earlier period. In part, it was a defense against the feeling of failure and the foreknowledge that their own generation, as students, would leave little to mark their passage through the university.

Still, the FECH calendar seldom omitted the annual pilgrimage to the grave of the young poet, Domingo Gómez Rojas. Whenever students looked into their own past for inspiration, it was to the 1920 period that they looked, even more than to the early 1930's, which were closer to their own time and which was a period when the action of students had been truly revolutionary. Over and above the commitment to party dogma, the disillusion, and the indifference, there existed the idea of a set of guideposts, a set of canons that governed and inspired student action. These were not often articulated, but they were recognized as going back to the very beginnings of the student federation and having been realized most completely in the 1920 period. They included the courage to have and to defend ideas, a readiness for self-sacrifice, loyalty in friendship, love of country, a sentimental identification with the working classes, and solidarity with the youth of other Latin American countries and the world at large.

The projection of the competition among national political parties into the student milieu served not only to confuse and circumscribe the organizational objectives of students. It blunted purpose and weakened the entire fabric of the organization. The contenders for control of the FECH had become so consumed by narrow partisan rivalry that they failed to realize that the prize for which they were struggling was a flaccid and moribund organism.

None of the informants of this period had any but the vaguest recollection of ever having seen a set of bylaws for the FECH during the years that they were active, and throughout this period the FECH lacked a legal corporate identity. Each election represented a crisis in which the life of the organization hung in the balance. The intrinsic weakness, stemming from the brief period of control actually exercised by each set of officers, was compounded by the fact that the outgoing group did not hesitate to abscond with whatever organizational records they possessed in order to make things difficult for their successors. Not only was there little concern about giving the FECH a firmer formal footing, but much of what was done served only to undermine the already precarious structure for mobilizing and co-ordinating the use of student resources.

The chief difference in the *formal* setup of the FECH organization between the popular front years and the 1920 period lies in the weakening of its links with individual students and the separate university schools. In the earlier period, students paid dues directly to the FECH through elected class delegates who were responsible for keeping a record of members in good standing and serving as a link between class members and the FECH leadership. In the late 1930's no student was linked directly as an individual to the FECH. There were no *class* delegates to the FECH directorate but simply two delegates from each school. This meant not only that there was a lesser sense of identification with the FECH on the part of the individual student, but also that those in the first years had small chance of getting direct representation in FECH councils. With delegates elected on a school-wide basis, it was chiefly the older students with established political ties that came to fill these offices. The student no longer chose his representatives from among the relatively small number of his classmates, with all of whom he was likely to have had some personal acquaintance. He had the opportunity only to vote for the school-wide candidates supported by the dominant political groups in his school.

The school presidents remained key figures, not only in their own schools but in the FECH as well. The school organizations enjoyed almost complete local autonomy and, in fact, handled most of their own problems with the university administration directly. The FECH was called on for support only when the situation seemed to require more powerful pressure than could be mustered locally. Since in most cases the school delegates and school presidents were militant members of some party, how closely a particular school worked with the FECH depended very much on which party happened to be in control of the top FECH offices. Still, the school presidents were thought of as more directly responsive than the FECH to the needs of their own students and to the university, rather than political, problems. When schism threatened, it was the school presidents who stepped in as arbiters.[57]

The executive offices of the FECH were no longer filled from among the elected school delegates. Election to the presidency and vice-presidency was by direct vote. Any student or alumnus who had not been out of the university for more than two years could occupy these posts. For these top offices the competition was ruthless. The campaigns—manifestoes, speeches, trading in votes, slander, blackmail, and fraud—probably consumed more of the organization's time than any other single activity. If, in the 1920's, it would have been inconceivable for a student to present himself as a candidate to FECH office in the name of a political party, between 1936 and 1940 to claim to be an "independent" was to admit to being a reactionary without the courage to say so openly. A candidate without a party was an anomaly, except in contests for the lower-echelon school offices or for posts in a few of the less politicalized schools.

In short, student attention, particularly at the top leadership level, was so consumed with the concern for advancing the cause of particular parties, that it occurred to only a few cool heads that the struggle to control the FECH was pointless if the FECH was to be no more than an isolated clique of political tyros cut off from the main body of students. Some lip service was given to the ideal of student unity and university reform, as has been seen, and certain token efforts were made in this direction. However, throughout there was no real truce in the struggle for control and political advantage. Unlike the student federation of 1920, whose main activity was *outward* and propagandistic, the FECH was now turned *inwardly* upon itself, engrossed and spent by its own internal trauma. No *Claridad* was bringing the voice of students to thousands in Santiago and the provinces each week. While surely there was fervor and passion in the hearts of those who were striving in behalf of one party or another, externally the voice of the students was heard as a hollow and dissonant echoing of tired slogans. The left in Chile had acquired more powerful and more authoritative voices than those of university youths.

Basically, the criteria of membership remained unchanged, although even here there was some tendency toward introducing limitations. All students in establishments dependent on the University of Chile in Santiago as well as alumni of the first two years after leaving the university had the right to vote and hold office. Students in Valparaíso and Concepción now had federations of their own. Students in the Catholic University in Santiago occasionally joined in some FECH-sponsored events, such as the student convention in 1939, but this was relatively rare. As the university expanded the scope of its activities, controversies arose as to whether some of the new establishments really qualified as teaching centers at the university level. These squabbles arose entirely out of political considerations. A new school that was suspected of having sympathies for a given party could count on the opposition of the rival political bloc.

The limitations which the new situation placed on FECH action did not go entirely unperceived by thoughtful student leaders of the time. One of the informants analyzed the shift from the all-encompassing, outgoing action of the 1920 FECH to the more circumscribed and internally focused activities of his own time so adroitly that a long quote from his remarks will serve to make the point here:

> I should tell you that at the moment that I was elected President of the Student Federation a spirit of intense political exaltation reigned among popular groups in the country. The nation had organized itself in an active, Popular-democratic movement with the popular Front as an instrument of action. . . . At that moment, the control of political and social activity in the country was decidedly in the hands of the political groups. . . . All that the Student Federation could do was to support fervently general democratic and civic principles, without being able to make its action weigh in reality within the nation, since all real power was in the hands of the political parties and the trade and labor associations. The Student Federation of 1920 . . . acted in a country that was not yet very much differentiated and structured. Then it acted as a sort of antenna picking up the diffuse popular fervor that had not been canalized into the organic channels of political parties or other interest groups. The Federation was then the instrument of populist action. The Federation over which I presided had to resign itself to being a more strictly and exclusively student oriented organism, and it was in actuality just that. . . .

Thus the ascent and expansion of leftist parties in Chile did not mean an expansion of the power and influence of the student movement. It was not simply that students abdicated their former role of ideological innovators and orientors of popular opinion; nor were they simply the victims of more mature and experienced political heads. This was, rather, a set of new conditions in which university youth *looked outward for guidance* in political affairs. In a sense, the existence of a powerful political machine that was much better equipped than the FECH to lead the masses in their demands for economic and political equality *freed* students for tasks closer to their own interests. There were still some intransigents among Communists, Socialists, and especially the Nazi contingent who felt that students must be in the vanguard of the revolution, or who argued in favor of direct action. However, these firebrands were among the most disciplined party people in the university. There had been a lowering of sights, not only, as has been seen, with respect to the scope of aims and activities, but also in the range of areas in which it was thought legitimate for students to initiate action independently.

Instability and improvisation still prevailed in the matter of resources. If anything, the situation became worse during this second period. The FECH had no permanent quarters throughout the years from 1936 to 1940. It shuttled from one corner to another, with frequent losses of the meager equipment and furnishings that were accumulated with great difficulty. A well-equipped clubhouse that the FECH obtained in 1939 through the good offices of the Socialist mayor of Santiago was soon lost. The organization's lack of corporate status created many difficulties in handling financial transactions. There was no formal or systematic collection of dues from the membership. Occasional levies among students on a voluntary basis provided some funds, as did dances and other social and sports events. Students continued to celebrate the spring festivals, but there were now competing sponsors, and the FECH had to seek the collaboration of more securely financed organizations that took correspondingly large shares of the profits for themselves.

The rector was the chief source of financial support for student endeavors. The university contributed substantial sums to be distributed as grants-in-aid to needy students through the FECH during 1938. In 1939, the university supported many of the cultural and artistic activities initiated in that year that proved to be the forerunners of the present School of Theater Arts, ballet company, and symphony orchestra of the university.[58]

Command over manpower was strongly influenced by political loyalties. The most active students were the most politicized, and they threw their weight and efforts behind leaders from their own political cliques. Delegates to the directorate who were in the defeated minority, not only frequently failed to show up for any meetings at all, but could be counted on to make an all-out effort to thwart and frustrate the efforts of the group in power. There were, of course, some incidents that brought a united response from students of all political leanings. However, by and large, the central command lacked firm control over material resources and could hope to mobilize mass support only through bargaining with other factions or winning the good will or enthusiasm of the politically uncommitted.

No formalized, permanent setup existed for exchanging or co-ordinating the use of resources with political parties or labor unions. The FECH normally appeared side by side with the popular-front parties and the labor unions in public demonstrations, parades, and rallies. However, here again the characteristic note was one of improvisation—the FECH was just one of a large number of organizations that were swept along in the upsurge of popular fervor aroused by the popular front and the promise of new and better times held out by Aguirre Cerda's candidacy. Whatever material contributions the parties made to students were channeled through their militants within the university. The FECH, as a unit, had no control over this. No financial help of any consequence seems to have been given by the parties to the student political groups; their support was given primarily around the time for FECH elections, when the party presses and other propaganda machinery were put at the disposition of the party's candidates to student offices. Whatever monies these groups had at their disposal seem to have been raised primarily through personal subscription among students themselves, rather than through contributions from party war chests.

Fundamentally, there had been little change in the relationshp between the student organization and the university administration. The rector of the university, Juvenal Hernández, was a young man still in his thirties. He was a Radical party member, a supporter of the popular front, and known as a moderate reformist within the university. He had been elected to the rectorate over the opposition of the Alessandri government. From time to time, he came into conflict with students, but relations between the rector and the FECH were, on the whole, cordial.

In keeping with the liberal tradition of the university, all political groups were allowed to have free expression there. The free play of ideas that this policy theoretically promoted was not infrequently transformed into the free play of brickbats, blows, and insults. Still the policy was not abandoned and has been maintained even in later years when it has become more controversial.

The open attitude of the rector toward proposed reforms took much of the drive out of student demands. The root problems of the university—its financial dependence on the government, its lack of material means, the limited curricula in some schools, and the poor quality of the teaching staff—could not really be resolved without a major overhauling of the university that was dependent on finding new sources of income and trained personnel. Some of what appears as lack of vision and low aspirations among student leaders was simply a realistic adjustment to the existing possibilities.

The FECH, as an entity, had no direct relation with the political parties. That is to say, there were no formal links between the central command of the FECH and the political parties. Rather, the youth sections of the different parties had enclaves in the university which *cross-cut* the federation and worked within it for control of the student organism. There were Communist cells, wings of the Socialist brigade, and semi-militarized units of the Nazi group in all of the major university schools and in many of the lesser ones. The University Radical Group (GUR) was a relative newcomer within the university, where it weighed much less as a political force than did the Radical party within the national political picture. Outside the university, the Radical youth organization took the lead in the various youth fronts, and *comandos* formed to promote the popular front and Aguirre Cerda's candidacy to the presidency. In part, the Radicals owed their prominence in these groups to the Communist tactic of pushing the Radicals to the fore, but in these years the national organization of Radical youth achieved considerable strength and was influential in prolonging the collaboration between the

Communists and the Radical party. The Catholic Falange was the only other organized political group of any consequence in addition to these.

Thus, the political parties were no longer external forces or social objects with which the FECH could ally, combat, or try to influence. *The parties were in the FECH and of it.* The FECH fight in 1920, challenging the right of acknowledged Radical party men or Masons to hold FECH office because they were subject to external discipline, would have seemed to the 1940 student a throwback to a remote and ingenuous political infancy.

The traditional friendship and solidarity between students and workers was maintained through these years, but, again, the relationship was loose and informal. The powerful Confederation of Chilean Workers (CTCH) joined with the political parties in the popular front. The FECH supported labor in the prolonged strikes during 1936 and could be counted on generally to come out on the side of labor in any conflict. Actually, as the Confederation gained strength, workers had little difficulty in getting favorable resolutions of their demands, especially once the popular front came into power. The hectic internal scramble among factions was draining the vitality of the FECH; it had little to give the worker, and workers did not feel the need to look outside their own ranks for leadership.

In summary, there had been, between 1920 and 1940, some fundamental changes in the patterns of action of the student organization and a basic reshuffling of students' beliefs about the meaning and objectives of their own efforts. Almost all of these changes stemmed directly from the penetration into the student milieu of new political parties that had come to life in Chile during the depression years. Of the parties that had important contingents within the university, only the Communist and Radical parties went back beyond that time, and the Communist party itself did not achieve stature as a broadly based political force in Chile until well into the 1930's. The new FECH was not simply infiltrated by political factions; it was not just an organism that had internalized some foreign and hostile body. The conflict was in the hearts and minds of individual members. The FECH became a tool and a prize to be captured; its values and traditions became symbols that were more manipulated than served. Nevertheless, the dismemberment of the FECH was not a calculated operation by cold-blooded political machinators. It was the work of dedicated men, who passionately believed that the long-range needs of students and the nation, if not mankind itself, were best served by the program of a particular party.

The Party Men at Work

The number of students in establishments dependent on the University of Chile had not changed markedly between these two periods. In fact, between 1920 and 1940 there was a small decline in the total student population that was not entirely attributable to the temporary separation from the university of the School of Fine Arts and the Conservatory of Music. Three new faculties were added between 1925 and 1940: Agronomy, in 1927; the Faculty of Economic Sciences, in 1935; and the Faculty of Animal Husbandry and Veterinary Science, in 1938. These additions, however, did not genuinely represent new schools or imply an increment in the student body. They were primarily administrative rearrangements.

The failure of the university to sustain the steady rate of growth it had displayed since the turn of the century is without doubt linked to the political and economic reversals suffered by Chile in the years between 1925 and 1935. From 1940 onward, the university entered upon a new and vigorous period of expansion that it has maintained to this day. However, in the opening years of the popular front, the university had changed little from what it had been fifteen years before.[59]

Women now made up nearly a third of the total student population. However, they tended to be concentrated in certain schools; outside of the School of Nursing, the School of Obstetrics and Child Care, and the School of Social Service (all of them with wholly female student bodies), women were present in large numbers mainly in the Schools of Dentistry, Pharmacy, and the Pedagogical Institute. They figured hardly at all in FECH activities. The schools with large proportions of women were the least politicized.

Although the age range of students had not varied markedly, there were fewer student leaders who continued their activity in the student organization beyond the years when they were actually enrolled in the university. There was very little participation by alumni, even though, technically, alumni had the right to vote and hold office up to two years after they left the university. The leadership was younger and was siphoned off into the party organization as it left the university; with few exceptions, the leaders of this second period lacked the maturity and personal prestige (based on other than student achievements) that marked many of the leaders of the 1920 period.

Despite the long years of talk about "democratizing" the university and the sentimenal identification of students with workers, the university remained a middle-class institution. In a 1939 survey carried out among 269 students in nine of the major schools (Dentistry, Law, Architecture, Medicine, Engineering, Pharmacy, Commerce, the Pedagogical Institute, and Physical Training), at most twelve students could be said to come from working-class families.[60] Two gave the occupation of their fathers as "workers," and ten said their fathers were "artisans." The term "artisan" is used loosely in Chile to designate individuals who perform services requiring moderate skills on a more or less independent basis (for example, shoemaker, plumber, and so forth). The largest category of fathers' occupations was *comerciante* (seventy cases), another ambiguous term covering everything from the peddler to the well-established department-store merchant. The latter term, however, implies a clear claim to middle-class status, even though the material level of living may not differ much between many *comerciantes* and some *artesanos*. The remaining students were the sons of professors and school teachers, professionals, farmers, white-collar workers, and a few persons living on income from investments.

Yet the situation of most students was modest, and many suffered real privation. The same survey reported that only about a third of the students questioned had adequate diets and were living in quarters with decent sanitary facilities. The average price paid per month for food and lodging (less than 200 Chilean pesos a month, or about ten dollars) was in itself an indicator that most students living away from home were occupying substandard quarters and living on a deficient diet. The modest charges for matriculation and the costs of the few school supplies and special equipment required for some courses presented a grave hardship for many students. The fight against matriculation fees was not just a quixotic crusade seeking to throw the doors of the university open to the children of the proletariat. It was the hard-pressed and depression-ridden middle-class youth which was fighting for its place within the university.

In 1934, there were more than 200 foreign students in the university, mostly Peruvians and Bolivians. Many others followed in the popular front years, and by 1938 there were enough countries represented to hold a Convention of Latin American Students in Santiago with little more than the students from other nations actually enrolled in the University of Chile. The Peruvians, who were mostly *Apristas* and anti-Communists, by and large threw their support to the Socialist brigade within the university. The Central Americans and those from the Caribbean countries were, according to all informants, largely sympathetic to the Communists. However, no group of foreign students operated as a bloc within the student organization. The *Apristas* were probably the most influential because of the intellectual stature and international renown of the elder statesmen of the movement, such as Haya de la Torre, Luis Alberto Sánchez, Manuel Seoane, and José Carlos Mariátegui.

The turnout for major FECH elections is a deceptive indicator of student involvement in the organization. About two in three of the enrolled student body voted in the 1937 election, but the number actually active in FECH affairs was much smaller. It was primarily the delegates of the same party as the victorious president that collaborated in FECH activities; the rest simply did not attend meetings. Attendance figures for twenty-eight meetings of the FECH directorate held between mid-1936 and mid-1937 show that more than half of the delegates attended fewer than seven of the twenty-eight meetings.[61] Of course, these figures were published with an eye to demonstrating the lack of responsibility and neglect of office shown by political opponents, but they reveal the extent to which organizational life was left in the hands of tightly organized political cliques. Probably at no time during this period did any of the major political groups have more than about 50 to 100 actively militant and disciplined members at work within the university. Of course, larger numbers were mobilized for demonstrations and mass meetings, but the see-sawing scramble for control of the FECH throughout the years from 1936 to 1940 involved no more than some 200 to 300 of the party committed. The high command, executive officers, and active members of the directorate at any one time numbered no more than a score, all of them prominent and dedicated party youth leaders.

Although the actual members involved in FECH activities and the social backgrounds of the FECH membership had varied little, the day-to-day conduct of student business was not quite the same. For the average student, life still centered around activities within the school. A good number of the apolitical schools were, for all practical purposes, unrepresented within the federation. These schools went through the formality of electing delegates, but these seldom or never attended meetings of the FECH directorates. The attendance figures for meetings of the directorate just cited show at least six out of the seventeen affiliated schools where neither of the two delegates attended even one-fourth of the meetings. Some of these schools were even overlooked in the barnstorming electoral campaigns for university-wide FECH offices. The politicos in the FECH not only did nothing for these students; they asked nothing of them and made only a token bid for their votes. By the end of this period, so much time was consumed with pre-electoral maneuvering and post-electoral wrangling that proposals were made to extend the term of each slate of officers to two years rather than one, so that they might have a chance to do something other than count the votes and begin the next campaign.

The schools for workers and the clinics and other services that had been maintained by the different schools and by the FECH itself during the 1920's were no longer in existence. There was intermittent talk of reviving these activities, but nothing much was ever done. Outside of the traditional, routine pronouncements of solidarity with the cause of workers in every conflict between labor and management or the government, students were doing nothing of consequence to help improve the situation of workers.

Behind everything stood the secretive cliques, where party strategy was mapped—the Communist cells, the Nazi units. Other less disciplined and more democratic groups operated more openly. Still, the atmosphere was conspiratorial. None of the party groups was as rigidly structured or controlled as their chief spokesmen or their enemies sometimes pretended. In the intimate world of university politics, where party lines were frequently crossed and recrossed, and where, in Chilean fashion, personal friendships often bound bitter political opponents, it was difficult to keep organizational secrets. The tendency was to look for political intent in every action, to distrust gestures of good will, to exaggerate the cynicism and the desire to manipulate events of opponents, and to justify the same behavior by one's own group as a realistic adjustment in the face of the boundless perversity of the enemy. It was an experience that in many led to a corrosion of ideals that is still being felt in Chilean politics.

The student leader informants of this period all affirm that they received scrupulously fair treatment from professors and university officials. However, every one of them (especially the FECH presidents) lost at least one or two years of time in the university as a direct consequence of their involvement in student political affairs. All agree that their academic records would have been much better had they been more attentive students and less responsive to the lure of politics. Being a top FECH officer and party youth leader at the same time was a full-time job, and student leaders received no special privileges in meeting the heavy schedules of classrooms and practical work required in the major professional schools in Chile. It was impossible to keep up both activities, even in the Law School, which has a relatively light schedule of classroom hours. In the 1920's, when the top figures had most often been outstanding alumni with their university careers behind them, leaders had less often faced this kind of academic setback.

For a time, being a good student had been regarded as extremely poor taste in advanced political circles. However, the switch that took place around 1936—toward giving university and student problems priority in the hierarchy of FECH aims—brought with it a revision of this viewpoint. The Communists, through the United Anti-Fascist Group, announced that a good student leader must also be a good student. Almost all the leader informants of the time seem to have been above-average students who consciously chose between achieving narrow academic excellence and acquiring the rounded experience afforded by student leadership. Though they have almost all passed anonymously and without great glory into FECH annals, none expressed any deep regret over having made the choice as they did.

Every single informant for this period figured prominently in the leadership of some party youth organization. None of them seems to have experienced then, or to perceive at this distance in time, any conflict between his responsibility and loyalty to fellow students and the party discipline he accepted. The most militarized group was the Nazi movement, in which there were no elective offices. The Nazis had groups, designated as battalions and assault squads, secret efficiency ratings, and decorations for wounds received in action. The movement demanded unquestioning loyalty and obedience, and it carried most of its major leaders in the university to a brutal death.

The Communists were also a disciplined group, but the popular front period was one in which the party opened its doors widely. For a time, the Communist youth functioned "independently" of the party, so that you could be a member of the youth group without being in the party. Students, except for the small group initiated into the inner party circles, had no duties to perform outside the university. The party sought throughout these years to sustain a surface atmosphere of legality and democracy—to avoid the stigma of belligerence or intransigence that might alarm their Radical collaborationists. Proposals for action were hammered out in the Communist cell, carried on for discussion in the United Anti-Fascist Group, and from there to the floor of the FECH. The soft line taken by the party and its avowed dedication to student and university problems as against political problems eliminated many possible sources of conflict.

The remaining groups—the Socialists, the *Falange,* and the Radicals—operated in a more open and democratic fashion. Moreover, the Socialists and the *Falange,* being relatively new parties, had very young men, some of them only recently in the university, in the very top party posts. There was thus a complete identification with party and little sense of submission to some external authority for university leaders from these groups.

The university Radicals, who were perhaps most in a position to enter into conflict with the party hierarchy, found strong allies against the conservative elements within Radical ranks in the leftist wing of their own party. The Radicals were not a large group within the university, although the Radical Youth organization was important nationally. It was the least doctrinaire of the parties and reputed to be heavily infiltrated by Communists. There is no doubt that the Communists sought to capture key men in this and other parties, but there is considerable question about whether they were as successful as some ex-Communists and critics of the Radical party affirm.

Fundamentally, these men experienced no conflict between party loyalty and their obligations to fellow students because they were dedicated party militants. Within each party, there was some mechanism for determining policy—the majority of them according to some surfacely democratic procedure, in which the university group had a voice and often a vote as well. Once policy had been set, it was up to student leaders simply to accept the will of the majority of their fellow party members. With regard to university matters, the university party groups enjoyed a great deal of autonomy. Since they were in the FECH as party men, there were, in effect, no FECH aims independent of those worked out for the FECH in party councils.

The Party Militant

As was the case with the 1920 generation, complete biographical information was obtained for only eight of the outstanding student chieftains of the late 1930's.[62] These include four men who occupied the FECH presidency. Again no statistical claims can be made regarding the representativeness of the men interviewed. We have called this group of eight leaders "party militants." As with the "agitators" of the 1920's, the label covers a wide variety of political-action groups which may loosely be called parties. Even the one or two who remained aloof from the major political party cells within the university were not individualists or independents. They were also "organization men" engaged in a group political effort to win power within the narrow orbit of the university.

Were the shifts in organizational forms that have been described reflected in changes in the personalities of the men that moved into positions of ascendancy within the student organization? This study can give only an inconclusive answer to this question. Still, taken together with the companion material in Chapters 1 and 3, the discussion that follows constitutes a small addition to the growing body of empirical materials on personality and political attitudes and behavior.

The average age of these eight 1936–1940 leaders was forty-two in 1956. They were university professors, lawyers, physicians, architects, construction engineers, and sales executives. They were all fairly successful men who had the best years of their professional lives before them. Six were married and had children, one was single, and one was divorced.

Like their predecessors of the 1920 epoch, these men came almost entirely from solid middle-class families—about half of them from provincial cities. Their fathers included an engineer, an accountant, several proprietors of small businesses (two restaurants, one bakery), and a shoe manufacturer. One or two of the fathers had started out modestly, as mine workers, but by the time their sons were of university age the families had a fairly secure middle-class footing. Of the eight, three were the sons of immigrants—two of Spanish and one of Yugoslav origin.

With one or two exceptions, neither the father nor the mother in these families had received much formal schooling. By and large, these were definitely not intellectual families. In fact, there was no evidence in the interviews that set off these families as a group from the Chilean middle-class norm. It will be remembered that the families of the 1920 leaders were marked by the moderate nonconformism of the father's political and social views, as well as by the somewhat exotic origins of the foreign-born among them.

The post-university careers of this second group of student leaders had been markedly different from those of the "agitators." None of the eight could be called professional politicians; only one of them was politically active at the time of the interview, and he functioned almost exclusively within his professional circle. These men were absorbed in professional rather than political roles; whatever social and political ideals they continued to hold they sought to express through their occupational activities.

On the whole, the same tone of realism and objectivity about the self that prevailed in the 1920 materials was present. Past failures and felt inadequacies were introduced without elaborate rationalization or effort at self-justification. Few of these informants failed to characterize themselves explicitly as realists. All professed a concern for social and political problems that went back to their youthful days. If they were practical men of affairs, in their own view they were still guided by strong ideals and a sensitivity to human problems.

The two informants who were outstanding Communist leaders as students showed the most interest in the theoretical discussion of political problems. Both remained Marxists. One, a lawyer who was expelled from the party in recent years, confessed that he felt himself politically isolated. His criticisms of the party were cautious and directed primarily at questions of ineptness in leadership and tactics. He hinted that he would return to the party if the way were made clear.

The second ex-Communist abandoned the party early in the game, when the party's complicity in Hitler's rise to power came to light. He was active in Trotskyite and Socialist groups for a short time but has not been active politically for nearly twenty years. He had found compensating activities in the field of social medicine in the creation of community self-help projects for improving sanitation and health practices in worker neighborhoods. He had sought to do this solely on the strength of national and local resources, rejecting assistance proffered for such projects by United States foundations.

Four informants in this generation have had no important political activity since they left the university. Two of them were "independents" within the United Anti-Fascist Group that functioned in the School of Engineering, where the movement was almost exclusively oriented toward the containment of the Nazi group that flourished there. Of the remaining two, one was nominally a Falangist and the other a Socialist. Neither was drawn into leadership positions in the FECH by strong political convictions. They were sympathizers of these parties and were absorbed into the mold of rigid partisanship that prevailed in the FECH during their time in the university.

Another Falangist and another Socialist, both of them leading party men in their university days, made up the full roster of this group of informants. The Falangist still considered himself a party man, although he held no formal position within the party at the moment. In his opinion, he was serving the party's cause more effectively by taking a leading role in his professional association. The Socialist held a number of political appointments after leaving the university but seemed to have drifted away from the party. A lawyer, he became interested in maritime and commercial law after extended work abroad in the consular service.

Although by somewhat different avenues, all of these men arrived at remarkably similar positions. Unlike the 1920 leaders, whose youthful differences seemed to have lasted through the years and to persist as meaningful elements of personality, the careers of these men seemed to have converged toward a common focus. Almost all were without party; whatever ideological labels they may affix to their current views, they could all, with fairness, be classified as moderate leftists. However, this leftism was largely of the do-nothing variety usually ascribed to United States liberals; some of these men did not even bother to vote. All seemed wholly engrossed in professional pursuits or in the conduct of business.

Nevertheless, their political perspectives continued to reflect their youthful ideological commitments. The two former Communists offered an essentially Marxist analysis of national problems. Both regarded Marxism as the only scientific theory of society. Both felt that the Chilean left was in a sad state of disintegration and disorganization that was chiefly attributable to poor leadership. In the meantime, they said, the right had consolidated its forces and was in a position to challenge the hard-won gains made by the left since the late 1930's.

One of these ex-Communist leaders focused on the problems of excessively large landholdings and foreign imperialism in Chile. According to him, the subdivision of lands, as a solution to the problem of the massive concentration of landholdings that exists in Chile and elsewhere in Latin America, was a foolish scheme. Under capitalist conditions, small property gravitates toward larger property, just as small industry tends to become big industry. Marx himself, he pointed out, condemned small property. The only scientific approach to economics derives from Marx. That is why, he felt, organizations like the United Nations Educational, Social, and Cultural Organization UNESCO and the Economic Committee for Latin America (CEPAL) were bunglers that could no nothing to reshape the fundamental, structural weaknesses of Latin American economies. The Chilean Communist party, he asserted, had as deplorable a record on the issue of land reform as all the other parties in Chile. Also deplorable was the failure of communism to link with United States groups that suffer from imperialism as well as those middle-class groups in Chile and other countries that had competing interests with the expansive forces of United States big business. In this respect, he declared, communism in other countries has learned little from the experience and sagacity of Mao Tse-tung.

The Chilean executive, he argued further, is much too powerful. There are no balancing powers in local government, and the president's excessive attributes are often reinforced with extraordinary faculties granted by servile legislatures. In his view, the Chilean citizen is free only during the brief moment that he steps into the ballot box to choose his next dictator.

The former Socialist youth leader had forsaken the idea of a classless society. He now saw stratification as inevitable and functional, not only in group task performance, but in the moral and intellectual qualities of men. He took what he called a *modern* Socialist position. The state must plan, control—must intervene. It must see economic and political justice done, but not in such a way that individual dignity is injured. There has been in Chile a demogogic excess and intoxication with socialistic ideas. The contradictions are evident—item one of a party program will call for a relentless fight against imperialism, item five will talk about attracting foreign capitals. Some ground will have to be yielded on this point, he said, because foreign capital is in fact indispensable.

On the whole, these men did not look to present political parties for a solution to Chile's grave economic problems. None of the parties offered a way out, said one of these leaders, who was a *Falange* member in the university and was still sympathetic to that group. The country needs a regeneration of the traditional parties. Democratic life is impossible without parties. The country must hope that a solution to its problems is possible, even though it is hard to tell whether Chile has already touched bottom economically or is still on the way down. No single group can be held responsible for the country's economic plight. There has been inflation no matter what party was in power. He did not believe that any single group has controlled or controls power in Chile. Power is everywhere and nowhere. All who have won political power find themselves in the same boat; they can't create more out of nothing.

A more optimistic view was taken by the two engineers who were at the head of the anti-Nazi movement in the School of Engineering when the Nazi movement was at its most powerful. The similarity of views of these two men is less surprising when one considers that they have been close friends for a long period of time, and both admitted that it was difficult for them to be friendly with persons who did not share their opinions. Both put great stock in Chile's racial homogeneity and the native talents of Chileans. Both saw selfishness and lack of civic spirit as the fundamental faults. One, who has traveled in the United States extensively, complained that Chileans look out for themselves and care nothing for the country. The other asserted that the problem is that there are too many capable people in Chile fighting over the little that is to be had there. The country is not to be judged too harshly, he said; no nation has solved the problem of poverty. The country is young; it can only go up, concluded the other.

The equanimity of these responses and the calm, analytical note taken by the majority of informants must be weighed in the face of the deep economic crisis that faced the nation during the year of field work. Certainly there is selectivity in focus and approach that reflects ideological preferences. However, if the diversity of approaches and definitions of the nation's problems suggests confusion, consider that these men are discussing an extremely complex situation that has defied clear analysis by experts. It is at the same time the kind of situation that carries a terrible urgency and an ultimate sense of stalemate and despair, for the country has been caught in a vise of impotence with respect to inflation throughout the entire lifetime of this generation. In short, it is the kind of crucial political and economic issue that invites the projection of personal tensions.

There was, of course, a certain amount of such projection in these answers. The Marxist was eager to demonstrate that his interpretation of doctrine on the vital issue of land reform is more faithful to the spirit of Marx than that of the Communist party. The moderate Socialist expressed his newly felt reservations about socialist goals as a preoccupation for the preservations of individual freedom and dignity. The two leftist independents seized the opportunity to reaffirm their patriotic belief in the racial superiority of Chileans. Still, any solution of Chile's inflation must deal realistically with the modernization of land tenure and the social institutions of agriculture, with the preservation of civil liberties during the process of economic reforms and an evaluation of the human resources of the country.

The content here is less significant than the tone of the responses. If there was confusion present, it did not seem an evasion of reality responding to some personal need. There was a balance of popularized social analytical expertise and informed judgment that suggested an individual mind at work in most of the opinions. There was no vindictiveness and spleen in these answers; no facile solutions were offered; no one group or person was singled out for blame. In this respect, these men are very like their counterparts of the 1920 period. Thus, again, in a country where political passions are thought to be prime movers of public events, and among men who at some time in their lives have been intensely caught up in the partisan struggle, political materials revealed little evidence of displaced aggression or irrational animus.

Of these eight men, only one had a non-Catholic upbringing (his father was a Protestant minister). Almost all of them turned from the church in adolescence. Only one or two were nominally Catholic at the time of the interview. Three were principled atheists; three expressed a vague belief in some superhuman regulating force and professed a tolerant viewpoint on religion. Except for the Protestant minister's son, none of the men had fathers with a religious bent. Even in fairly Catholic families, the man of the house did not, and was not expected to, fulfill details of religious observance. In others, the fathers thought of themselves as freethinkers. It was the mothers and other family women who kept alive the links of the family with the church. The break with Catholicism occasioned little familial conflict for these men beyond occasional recriminations and entreaties from the mother. This pattern appears to be so common among young middle-class males as to have acquired the sanction of usage and familiarity.

The most suggestive difference between the men of these two generations is encountered in their attitudes toward parents. On the whole, these eight men showed the same high level of objectivity toward parental figures that was displayed by the 1920 leaders. Here, again, a fairly rounded appraisal of both parents, including both good and bad points, was given in the majority of cases. Parents were neither lionized nor vindictively caricatured.

However, in contrast to the 1920 group, there was strikingly little expression of distance or of rejection and minimization of the father in these interviews.

In the 1920 materials a common note of the father-images projected was one of weakness—the fathers were described as good, as well-intentioned but ineffectual and pusillanimous men. Some of the fathers of this second generation of leaders were pictured as impractical and quixotic by their sons, but the dominant note was one of severity and correctness. Fathers of this group were more often than not characterized as well organized, serious, tenacious, obstinate, firm, and *hard*. The mother did not emerge here as the dominant, stabilizing force within the family; she was overshadowed by the male head, even when she shared his strength of will.

Despite the emergence of the fathers as strong figures, there was little evidence of latent conflict between father and son in this group. There was frank, principled rejection—in one instance, father and son almost came to blows when the son refused to submit to bodily punishment as an adolescent. However, it is not the principle of parental authority that is questioned as much as the precise instances of its applications.

This observation invites the hypothesis that when the dominance conflict between father and son is resolved by a fundamental submission to parental authority, the tendency will be for the son to find the acceptance of the role of disciplined party militant more congenial than that of rebel individualistic agitator. When, by contrast, the father is never fully accepted as an authority figure, political behavior is much more likely to follow the pattern that characterized the 1920 generation. Previous efforts have been made to connect childhood relations with parents to aspects of political outcomes associated with similar childhood experiences.[63] It remains of interest that this particular feature should distinguish men who, despite a generational difference, are so alike in social origin and biography.

Leaders of this second generation of students also expressed much the same sentiments about friendship as did their 1920 counterparts, with perhaps a somewhat less poignant sense of frustration and isolation than was revealed by the older men. The desire for unconditional acceptance and the insistence on complete sincerity, disinterest, and unpretentiousness as the basis of true friendship are repeated here. Few, if any, existing friendly relationships fulfilled this idealized image for informants.[64] Yet few of these men gave the impression of being cut off from meaningful social contacts outside the familiar circle to the extent observed in the earlier group. More often than the sexagenarians, these men spoke of variety in the types and levels of friendship, the rewards of friendship, and the significance of friendly relationships in their lives. Yet a note of loneliness, of an unsuccessful search for unquestioning acceptance came through in these interviews as well.

The assumption that the sharp differences in the structure of the student organization in these two epochs meant that men of contrasting personality would come to the fore in each of the two periods is not well supported by these data. The dimensions of family background and personal attitudes that have been explored here reveal only one noteworthy point of divergence. If there were ever any fundamental differences in the personalities of these two generations of student leaders, they have been blurred by time or simply do not show up in our small sample.

Summary

Significantly, this account of a second period in the organizational life of the Student Federation of Chile ends, like the first, with the organization divided and moribund. Thus, in a sense, this study cannot be said to be an examination of evolution and change in the development of a single organism that has preserved its essential identity. It is, rather, a study of different *forms* of organization produced within the university milieu under varying circumstances.

Without a doubt, the most important external change affecting the FECH between 1920 and 1940 was the emergence in Chile of vigorous, broad-based parties of the left. The parallel development of a strong Nazi movement and a liberal Catholic force, in part as a reaction to the dramatic gains by the Marxist left, provided the framework for a political struggle that was perhaps more sharply crystallized within the university than anywhere else. When Chile became a successful testing ground for the popular front, there was reproduced within the nation on a small scale the global conflict of ideas and power drives that came to a head in World War II. This struggle was carried through in microcosm within the student organization. The analogy, of course, cannot be pushed too far, for the progress of this contest and its outcome at these different levels were far from identical.

The contrast in the enthusiasm awakened nationally by the popular front and the intensification of the Communist-Socialist struggle that it brought in the university show how the student organization was at once intimately involved in the political machinations of the time yet firmly excluded from the real centers of power. In a practical sense, the concept of the popular front had little applicability within the university. There, Communists and Socialists were the major political forces and were about evenly matched; each group was strong enough to feel that it could alone muster the votes and other support necessary to control the FECH. Within the university, Socialists were not seriously threatened by the success of Communists in winning the collaboration of Radicals. In short, it was neither necessary nor congenial to the true party initiates in the university to give more than formalistic approval to the popular front idea. This was not the first or the last political pact made outside the university that has not been fully honored by students—either by their own choice or on instructions from party policy-makers.

The ostensible unity of the parties on the national plane meant, however, that the struggle within the university had to be framed in nonpolitical terms—hence the emphasis on reform and student problems. The emergence of the new parties and the successes of the popular front thus had three chief effects on the FECH: (1) The FECH became internally crosscut by political factions more responsive to partisan interests than to FECH values in themselves. (2) The FECH was displaced as an innovating and orienting force providing political leadership to popular groups. (3) The political struggle within the university became a contest between the two major parties to appear as the champions of student interests and university reform.

The new political groups represented ideological currents that were also relatively new within the university. Communist and Socialist ideas were, of course, known among students even before the 1920 period, but the serious study of Marxism and Leninism and the popularization of Marxist-Leninist thought among students came only in the 1930's. Perhaps more important than the economic and political doctrines of the Communist ideology, in terms of its broad effect on the student organization, was precisely its emphasis on organization. Whether or not one accepted the materialist view of history, the potentiality of the weapon of organization as portrayed in Leninist writings struck home. The Nazi group justified its own paramilitary structure as a defense against the organized force of Communists. The conspiratorial party became the order of the day.

With the dominance of the political cabal within the student organization came a shift in attitudes and practice that produced marked differences between the 1920 FECH and its 1940 counterpart. The FECH became an *object,* a tool to be won, rather than a set of values to be served. Manipulativeness and indifference to long-range objectives were tacitly accepted in a leadership that was guided by expedience. In the absence of any unifying and moving statement of aims and in the face of the gradual alienation of the unpoliticized mass of students, two sets of values were agitated to enlist the support of students who were not responsive to partisan appeals. One of these was the banner of university reform and student welfare; the second was a vague set of canons inherited from earlier student generations, which broadly called on students to take a serious view regarding their own intellectual growth, as well as the development of the university, and to cry out courageously against social and political injustice wherever it existed. However, the FECH of the popular front era, outside of the university, was a follower not a leader. It echoed what went on outside; it did not present a united face or voice outwardly. When the political groups that had benefited most from student support came to power, the FECH role beyond the orbit of the university was circumscribed rather than broadened.

NOTES

1. Refer also to Julio César Jobet, *Ensayo Crítico del Desarrollo Económico-Social de Chile,* (Santiago: Editorial Ercilla, 1936); and Ricardo Donoso, *Alessandri, 50 años de Historia Política* (Mexico: Fondo de Cultura Económica, 1952).
2. Guido C. Macchiavello, "La Universidad desde 1927 al 1931" (Term Paper, School of Political and Administrative Sciences, University of Chile, 1953).
3. The status of the parties was such that in 1930 a new legislature was named by

executive decree after a meeting of representatives of the government at a watering place in the south of Chile. A constitutional provision permitting the parties to waive electoral contests when they agreed on the candidate for a given department was invoked to give legal footing to this "thermal Congress," as it became known. Luis Galdames, *Historia de Chile* (Santiago: Empresa Editors Zig-Zag, 1952), p. 557.

4. Townsend y Onel, *La Inquisición Chilena* (Valparaíso: Imprenta Augusta, 1932); Guillermo McInnes Mitchell, *La Checa Ibañista* (Santiago: Empresa de Publicidad Lepax, 1931).

5. P. T. Ellsworth, *Chile: An Economy in Transition* (New York: The Macmillan Company, 1945).

6. Frank Whitson Fetter, *La Inflación Monetaria en Chile.* The years from 1924-1930 saw the final entrenchment of United States capital and the displacement of the British in Chile. Jobet, *op. cit.*

7. Enrique Zanartu Prieto, *Hambre, Miseria, e Ignorancia* (Santiago: Editorial Ercilla, 1938). Also, Javier Vial Solar, *El Diluvio* (Santiago: Editorial Ercilla, 1934).

8. Details of student activities for the years from 1928 to 1935 are drawn in large part from Roberto Alvarado, "Tesis Sobre la Historia del Movimiento Estudiantil Chileno" (unpublished manuscript), and from extended conversations with Dr. Alvarado, Professor Aníbal Bascuñan, Professor Adolfo Tapia, Julio Barrenechea, and Ignacio Palma, all outstanding leaders of the student groups that sprang up about this time. Refer also to Raúl Marín Balmaceda, *La Caída de un Régimen* (Santiago: Imprenta Universitaria, 1933); Enrique Molina, *La Revolución, Los Estudiantes y la Democracia* (Santiago: Imprenta Universitaria, 1931); and Clarence Haring, "The Chilean Revolution of 1931," *The Hispanic American Historical Review,* Vol. 13 (May, 1933).

9. According to one account, 200 breakfasts were sent to the beleaguered students from the exclusive Club de la Unión by the Minister of Finance. Marín Balmaceda, *op. cit.,* p. 46.

10. The labor unions had fallen into disorganization during the years of the dictatorship except for an official group, the Confederación Republicana de Acción Cívica (CRAC). See Tulio Lagos Valenzuela, *Bosquejos Históricos del Movimiento Obrero en Chile* (Santiago: Imprenta el Esfuerzo, 1941).

11. The APRA in Peru was the outgrowth of student movements from about 1919 to 1923 that parallel closely student activities in Chile in those years. *Apristas* had been in touch with Chilean students and intellectuals since before the formal proclamation of this Americanist movement in México in 1924. The movement did not achieve the following in Chile that it might have had partly because of its focus on the integration of the indigenous Indian cultures into the mainstream of Latin American life. Since this problem was much less vital in Chile, this emphasis proved a barrier to its spread. However, the *Aprista* position on anti-imperialism, Indo-American unity, and an independent, American application of Marxist theory has had enormous influence among students throughout the hemisphere. See Víctor Raúl Haya de la Torre, *Treinta Años de Aprismo* (Mexico: Fondo de Cultura Económica, 1956); and Harry Kantor, *Ideología y Programa del Movimiento Aprista* (Mexico: Ediciones Humanismo, 1955).

12. Refer to chap. 1, "The First Hundred Years of Independence" and "The Institutionalization of Protest."

13. *El Mercurio* (Santiago), March 22, 1932.

14. Lagos Valenzuela, *op. cit.* Aristodemo Escobar Zenteno, *Compendio de la Legislación Social y Desarrollo del Movimiento Obrero en Chile* (Santiago, 1940).

15. Jorge Grove, *Descorriendo el Velo* (Valparaíso: Imprenta Aurora, 1933); Alfredo Guillermo Bravo, *4 de Junio: El Festín de los Audaces* (Santiago: Empresa Letras, 1932); Galdames, *op cit.,* pp. 566 ff.

16. A statistical analysis of the vote by party appears in Wilhelm Mann, *Chile Luchando por Nuevas Formas de Vida* (Santiago: Editorial Ercilla, 1935), I, 121.

17. Galdames, *op. cit.,* p. 571.

18. Juan Crocco Ferrari, "Ensayos sobre la Población Chilena" (Thesis, School of Economics and Commerce, University of Chile, 1947).

19. *Geografía Económica de Chile* (Corporación de Fomento, Santiago: Imprenta Universitaria, 1950). See also, Salvador Allende, *Realidad Médico-Social Chilena* (Santiago, 1943).

20. "Estadística Chilena," *Dirección General de Estadística,* XIV, No. 11 (November, 1940).

21. Crocco Ferrari, *op. cit.* See also, Ellsworth, *op. cit.;* and Oscar Bermúdez Miral, *El Drama Político de Chile* (Santiago: Editorial Tegualda, 1947).

22. Comisión Económica para América Latina, *Antecedentes sobre el Desarrollo de la Economía Chilena (1925-1952),* (Santiago: Editorial del Pacífico, 1954).

23. Julio César Jobet, *El Socialismo en Chile* (Santiago: Congreso por la Libertad de la Cultura, 1956). Refer also to Ricardo Cruz-Coke, *Geografía Electoral de Chile* (Santiago: Editorial del Pacífico, 1952); and Lagos Valenzuela, *op. cit.*

24. Jorge Gonzáles von Marees, *Gonzáles von Marees se Dirige a los Chilenos* (Santiago: Talleres Gráficos Portales, 1941).

25. "El Movimiento Nacional Socialista de Chile," *Biblioteca Nacista,* No. 1 (Santiago, 1932).

26. Eudocio Ravines, *La Gran Estafa* (Santiago: Editorial del Pacífico, 1957).

27. Lagos Valenzuela, *op. cit.*

28. Chamudez later left the Communist party and traveled to the United States. He served the United States Army in the European theater as photographer and became a United States citizen. After the war, he returned to Chile, where he was reinstated as a citizen by a unanimous vote of the Senate. See Marcos Chamudez, *Cuidado no me Desmienta* (Santiago: Editorial Alonso de Ovalle, 1954); and Ravines, *op. cit.,* pp. 98 ff.

29. *La Opinión* (Santiago), February 22, 1936.

30. The known fact that the Radical party is closely linked with Freemasonry in Chile suggests that the Masons had their part in the building of the Chilean popular front as they did in countries such as Spain. See José María Gironella, *The Cypresses Believe in God* (New York: Alfred A. Knopf, 1956).

31. In addition to Ravines, *op. cit.,* consult John Reese Stephenson, *The Chilean Popular Front* (Philadelphia: University of Pennsylvania Press, 1942).

32. Most of the factual data and statistics on the CTCH are taken from Lagos Valenzuela, *op. cit.*

33. Stephenson, *op. cit.*

34. Enrique Burgos Vara, *A Los Radicales de Mi Patria* (Santiago, 1938).

35. *Clamor* (Santiago) No. 1–18 (1938).

36. Gonzáles von Marees, *op. cit.*

37. *La Senda del Sacrificio* (Santiago: Editorial Nascimento, 1940). This is a commemorative volume, giving the National Socialist version of the events. It contains photographs and short biographies of those who died. See also Ricardo Boizard, *Historia de una Derrota* (Santiago: Editorial Orbe, 1941).

38. *Vanguardia Popular Socialista: Breve Explicación de su Doctrina* (Santiago, undated). The VPS denied racism but added that "we do not accept racial minorities that resist mingling and assimilation with the Chileans."

39. A notable achievement was the creation of the Development Corporation (CORFO), the first governmental agency of its kind in Latin America. See K. H. Silvert, "The Chilean Development Corporation" (Ph.D. diss. in Political Science, University of Pennsylvania, 1948).

40. Arnold Toynbee, *Survey of International Affairs* (Oxford: Oxford University Press, vols. for 1930, 1933, and 1936).

41. The two official party pamphlets cited in notes 25 and 38 of this chapter provide a full exposition of the credo of the Chilean Nazis.

42. *La Opinión* (Santiago), May 5, 1936.

43. *Proyecto de Grupo Unico Antifascista Propuesto por el Secretariado General de Avance* (Santiago: Grupo Universitario Avance, undated); *Boletín del Sector Comunista Universitario* (September, 1937).

44. In May, 1936, the Nazis were forcibly driven out of a Law School meeting to nominate candidates for the 1936–1937 period. Nazi raids and counter-attacks by others occurred repeatedly until the police massacre of young Nazis in September, 1938.

45. *FECH*, Organo Oficial de la Federación de Estudiantes de Chile, I, No. 4, 1934.

46. *Frente Popular* (Santiago), June 22, 1938.

47. *Boletín del Sector Comunista Universitario* (September, 1937).

48. *Segundo Congreso Mundial de la Juventud* (Edición de la Universidad de Chile y de la Federación de Estudiantes de Chile, undated).

49. *Antes que Palabras Hechos* (Editado por la Secretaria Nacional del Partido Socialista, undated).

50. *Flecha Roja,* Organo de la Falange Universitaria (Santiago), 1940.

51. Informants who took part in the conventions and newspaper reports of the time agree in this assessment of the temper of the meetings. Consult especially *Revista Universitaria,* Organo de la FECH, I, No. 3 (1939).

52. *La Opinión* (Santiago), May 5, 1936.

53. The reference is to the victory of the popular front presidential candidate, Pedro Aguirre Cerda.

54. *La Opinión* (Santiago), May 5, 1963.

55. *FECH,* Organo Oficial de la Federación de Estudiantes de Chile, I, No. 4 (1937).

56. *Revista Universitaria,* Organo de la FECH, I, No. 1 (1939).

57. *Torque* (Santiago), September, 1939.

58. Personal interview with Juvenal Hernández, Rector of the University of Chile from 1932 to 1953.

59. Luis Galdames, *La Universidad de Chile (1843–1934)* (Santiago: Universidad de Chile, 1934).

60. *Revista Universitaria, Organo de la* FECH, I, No. 3 (1939).

61. *FECH,* Organo Oficial de la Federación de Estudiantes de Chile, I, No. 3 (1937).

62. A total of fourteen leaders of the 1936–1940 period were interviewed. Data on the principal student events of the time and on organizational structure were obtained from all informants, but only eight went through the full schedule on personal background and present attitudes.

63. Early research linking authoritarianism and submissiveness in political behavior to patterns of authority in the family was conducted by the Institute for Social Research. Max Horkheimer, ed., *Studien ueber Autoritaet und Familie* (Paris: Librairie Felix Alcan, 1936). The general theme of this work, later carried forward in T. W. Adorno *et al. The Authoritarian Personality* (New York: Harper & Brothers, 1950), was that the modern family with its irrational authority structure permanently scars the child's ego. According to Horkheimer ("Authoritarianism and the Family Today," in Ruth Anshen, ed., *The Family: Its Function and Destiny* [New York: Harper & Brothers, 1947], p. 365), "... the modern family in fact produces the ideal objects of totalitarian integration." *The Authoritarian Personality* found that submissiveness and coldness in family relationships were marks of the potential fascist. One pattern found among unprejudiced individuals parallels closely that found among the "agitators" in this research. "The unprejudiced man, especially, seems oriented toward his mother and tends to retain a love-dependent nurturance-succorance attitude toward women in general, which is not easily satisfied. Such an orientation toward the mother, together with the conception of the father as 'mild and relaxed,' makes it possible for the unprejudiced man to absorb a measure of passivity in his ideal of masculinity" (p. 388). A United States study of Socialist students (Maurice H. Krout and Ross Stagner, "Personality Development in Radicals," *Sociometry,* II [1939] 31–46) who were contemporaries of the popular front generation in Chile, reported that these "radicals" referred to their mothers as strict, indifferent, or inconsistent. There was also evidence of incomplete identification with fathers. Harold Lasswell's *Psychopathology and Politics* (Chicago: University of Chicago Press, 1930) illustrates with extensive case histories the complexities of tracing the connections between early family relationships and adult political behavior. Gabriel Almond (*The Appeals of Communism* [Princeton, N.J.: Princeton University Press, 1954], p. 293) speaking of former Communists, many of them contemporaries of the subjects of the present study, remarks: "There were family situations in which the father was authoritarian and the mother weak, where it appeared that the party symbolized a revolt from the father. Among the American first generation native born of foreign parents a quite frequent constellation was one in which the father was weak and the mother dominant, and in which joining the party appeared to symbolize revolt from the mother and a search for a strong father."

64. Krout and Stagner, *op. cit.,* found that radical students had fewer intimate friends than more conventional students.

Chapter 3

The Guildsmen vs. the Political Activists (1956–1957)

Reform in the University

The years between the popular front victory in Chile and this final period were not as dramatic politically as were the years between 1920 and the front's triumph at the polls. All changes of government occurred peacefully by free elections in which violence and bribery had a minor and diminishing role. It was a period of gradual industrial expansion, offset by long-term inflationary pressures that no government has been able to contain. There were no rude shocks or changes politically or economically, but rather a gradual buildup of pressures marked by sporadic incidents of violence that betray the serious stresses present within Chilean society.

However, in these years students finally won some of the basic reforms in the university that had been talked about since 1918. The FECH was also able to consolidate its position within the university, obtaining legal sanctions for many of the privileges that students had exercised on an informal basis for several decades. These events have meaning for an understanding of what is happening in the university today.

The schism within FECH ranks after the 1940 election was the logical outcome of the bitter internal rivalry that had been rampant in student circles since the early 1930's. The gradual alienation of the mass of students from the warring cliques that dominated FECH action meant that both claimants to the federation presidency in 1940 met with the indifference of students.

139

Neither the leftist wing nor the anti-Communist faction was able to muster any real support in the university.

Efforts to inject new life into the FECH were repeatedly stalemated in the next few years.[1] The elections of 1942, 1943, and 1944 all produced the same discouraging results—in each case the elected officers proved ineffectual or incapable of working together. By 1944 there was a formal movement under way to scuttle the FECH. Groups in the School of Engineering and in the Pedagogical Institute voted a "blue ballot," calling for the elimination of the FECH and the formation of a co-ordinating committee of school centers.

While the federation continued in this low state, a number of schools in the university were energetically pressing for reforms of various kinds within the university. This surge of reformist feeling seems to have been at once a reaction to the sterility of FECH action and to the fact that some old problems within the university had grown to intolerable proportions. In some schools the reforms demanded and achieved were more limited than in others. The movements in the different schools reached a climax at different times and developed fairly independently of one another. The School of Architecture, the Pedagogical Institute, and the School of Engineering won the broadest and most lasting reforms. The Schools of Medicine, Law, and Agronomy achieved more limited changes in staff, curricula, and academic requirements.

Although each of these movements grew more or less independently, they were all linked by a particular set of sentiments and aspirations modeled on the Córdoba Reform movement (mentioned repeatedly in this discussion). Between 1944 and 1947 students poured forth articles, manifestoes, and speeches expounding the theory and principles of "The Reform." Stated broadly, students demanded revisions in curricula that would bring their training more realistically in line with their future professional needs and the needs of the nation. They sought the elimination of incompetent professors and outmoded methods of instruction. They demanded a more formal voice in all university councils.

On these university-focused goals there was general accord. Students found support for many of their demands in the ranks of the younger professors and assistants, as well as in the university council. This support was not always disinterested. Professional jealousies and ambitions and religious and political prejudices within the academic community blurred the issues. The university was convulsed by a long series of strikes, stormy meetings between students and university authorities, indignant resignations by professors, and accusations of duplicity and weakness from those displaced in the process of reform.

At first, no political group was in control of the movement; in the Pedagogical Institute Communists and Catholics fought side by side on the issue of reform. The FECH backed the movements in the different schools but never took over their direction; the federation was not sufficiently organized to undertake proposals for university-wide reforms until nearly 1946. However, inevitably, the movement split politically.

Two main issues divided reformist students. One of the chief elements in the Córdoban concept of the university is the view that the university is the chief receptacle, elaborator, and creator of the national culture. The university must seek to shape distinctive national and "American" cultures that truly reflect the spirit and mentality of modern America. The Córdoba Reform movement quickly acquired a nationalist and Americanist cast, which was broadly against all foreign influence and specifically anti-United States. However, Catholic groups sought to reaffirm the Catholic and Hispanic tradition as the fundamental core of Latin American cultures, while the leftists, heavily influenced by the *Apristas,* tended to glorify the indigenous Indian cultures and to seek some new cultural synthesis authentically expressive of man in the southern part of the hemisphere. This debate transcended the university and engaged intellectuals throughout the region.

The Córdoba program further affirmed that the university could not be simply a secluded harbor for study and research or a factory turning out professionals and technicians. The university must seek to serve the whole nation, not only by working to enrich the cultural opportunities of popular groups who are not pursuing studies at the university level, but by providing orientation and guidance to the nation with respect to major social and political problems. The university could not be an idle spectator; it must seek to define and defend the fundamental and enduring values by which the nation lives. On this score, students divided on the *degree* to which this responsibility should involve and commit student attention. The Catholics and more moderate elements wanted student pronouncements limited to broad declarations of principles, while the more politicized groups insisted that student action be firmer, more direct, accepting the challenge of small as well as large issues. This has been, of course, a long-standing cleavage in student opinion. The history of the FECH may, in fact, be seen as a series of cyclical shifts from extreme political activism to an almost exclusive concern for student and university problems.

With the reform movement in full swing in several schools, a national student congress was held in Valparaíso in May, 1945. The congress had been called by the Student Federation of Valparaíso, the organization of the students of the University of Chile in the port city. The Catholic University and the University of Concepción also sent delegations. There was some talk of forming a national confederation of students, but the congress itself could reach no agreement and wound up with factions meeting separately.

Still, a direct election of FECH officers, in which a majority of students participated, followed the Valparaíso meetings. A reform front, backed by Communists, Radicals, some *Apristas,* and independent leftists, took nearly 2,000 votes in this election. A Catholic Reformist group polled 947 votes; another group of independents took 723 votes; and the Socialists polled 291.[2] Most of the candidates, including those of the winning slate, were known as political independents. All the groups had campaigned on a platform promising a high priority for student welfare and university reform. All promised elevated and constructive criticism without political partisanship on national problems.

The reform front candidates proved to be one of the most effective and successful FECH administrations of all time. The list of their accomplishments is especially impressive, considering the low state in which they found the student organization. In one year the FECH obtained a new constitution and achieved corporate status before the law for the first time since 1920. The FECH was put on a more secure financial footing when the university agreed to assign a proportion of the matriculation fees collected each year to student activities. Several issues of *Claridad,* a student newspaper, appeared over a period of months. A Reform commission, including professors and students, addressed itself to the question of university-wide reforms. The basic structure was laid for a university press in which the FECH was to be an important shareholder. A new Popular University was established early in 1946.[3] A series of radio programs also sought to link the university with a broader public. Former FECH presidents laid the groundwork for the Andrés Bello Foundation, an alumni association of students of the university, named after the first rector. During this year, FECH presidents and two student-elected delegates were granted a voice in the University Council, the ruling body of the university.

Despite this enviable record, the university reform front lost the following election to the Catholic and independent opposition. The cleavages in student ranks persisted in spite of the great advances made in strengthening the formal structure of the organization. The outcome of this election was related to political events at the national and international level. Communist gains in the 1945 parliamentary elections and their success in wresting control of the Chilean labor confederation (CTCH) from Socialists had begun to disturb the complacency of the other parties. Political changes that seemed remote from student interests were again making themselves felt in the university.

The sudden death of President Aguirre Cerda late in 1941 brought to the Chilean presidency a candidate representing a compromise within the left and between the left and the opposition. President Juan Antonio Ríos was committed to a continuation of the economic policies of Aguirre Cerda's government but was looked to for a firm stand against what front critics called "the demagogic indulgence and pampering of labor and popular groups."[4] By 1942, only Chile and Argentina among the Latin American nations had not broken with the Axis powers. Until the Nazi attack on Russia, the Communists remained adamantly neutralist, and there was undoubtedly a respectable body of pro-Axis feeling among Chile's Germanic population as well as among the vestiges of the Chilean Nazi movement that had survived the ill-fated *putsch* of 1938. Some also felt that Chile's long, exposed coastline made a gratuitous declaration of war a foolhardy gesture, considering the fact that both Germany and Japan had powerful navies in vigorous operation. There was a secret mutual defense pact at the top military levels between

Chile and the United States, but the United States was pressing for an open break with the Axis and for more stringent curbs on Axis agents said to be operating in Chilean territory.[5]

A speech delivered in Boston in 1942 by Sumner Welles offended Chilean sensibilities on the point of neutrality. Welles was reported as having insinuated that Chile was stabbing democracy in the back. The United States ambassador had to placate the storm of resentment and protests, meeting personally with a delegation of students to explain that no offense to Chilean sovereignty and self-determination was implied.[6] When the break with the Axis finally came in January, 1943, there were great public manifestations in support of the Allies, and a moratorium on strikes was declared as Chilean labor's contribution to the Allied cause.

The Communists fared much better by remaining outside the front government and subsequent leftist coalition cabinets than did the Socialists, who took a leading role in the Aguirre and Ríos governments. Throughout the war years, the Communists continued to gain at the polls and within the labor confederation at the expense of the Socialists, who seemed incapable of maintaining a united front. The end of the war brought a change in political climate.

President Ríos' death in June, 1946, required still another presidential election. Gabriel Gonzáles Videla, with Radical and Communist support, won out by a small margin over the Conservative candidate, Cruz Coke. Since Gonzáles did not have a clear majority, he was forced to seek Liberal support in the legislature, where, according to constitutional procedure, final decisions in close races are made. Gonzáles launched his government with a cabinet including Communists, Radicals, and Liberals. The Communists were given the Ministries of Lands and Colonization, Agriculture, and Communications and Public Works. Soon the government found itself continually harassed by strikes, and for the first time the Communists made a determined bid to organize farm workers. The split in labor broke out into violent clashes between Communists on one side, and Socialists and anarchists on the other. There were a number of beatings and assassinations on both sides. The continued gains in parliamentary elections by Communists (1941 and 1945) and their new strength and influence in the labor movement and the government alarmed both Liberals and Radicals. These two parties withdrew from the government, and Gonzáles Videla finally asked the Communists to step down and proceeded to form an entirely Radical cabinet. As Communist pressures mounted, chiefly via continued strikes that crippled major industries, Gonzáles formed a "concentration" cabinet, including most of the major parties other than the Communists. In October, 1947, diplomatic relations with Russia and Czechoslovakia were broken, the government declaring that the labor unrest that plagued Chile could be traced directly to Moscow. In September, 1948, the Law for the Defense of Democracy, outlawing the Communist party, was passed. Communists were stricken from the electoral rolls, and hundreds were interned in improvised camps under military administration.[7] The same shift in mood was evident in the sphere of student politics. The Independents who had won the student federation election from the reform front in 1946 were guildists *(gremialistas)*; that is, they promised an apolitical FECH that would place student interests above all other considerations. They were anti-Communists as well. This politically moderate line was maintained for several years. Thus, in November, 1947, the FECH supported government charges that strikes in the southern coal fields were part of a subversive plot by Communists. However, the student committee that visited the area went on to describe the hard conditions under which the miners lived as well as the abuses to which they were subject from employers, police, and local government authorities.[8] A 1948 convention also took a firm anti-Communist stand and reasserted the determination of the new student directorate to avoid demagogic pronouncements or serve partisan political causes. Voting figures, however, showed that the leftists and moderates in the FECH were still fairly evenly matched. In the 1948 election the Communists running alone polled 1,527 votes; the victorious *gremialistas* took 1,955 of the total 5,700 votes cast.[9]

Between 1949 and 1956 control of the FECH see-sawed between shifting coalitions of *gremialistas* and leftists. The electoral combinations within the FECH are responsive to shifts in party alignments at the national level but are not entirely determined by external influences. The scramble for the top FECH posts by politically oriented cliques is still the major characteristic of the organization. During these years the FECH campaigned most persistently against the Law for the Defense of Democracy and against progressive increases in the cost of living, particularly the cost of public transport in Santiago. There was violence over bus-fare hikes in Santiago in 1949, 1953, and again in 1957.

During that time the FECH also came out against the sending of troops to Korea, against an educational co-operation pact with the United States (the Bowers-Leighton pact), and against a military treaty with the United States. At the time of the fall of the Arbenz government in Guatemala, students burned the United States flag in the principal plaza of Santiago. The FECH supported a long and unsuccessful strike for reforms in the School of Medicine in 1954, and in 1955 led a massive protest in behalf of a group of Peruvian students who had been denied political asylum by the Chilean government. In 1955–1956 and 1956–1957, top FECH offices were in the hands of a Christian Democrat coalition led by university Falangists, but a majority of the FECH Executive Council and of the FECH Assembly of Delegates was controlled by a rival bloc of Communists, Socialists, and Radicals. At first glance, the FECH seemed to have progressed little indeed since the crippling schism of 1940.

Chile: 1956

In mid-1956, the twenty-fifth anniversary issue of *Topaze,* the justly famous Chilean political-satirical review, carried as its centerpiece a cartoon entitled "25 years of Social Conquests in Chile." Below this caption there appeared twenty-five identical drawings of Juan Verdejo, the central character in *Topaze,* who typifies the working-class Chilean. Verdejo, his thin frame planted firmly on feet grown grotesquely large from going shoeless, stared out from the page twenty-five times with the same sardonic grimace, lurking somewhere between derision and despair.

The *Topaze* cartoon stated wryly a feeling that troubled many Chileans that fundamentally *nothing* in the country had changed in the previous few decades. Some of the parallels that can be drawn between the three periods studied are most disheartening. In all three, Chileans faced grave economic problems whose basic nature remained the same. Despite the almost permanent feeling that the country had touched bottom economically, the situation continued to deteriorate, with small gains offset by larger set-backs. In 1920, in 1938, and again in 1952, the Chilean people elected chief executives who were acclaimed with great public fervor as heralding new triumphs for workers and the lower middle class. Except for Pedro Aguirre Cerda, whose premature death may have spared him a similar experience, these men failed to fulfill public expectations and soon fell into disfavor with the popular elements that had voted them into power. All of them, on occasion, found stronger support for their governments among opposition parties than among the parties originally backing their candidacies. Furthermore, during all three time periods, the governments had requested and been granted extraordinary faculties to deal with political unrest. In all three there were laws restricting civil liberties and frequent abuses of these laws. Sporadic violent encounters between police and civilians occurred down the years. In all three periods, governments were charged with complicity in the destruction of private property (usually printing presses) without respect for due process—*Numen* in 1920, *La Opinión* in 1936, *Horizonte* in 1956. Of course, much the same could be said about almost any nation in the region and beyond. It is because Chileans themselves often speak as though they had advanced further in these respects than seems truly to be the case that the point bears making here. It is because these conditions are enduring elements in the situation of action for the student organization that they must be kept in mind.

Chile's economic problems have not gone unsolved because of a lack of careful study and diagnosis. There have been excellent analyses of Chile's economy carried out by Chileans independently, by international organizations, and by Chileans under the guidance of visiting experts.[10] The crux of the nation's problems can be expressed in a single statistic: the cost of living index in 1955 had risen to 2,887, taking 1940 as the base year.[11]

Numerous alternative explanations for the nation's failure to curb inflation after eighty years of harsh experience were offered in the mid-1950's. One study carried out by the University of Chile's Institute of Economics attributed the seemingly unbreakable wage-price spiral chiefly to the intense competition among different groups in the country for a bigger share in the limited national product.[12] Because Chile is a country in which competing interests have relatively free play politically, all programs of reform have been applied selectively, half-heartedly, and with an eye on political consequences. However, in this political "impasse" each group had not held its own. Between 1940 and 1956, wages fell from 27 to 21 per cent of the national income, although workers are still 57 per cent of the economically active.[13] When, in 1956, on the recommendation of a mission of United States economic consultants, the government introduced a series of economic measures to slow down the acute inflation, it was again workers who were first asked to "tighten their belts." This only served to aggravate the existing large and legislatively sanctioned gap in the pay scale between *empleados* (white-collar salaried workers) and *obreros* (urban wage-earning manual workers). Farm workers were at the bottom of the heap out of the annual competition for wage adjustments and unprotected by any of the social legislation that covers other workers.

A second explanation for Chile's inflation offered by the Institute of Economics focused on the inertia of the inflationary process once in motion. The failure of taxes to satisfy government financial needs has made for chronic deficits that have been covered by successive emissions of paper money. New issues of money have always been followed by price increases, which in themselves contribute to new deficits and fresh pressures for new emissions. Chronic inflation has also had psychological effects. It becomes a spur to consumption rather than saving or investment, giving added impetus to the spiral of prices and demand.

The Klein-Saks mission, a group of United States economic consultants engaged in 1955 by the Ibáñez government to produce a co-ordinated plan for curbing inflation, recommended the now familiar "monetarist" package—curbs on credits, tax reforms, cutbacks in government spending, especially in dollar expenditures, and the freeze on wages and salaries that has been mentioned. Throughout 1956 and well into 1957, the chief issue before Chilean public opinion was the efficacy of these measures. Initial confidence was shaken by the inability of the government to hold the line on prices as readily as it had imposed the ban on wage increases. Successive price boosts on vital items provoked widespread protests as did repeated revelations of fraud, corruption, favoritism, and waste in the government. Taking stock of the effects of the Klein-Saks program in April, 1957, *Panorama*

Económico, a Chilean economic review, acknowledged that the measures taken had slowed inflation, steadied the dollar-peso exchange rate, simplified the controls on exports and imports, provided some needed tax reforms, and won increased confidence for Chile abroad. On the negative side, the report charged that the Klein-Saks measures had created unemployment (especially in the construction industry), brought about a contraction of investments, and contributed to the regressive tendency giving wage-earners a diminishing share of the national income.[14] However, even the limited success achieved by the government's moves to halt inflation was attributed by some to high copper prices in the years before the reforms were implanted. With the drops in the price of copper in 1956 and 1957, more trouble loomed ahead for Chile. The country was producing more for export but selling abroad for less; population growth continued to outpace expansion of the national income. Life expectancy at birth had increased dramatically from 31.5 in 1920 to 51.4 in 1952.[15] Still the economically active group remained relatively small, unproductive, and burdened with a large number of dependents.

Between 1940 and 1956 industry had overtaken agriculture as a contributor to national income.[16] Chile had become an exporter of steel. It was also satisfying internally a growing proportion of its petroleum needs. The cement and paper industries had also expanded. Some of this growth was artificial. Most industry remained in an incipient state of high costs and low productivity; it was monopolistic and protected. Outside of the successful steel industry—a showcase for the nation—standards of quality in relation to price left a great deal to be desired. Chilean industry, as a whole, was still geared to production for a limited and noncompetitive market.

Agriculture remained the most backward and unproductive arm of the national economy. It occupied 30 per cent of those economically active but produced only 13 per cent of the national income. Per capita earnings in agriculture barely provided a survival standard of living. Food imports had been eating up foreign exchange despite the country's favorable ratio of arable land to population.[17] If there is any area in which it could be said with some justice that nothing had changed in Chile in the years spanned by this study, it is that of agriculture. Reform plans, aided by international and United States financing, were operating in selected areas in 1956, but the choice lands remained in the control of a small elite and were still inefficiently worked by an impoverished mass of tenant and migrant farm workers. Chilean landowners had repeatedly been able to buy time; despite much talk, no serious agricultural reforms had ever been undertaken. No effort to organize rural workers had ever gotten off the ground.[18]

In September, 1952, General Carlos Ibáñez del Campo, perennial aspirant to the Chilean presidency for more than thirty years, swept into office with one of the largest pluralities ever scored in a Chilean national election. Ibáñez ran in that election with the support of the Farm Labor party *(Partido Agrario-Laborista)* (PAL) and the Popular Socialists, one of the two major surviving Socialist factions in Chile. In addition to PAL, which itself was a hastily formed and heterogeneous group, a large number of small groups professing loyalty to Ibáñez' aims emerged at this time. The symbol of Ibáñez' campaign was the broom, with which he proposed to "clean out" the Radicals who had been misgoverning Chile since 1938. The general also promised to repeal the Law for the Defense of Democracy (which outlawed the Communist party), affirming that Chilean democracy could not tolerate the reduction of any of her citizens to the status of political pariahs. At the time it was rumored that Ibáñez' campaign was receiving warm support and some financial help from across the Andes in Argentina, where the general had spent some years in exile. Ibáñez pledged to Chileans an austere and disciplined government that would take decisive action regarding urgent economic reforms and defend the national interest against foreign encroachment, chiefly from the United States.

The general's victory was regarded as a sign of the disgruntlement of voters with the established political parties. Political commentators soon began to speak of "the September Revolution." For the first time, a substantial proportion of the traditionally captive rural vote had gone over to a candidate opposed by Liberals and Conservatives.[19] Ibáñez was popularly acclaimed as "the General of Hope." Although he early lost the support of the Popular Socialists, and the personalistic groups backing his candidacy soon began to disintegrate or themselves joined the opposition, Ibáñez refused to accept the collaboration of rightist parties in the initial years of his term. However, the economic measures taken in early 1956 were pushed through the legislature with Liberal and Conservative votes added to those of the remaining loyal PAL deputies and senators.[20]

An attempted general strike by Chile's major labor confederation (CUT) against the wage freeze that was a major feature of the reform program was unsuccessful. The government moved with a strong hand against workers, using the Law for the Defense of Democracy (it remained in effect, notwithstanding Ibáñez' campaign promises) to break up labor agitation and isolate the more belligerent labor leaders by relegating trouble-making union chieftains to remote, nonindustrial areas. Bank employees who went on strike and postal employees who only threatened to do so faced demotions and transfers to undesirable locations.

Despite these stern measures, as 1956 drew to a close it seemed clear that the government would be unable to hold the line on the wage freeze in the face of the mounting prices of vital consumer items. Various projects for partial salary "adjustments" were discussed in the legislature, and some of the legal price increases were held back as long as possible. Late in the year, an increase in bus fares was announced and rescinded after two or three weeks of agitation and demonstrations captained by a few student leaders.

This disposition to compromise and bargain (as well as some of the protest) in the early months of 1957 was in part dictated by an upcoming legislative election in March of that year. That election would not only test public acceptance of the government's reform program, it was also to be a pre-test of party strength for the new presidential election in September, 1958.[21]

The election, which took place in normal, orderly fashion, was proclaimed as a repudiation of Ibáñez and a reaffirmation of faith in the traditional long-established parties. There were only minor changes in the Senate lineup, where 20 out of 45 seats were renewed. In the Chamber of Deputies, where all 147 benches were contested, Radicals, Liberals, and the Catholic *Falange* were the chief winners. The displaced, in addition to Ibáñez' backers, were mostly members of the Popular Action Front (FRAP), a coalition of Communists, Popular Socialists, the Socialist party of Chile, and a few minor leftist factions.[22]

Immediately after the March election, the roster of price increases that had been held up since the beginning of the year began to go into effect. When a 5-peso increase was announced in the 10-peso city bus fares, students renewed the protests and demonstrations that had been carried out on a small scale earlier in the year. The fact is that the capital's archaic transport system is heavily overburdened; long waits, overcrowding, and the discomfort of riding on antiquated and poorly maintained equipment are a continuous irritant to the public. Successive fare increases over the years have always provoked public protests in which students have almost always taken the lead. In the space of a few days the protest snowballed, culminating in bloody disorders in the port city, Valparaíso, and in Santiago. In the capital, at least a score were killed, more than a hundred injured, and the downtown shopping and business area was for several hours at the mercy of an enraged and destructive mob.

As these figures suggest, the government had responded to the protests with the resolution to "maintain order" at all costs. The first sorties by students, workers, and the idlers who are always ready to add to the tumult on these occasions had been met by police squads, swinging nightsticks and firing tear-gas bombs. On April 2, 1957, when a mutinous mob threatened to engulf police contingents in the capital by the sheer weight of numbers, the police were withdrawn and the army was called in. Martial law was declared for a week while the president sought extraordinary faculties from the legislature to deal with what was called a subversive plot to overthrow the government.

Despite the hard opposition in the Senate and the Chamber of Deputies of Radicals, Socialists and other members of the Popular Action Front, the government was granted these extraordinary faculties. The opposition parties charged the government with negligence and provocation; they defied the government to produce a single seriously injured policeman or soldier to match the scores of civilian dead and wounded; they provided conclusive evidence that the printing press which published the Communist daily and a number of labor newspapers had been destroyed by police with complete disregard for legal procedures.

A few months later, the increase in the bus fares was imposed with little or no resistance. Neither students, nor the unions, nor the political parties seemed disposed to carry on the fight. By then, the center of political attention in the nation was on the nomination of candidates and the alignment of voting blocs for the forthcoming election to the national presidency. Senator Frei was the nominee of the Christian Democratic party, a fresh fusion of the National *Falange* with the United Conservatives. The Radicals, in a stormy convention, had placed another senator, Luis Bossay, in the running. Two other senators, Jorge Alessandri for the Liberals, and Salvador Allende for the Popular Action Front, made up the roster of top runners.

Chilean democracy and the endurance of her people faced additional hard tests. *Topaze,* in its sardonic fashion, had prophetically published a solid black page, labeled "Outlook for 1957," at the beginning of the year. The continuing descent in copper prices and restrictions in United States buying that came in that year certainly pointed toward even harder times ahead for the nation. None of the aspirants to the presidency or the parties behind them offered any alternative solutions to Chile's problems beyond those partially put in practice by Ibáñez—at least none that could be expected to produce any immediate results.[23]

While the rest of the society gave the appearance of standing still, the university had experienced substantial changes. In 1956 there were nearly 13,000 young people studying in schools of the University of Chile in Santiago alone. This was about four times as many students as had been enrolled in 1940 and about half of the students in university establishments even though there were now seven universities in the country. Chile's major university had become a sprawling establishment, with more than thirty schools scattered throughout the capital, Santiago, and with outposts in Valparaíso and Concepción. The university had twelve faculties, each with its dependent schools and research institutes, a flourishing theater group, a ballet troupe, and a symphonic orchestra. It administered hospitals, museums, experimental farms, an astronomical observatory, and a radio station.

Although the university remained financially dependent on the government, it continued to enjoy virtual autonomy in its internal management. The rector was elected by all professors, and deans of faculties were elected by the professors of each faculty. The president of the Republic still had to approve these appointments, but any government would hesitate to oppose the will of the university's professors in this regard. The University Council, the maximum ruling body of the university, is composed of the rector, the deans of the faculties, the directors of primary and secondary education, and two representatives of the national government. Two student delegates and the president of the student federation had been granted voice, but no vote, in this council.

The major weakness of the university continued to be its chronic poverty, less as a result of the indifference of the government than of the perennial economic difficulties that plagued the nation. In other respects as well, the university reflected the widespread shortcomings of higher education in the region. Professors remained, by and large, working professionals, teaching as an avocation, as a sort of public service with certain honorific rewards. Few of them engaged in original research or kept up systematically with advances in their fields.[24] Students, as had been the habit for many decades, did little collateral reading, but simply memorized from lecture notes, often printed and used year after year. Despite the notion of Latin Americans that they are more sensitive to humanistic and cultural values than their neighbors to the north, university instruction in Chile, as elsewhere on the continent, still tended to be almost entirely of a narrow, professional, and utilitarian bent. The extent of decentralization and the relative autonomy of faculties and the schools within them by this time made for a certain amount of duplication of effort and jurisdictional squabbles over what school had exclusive rights over a given subject matter.

The university's 13,000 students still constituted no more than 1.5 per cent of the young people between seventeen and twenty-five years of age in Chile. The sons of working-class families had yet little hope of reaching any of the major professional schools. However, this was not because of anything inherent in the university itself, but rather a reflection of general economic conditions in the country and the desperate poverty of Chile's rural and urban masses. Student welfare services had been expanded, and the number of "scholarships" (exemptions from the nominal registration fees) had grown through the years. Still, the university remained a stronghold of Chile's middle class, who were themselves often hard pressed by need and who were able to stay in the university only with great sacrifice.

The FECH election in September, 1956, gave the top three posts to a coalition of Falangists and Liberals with independent Catholic support. The remaining four seats on the Executive

Council were split between the Radicals and the Popular Action Front (FRAP), a coalition of Communists and Socialists. In recent years FRAP had allied with the Radicals, in university elections, to form a University Progressive Front (FAU). In 1956 the Socialists refused to run candidates on a ticket including Radicals, apparently on instruction from the party hierarchy, which had decided that a workers' front excluding the collaboration of bourgeois elements must be built in Chile. Nevertheless, the FRAP and the Radicals continued to work together within the student federation and to control its action, even though the voting split in the election threw the major student offices to the opposition.

The first few weeks of the new student administration were eventful. The summer vacation period, from December to March, brought the first open clash among members of the Executive Council. The president and vice-president of the federation were outside the capital. Only the secretary, a Liberal, and the four FRAP and Radical members of the Council were on hand to direct FECH affairs. During the summer vacation period, it is practically impossible to mobilize students for any concerted action; the assembly of school delegates does not even meet during these months. Not uncommonly, the government takes advantage of this lull to push through unpopular measures for which it anticipates student opposition. On this occasion, an increase in bus fares and other essential articles was announced as the school year ended. The fact that the campaign for the March, 1957, legislative elections was in full swing and that one of the Radical members of the FECH executive was a candidate in that election provided additional incentives to action for the young politicos in the FECH.

During January and February, FRAP and Radical student whips led almost daily demonstrations against the price increases. Relatively few university students, outside of the small nucleus of the most militant Radical and FRAP supporters, were active in these demonstrations. The nightly skirmishes between student-led crowds and the police were ignored by the non-leftist press. Still, whether as a response to these and other protests, or as a political expedient in view of the upcoming parliamentary elections, the government at this time rescinded the increase in bus fares that had touched off the tumult.

Three numbers of the FECH newspaper, *Claridad,* were issued during the month of February. These were largely given over to denunciations of police brutality against the demonstrators and the accusations that the absent members of the FECH executive were traitors to the student movement. The squabbling among the FECH Executive Committee members subsided as the school year opened. The committee began meeting in regular fashion in the first weeks of March, 1957, just after the legislative elections. A deceptive cordiality reigned at these meetings, where the FRAP and Radical combination now outnumbered the opposition by four to two, since the Liberal secretary was under suspension. In the relative privacy of the Executive Committee meeting it seemed possible for the rival political groups to work in friendly fashion, at least on problems related to student welfare and interests within the university.

The first full meeting of the FECH assembly of delegates, the *directorio,* was held on March 26, 1957. The meeting drew a large crowd. One large contingent from a university school for medical aides came seeking FECH support against a decision of the University Council to do away with the school. The remainder came to take part in or watch the spectacle of a public showdown between the rival members of the Executive Committee. Though the session began with a semblance of order, once the round of accusations, counter-accusations, and recriminations was set off, the meeting rapidly deteriorated. It ended in a bedlam of screams, with Liberals and Falangists on one side of the hall shouting *"Chile sí, Rusia no,"* while the FRAP and Radical contingents replied with *"Chile sí, Nazi no."*

Three days later, students in the port town, Valparaíso, led the public in mass demonstrations that won a provisional repeal of fare increases there. The success of Valparaíso students in mobilizing popular support irked the pride of Santiago student leaders. A council of war was held in which representatives of all the political groups in the FECH agreed that a university-wide movement was in order. It was unanimously agreed to hold an emergency rally on the next night, a Friday, and to organize a major display of strength for Saturday noon. The plan was to make this a well-organized showing, in which university students would be the chief participants and maintain control. There was to be no violence but chiefly attempts to tie up traffic at strategic intersections. It was explicitly agreed that some of the more aggressive FRAP militants and the impetuous secondary school students would have to be curbed.

None of this worked out altogether according to plan. The Friday rally emptied into the streets in a noisy, disorganized, and violent demonstration. The next morning some 2,000 students and sympathizers gathered to march down Santiago's Alameda. The column was diverted by a police phalanx firing tear-gas bombs. The news from Valparaíso had apparently affected the mood of the public as well as that of students. The crowds of afternoon shoppers cheered the demonstrators on; office workers applauded and shouted encouragement from office windows. Stones flew, and buses were damaged. Parked cars were pushed into the middle of the streets as roadblocks by the demonstrators.

After this first substantial show of strength by students, the Minister of the Interior received the president of the FECH. The minister insisted that he could not revoke the fare increase and urged students to reconsider their position. He promised that students would be allowed to hold public mass meetings and to demonstrate in an orderly fashion without police interference. Students were requested to make known to the military commander of the area the time and streets through which columns of demonstrators would be marching.

By Monday night, there was a mutinous atmosphere in the capital. Half-tracks and tanks patrolled the streets. Secondary-school students, as well as those in evening commercial schools, both of which have independent organization, had joined in the protests. A turbulent mass meeting was held in front of the university, with the permission of the military commander of the area. That night produced the first death in the ranks of the FECH, a young nursing student was killed by police bullets during one of several altercations that occurred as the mass meeting dispersed.

The death of the young student, Alicia Ramírez, after the only mass meeting held under the tentative truce between the students and the government, put negotiations on a new plane. On Tuesday morning, April 2, when the impending new violence was already foreshadowed, student leaders met with the representatives of all the major political parties in order to work out some formula of compromise. The president of the Senate then approached the Minister of the Interior with an offer from students to call off their strike and all further demonstrations provided that the government (1) revoked the fare increase, (2) freed all those arrested, (3) determined guilt in the death of Alicia Ramírez, and (4) created a commission to study the problem of municipal transport.

By mid-afternoon, as the crowds in the midtown area became uncontrollable, the government was prepared to accept all of these conditions. The president of the FECH rode in a military jeep to FECH headquarters to obtain ratification of the terms of the agreement from the Executive Committee of the student organization. However, events ran ahead of the parleys. By the time the students returned to the Senate with the approval of the committee, and this was again brought up to the Minister of the Interior, the government had backed up and decided to deal with the rioters in a summary, military fashion. Martial law was declared, and the negotiations ended.

Nevertheless, the fare increase was later rescinded and a commission was set up to carry out a study of transport costs in the capital. The commission invited a student representative to sit with them, but students declined the offer saying that they refused to view the problem as simply a matter of cost accounting. Despite this, the government asked students to study the report of the commission, which attempted to arrive at an estimate of true costs on the basis of the best data that could be obtained on such short notice. Even after students had rejected the committee report, student representatives were invited to meet with government officials and finally with President Ibáñez himself in efforts to persuade them of the inevitability of the fare increase. These may have been no more than token gestures or clever public relations on the part of the government. The fact is that as soon as the winter vacation period came around near the end of July, the fare increase was imposed again with no public outcry. Efforts to rally labor groups and students for a new campaign of resistance failed to get off the ground. The movement was spent; the *directorio* was no longer meeting; examinations and the new student elections were in the forefront of student attention.

Party vs. Interest Group

The 1920 generation and that of the popular front had, each in its own way, a basis for hope and optimism. They could believe that Chile was moving forward adventurously toward new conquests—that imminent social and political reforms promised to revamp Chilean society and erase long-standing inequities. The young men in the university in 1956 had no such vision. President Ibáñez, dubbed by publicists during his campaign as the "General of Hope," had few supporters within the university. The Popular Socialist party was the only party with any university following that backed Ibáñez. However, the Socialist brigade in the university split over the party's decision to support the general, and the Socialists did not begin to gain new strength in the university until after the party had turned against him.

By 1956, the political shadowboxing that was carried on so intently by the handful of adepts within the university and by their mentors outside it only thinly masked the underlying sense of stalemate and frustration gripping many Chileans, young and old. In the university the prevailing attitude toward the FECH and politics was one of apathy, indifference, or precocious cynicism. The trend was against taking extreme political positions except opportunistically. There was a peculiar conservatism abroad in Chile—a moderation born of fatigue, boredom, and hopelessness. The fact that the conditions making for protest remained glaringly evident and produced sporadic incidents of violence made this conservatism more difficult to perceive. However, beneath the surface show of relentless political combat, the visitor sensed an ennui and defeatism more suggestive of some decadent European power than of a presumably "young" nation in one of the world's newly developing areas.

The 1956 generation of university students had lived from childhood until the presidency of General Ibáñez entirely under Radical-dominated governments. Most of them were in high school when, in 1948, the last of the loose and ineffectual leftist and Radical coalitions that had governed during World War II held office; they are contemporaries of the young soldiers who fought in Korea. They awakened to political concerns in the climate of the cold war and the Law for the Defense of Democracy, which technically outlawed communism in Chile. They reached the university well after the wave of reforms (1944–1947) that had signaled a new era of growth and expansion for the university and consolidated the FECH's position within it. The battle lines between reformist guildsmen *(gremialistas)* and the political party men in the FECH had been drawn long before this contingent of students arrived on the scene. Still, the basic cleavage among students in this final period was articulated in terms of this conflicting definition of the role of the student organization.

The constitution governing the Federation of Students of Chile in this period is not a document familiar to many students. It took the writer several months to unearth a copy; even the members of the top seven-man Executive Committee had only sketchy knowledge of its main provisions. Nevertheless, the statement of federation objectives in the present charter is indicative of the shift in mood from earlier periods; it could hardly be further in spirit from the Declaration of Principles worked out by students in 1920. The aims of the student organization, according to this 1954 statement of purpose, are:

1. To represent students of the University of Chile before university, educational, political, and administrative authorities of the Republic;
2. To work toward the solution of university problems—educational, administrative, financial, and social;
3. To work for the material and moral welfare of members;
4. To make known student opinion regarding economic, social, political, and educational problems which arise in the nation and internationally;
5. To promote the extension of culture both within and outside the university.[25]

The FECH here officially defines itself as primarily an organization working for the defense of the interests of students and the solution of university problems. Its role in national politics is by implication secondary and presumably limited to the expression of student views on major problems. In contrast to the 1920 Declaration, this constitution has a great deal to say about what the organization will *do* and nothing whatever about the principles or ideals that will guide that action. As will be recalled, the earlier Declaration was very vague as to program of action but took considerable pains to present students' concepts regarding society and man's place within it, as well as the specific responsibilities facing youth in the university. While the earlier Declaration was a blanket indictment of the existing social structure, the 1954 document attacks nothing and no one.

The very blandness and lack of substance of the statement of aims current in the 1950's reflects, in part, the division in student ranks between those favoring a nonpolitical, student-oriented organization (the guildsmen, or *gremialistas*) and those who leaned toward the contending set of goals and values presented by leftist students. The guildist position was in itself not entirely nonpolitical. Although it drew its chief support from independent or politically indifferent students, its leadership came from the Christian Democratic forces and liberal ranks within the university. The "independent" guildist vote reputedly came almost entirely from Catholics. The spokesmen for the "apolitical" guildists in the university are all prominent figures in university political groups. They do not rule out political activity as such but would limit FECH political action to the letter of the Constitution (that is, to broad statements of student opinion on current issues). In the words of a Liberal party youth leader, prominent in FECH activities:

> We believe in knowing and understanding our national reality, but this is to be applied only on broad lines. They [the opposition] want to use it [the FECH] constantly as a means of momentary political agitation. . . They want to carry to a maximum, to the least detail, this agitation, this knowledge, this concern. This is an abuse of the possibility that students have for carrying forward their political action. We believe that University politics should aim exclusively at orienting, exclusively at student welfare; it should promote guild feeling with the University.

This Liberal leader went on to say that the leftist groups ostensibly do not oppose these efforts to work for urgent student needs, but that since the student organization has limited means, the choice of taking a more combative political stance inevitably drops student welfare projects to a sorry second place.

Speaking for the Catholic *Falange* and United Conservatives, another guildist leader explained the position of the *gremialistas* in these terms:

> To me the ideal thing would ·be what I told students during my campaign. . . the Federation has to change. What happens in our

sessions? The Marxist rises and says, "Friends, we are against all this injustice that exists in the world, we must carry forward the bloody revolution." But I have asked them whether they have any statistics on the number of students from the provinces who have no money to pay for their lodging. And they do not know; they don't even know the students from the provinces in their own classes because they do not bother to become acquainted with their fellow students. Our ideal and what I would like is for someone to come with statistical data and concrete solutions for the problems of student housing; that is what we believe these organizations are born for, to serve students.

At loggerheads with these guildists were the Communists and Socialists (FRAP) and the Radicals. The FRAP and the Radicals vied for the support of leftist students but generally banded together against the Christian Democrats and Liberals. The FRAP and Radical position had the advantage of being in the grand tradition of student activism; it struck a sentimental chord that its exponents did not fail to exploit. Although the Marxists have little respect for the romantic generation of 1920, even they occasionally (but more commonly the Radicals) invoke the heroic feats of the 1920 youths as a model of student political action. One of the more articulate FRAP leaders had this to say with respect to FECH objectives:

. . . the Popular Action Front has emphasized the intimate relation that exists between the life of the nation and the problems of the University. In our judgment it is not possible to speak about University reforms without assuming some fundamental transformations in the nation. . . . Because of the high registration fees, the entrance examinations, the length of the courses, the lack of scholarships, and the economic crisis, the University is becoming exclusively a house for the middle class and primarily for the upper middle class. The University FRAP does not look at the problems of the University as isolated from national problems. For us, to talk about the University budget is to talk of the problem of our copper, our nitrate, of the redistribution of the national income, etc. . . . There is no University problem that does not have some political content.

There is some division in the ranks of university Radicals on this issue, but the dominant viewpoint is close to that of the Marxist left. According to one Radical university chieftain:

We believe that the University student—and this may seem strange to you in the U.S.— should have political ideas and should be a member of a political party. . . . Because through political parties one enjoys a certain plan of action; one has a program, an ideology. . . . For us, the University student who does not have political ideas and act in a political party is a bad citizen and does not meet his obligations. Because tomorrow that student will have to act in different areas, and he will have an important role in society. . . . We believe that the FECH's role—and that is what we fight for—is to be, if you will, a receptacle of the needs, of the economic and social problems that exist around it. We believe that the University should reach out to society.

These are the terms in which the issue is posed at the value level. Actually neither contingent challenges the need for students to act both in defense of their own interests and in the broader political sphere. It is a question of priority or degree; as a matter of practical, workaday politics, each group in the university tries to appear more "guildist" or more social minded, as the occasion dictates. At bottom, the mass of students seemed as indifferent to the exhortations of guildists as to those of the political activists among federation leaders.

Although one heard frequent, bitter talk among students and alumni about how weak and riddled by politics the FECH was between 1956 and 1957, the organization was then on a stronger formal footing than in either of the two time periods that have already been analyzed. The FECH had legal status as a corporate entity; it had stable, formalized links with the university administration and the cordial endorsement of the rector and other university authorities. It enjoyed a steady, assured income collected as part of university matriculation fees as well as occasional contributions for special projects. All of this had been inherited from the dynamic reformists of the middle 1940's.

The 1954 constitution vested executive powers in a seven-man committee. The chief decision-makers of the student organization were in this Executive Committee, made up of the FECH president, vice-president, the secretary, and four members at large. These posts were filled in university-wide elections; the candidates for these offices, practically without exception, were leaders of the political party groups in the university. The committee is responsible for preparing the agenda for meetings of the FECH Assembly (the *directorio*) and for carrying out the decisions of that body. Since the Executive Committee members are captains of the political cliques at work in the *directorio,* and the lineup of political force is similar in both bodies, for all practical purposes the Executive Committee has the first and final say on all issues. *Directorio* meetings are, in a sense, only Executive Committee meetings with a broader audience.

The *directorio* is made up of the presidents and delegates of the federated schools. There were twenty-five federated schools in 1956 and 1957. Each school had delegates in proportion to its enrollment, with a minimum of two delegates per school. The Pedagogical Institute, and the Schools of Law and Medicine, with twelve, nine, and seven delegates, respectively, were the schools with the largest representation. This assembly was the chief stage of political action in the FECH. The *directorio* held weekly meetings during the school year, although there was often difficulty in raising the quorum of thirty-four delegates (one-fourth of the total).

The *directorio* performed three chief operations of political significance: (1) it emitted resolutions or *votos* stating the position of the FECH on given issues; (2) it declared university-wide strikes; and (3) it approved projected street demonstrations in support of FECH demands. Any resolution or action taken by the *directorio,* presumably the authoritative voice of all students in the university, is expected to have a greater public impact than the statement or act of any single party youth group.

The 1954 charter also provided for a number of departments or commissions (Student Welfare, Publicity, Cultural Extension, University Reform). A member of the Executive Committee technically heads each of these, with each other member of the Executive Committee naming a representative to each commission. In the year under study, these commissions were largely inoperative. It should be observed, however, that this practice of naming commissions on the basis of the existing representation in the Executive Committee *carried through the political split at the top to every working arm of the organization.*

Since 1946, the FECH president and two delegates selected by the *directorio* sit in on meetings of the University Council, the highest ruling body of the university. Although politics inevitably weighed in the selection of these delegates, these offices were taken quite seriously by students at large and those who acted as delegates. They were usually outstanding students, commonly *egresados* (those having completed course work but not receiving their degrees) from major professional schools such as Law or Medicine. Students had been admitted to the council on the basis of a broad interpretation of the existing University Statute which provides that students shall be represented before university councils in all matters concerning their welfare. Student delegates had a voice but no vote in these sessions.

The FECH charter provided for the disciplining by the *directorio* of lax presidents or delegates of federated schools. However, despite the fact that technically a majority of delegates had disqualified themselves (through nonattendance at meetings) by the end of the 1956–1957 term, no action was taken against them. It would be even more difficult for the FECH to disqualify a school president for neglect of his duties as long as he took care of his responsibilities within his school. The FECH had little moral authority over the mass of students. According to all informants, the majority of students in federated schools are indifferent to FECH affairs and feel no sense of obligation to the central organization.

The predominance of the party political groups within the FECH is formally acknowledged only in the electoral statutes; the constitution itself gives no clue that the FECH is at once a federation of schools and a federation of warring party organizations. On the all-important question of nomination to office, however, the power of the parties is bared. The signature of the president and secretary of any *political* group that has representation in the Executive Committee or *directorio* is sufficient to nominate a candidate to any FECH office. Without these, it takes the signature of ten delegates or two hundred students to name a candidate to the Executive Committee, or of one delegate from the school or twenty students to place someone in the running for the *directorio*.

In many ways, the patterns of FECH action remained unchanged since 1940. The parties retained their grip on the top FECH posts. It was the presence within the university of a powerful voting bloc of moderates—Liberals, United Conservatives, and Falangists, backed by independent Catholics—that in 1956 gave the FECH a new stamp. This group was not as effective within the organization as their leftist antagonists—Communists, Socialists, and Radicals. But their mood of restraint, their disposition to negotiate rather than protest, and their professed commitment to a rational and technical approach to problems seemed more representative of the mood of students at large. In fact, even among the leftists at that time the style of leadership being cultivated was that of the "technician." The model of the leader had shifted dramatically since the 1920 days—fiery oratory met with impatience and derision. The rising star was the "manager" of student interests—the successful negotiator, planner, and organizer.

The federation was still technically the organization of all students of the University of Chile in Santiago and university alumni for two years after graduation. However, the FECH now enjoyed a "closed shop"; students automatically became members on enrollment. However, there were now five other universities in Chile in addition to the Valparaíso and Concepción outposts of the University of Chile. Although the FECH still held on to the name "Student Federation of Chile," it at best covered about half of the young Chileans in university establishments. The FECH was still the organization technically representing the largest student bloc, but it was no longer the unrivaled spokesman for all university students in Chile.[26]

Although on the surface the FECH in 1957 reclaimed its traditional role as a spearhead of popular protest, in fact, students stepped into the leadership vacuum only half-heartedly. The impotence of labor and political leaders thrust students momentarily into the foreground of popular protest. The FECH was offered a prominent place in several joint commands including political and labor groups that were organized to resist the wave of price increases. Student delegates participated on an equal footing with labor leaders in these discussions; they were heard with deference and given a considerable share of power and responsibility in the proposed organizations. Yet none of these efforts produced any concrete results. Neither the unions, nor students, nor the political groups behind them showed much real determination. It was not just that student leaders were divided politically or were chiefly attentive to party directives. There was no real backing from the mass of students for this kind of action. The demonstrations, culminating in the April, 1957, rioting at their height, involved at most some 1,500 of the approximately 12,000 students in federated schools. Students themselves were quick to repudiate the violence and vandalism of the mob, and in fact tried to curb the looting and helped turn back a column that was bent on staging a protest at the doors of the presidential palace. No one seriously accused students of having engineered the tragic events. It seemed clear that student leaders, as well as the political parties and the government, had been caught by surprise.

The FECH of the popular front days was circumscribed in its aims and range of action by political factionalism and by the fact that there were powerful parties and a vigorous labor organization monopolizing the leadership of popular groups. The FECH action in 1956 and 1957 was still frustrated by internal political conflict, but limitations on the scope of activities were to a greater degree *self-imposed*. Although the charter definition of the political role of students (namely, to make known student opinion on broad questions of national and international policy) was not observed to the letter, it was only the hard nucleus of political activists within the organization that fought to give the FECH the appearance of being a politically potent and combative force.

The FECH links with organized labor in this last period were thus informal and sporadic. The major confederation of Chilean labor unions, CUT (the *Central Unica de Trabajadores*) had suffered a series of crushing defeats at the hands of the government; the Law for the Defense of Democracy had been applied against Communist as well as non-Communist labor leaders. Like the FECH, CUT was internally split by political factions and personal cliques. In addition, there were rivalries between CUT and non-CUT unions as well as tensions between white-collar and worker organizations. The labor press itself lamented the widespread disillusion and unresponsiveness of the rank and file and the lack of unity and combativeness among wage earners.

Labor had almost always been able to count on the backing of the FECH and FECH leaders have almost always stood ready to provide a rallying point for workers when labor leadership has failed or been under heavy attack from the government. Yet the internal divisions in both labor and student ranks made co-operation on an *organized* basis impossible. Students retained some sentimental notions about solidarity with the working class and some illusion that working-class people looked to them for leadership; however, these were not translated into any effective action on the part of the FECH as an organization.

The relationship between the national parties and their militants at work within the university is also not so simple or one-sided. Student leaders are not merely dupes and shields of more mature politicians. Party members in the university are only a fraction of the young people in the youth organizations of the several parties, which usually include party supporters between fourteen and thirty years of age. On university questions proper, the student groups have almost complete autonomy. Even on national political issues, students sometimes take a stand opposed to that of their parties. The Falangists in the university repudiated their party's support of the measure granting special faculties to President Ibánez after the April, 1957, rioting. The Liberals and Conservatives in the university supported student demonstrations against bus fare and other price increases even though their parties were backing the government on this score. University Radicals stood fast against the Law for the Defense of Democracy, which was sponsored by their party. Except for the Falangists, student leaders in these parties complained more about indifference and petty opposition from the party hierarchy than about any strong pressures from above.

The Communists and Socialists are probably the most disciplined groups, although even here the classical image of the totally committed revolutionary is inappropriate. None of the parties has been fully successful in drawing students into broader party functions. University Communists, like the militants of other parties, are assigned few tasks outside the university. To say, then, that the student organization is "captive" or riddled with political factions is not to say that it is a passive instrument of older and more experienced politicians. The FECH is really in the hands of *students with strong political convictions,* who have a strong sense of dedication and allegiance to their parties. The university political groups enjoy considerable independence within the broad framework of basic party policy and organization. They are in a position to influence party decisions through their dominance in the youth sections and by allying themselves with sympathetic elements in the party hierarchy. They ordinarily experience no conflict between their loyalty to party and their responsibilities to fellow students because they believe their parties offer acceptable solutions to the problems of youth and the nation.

The parties make no direct contributions to the FECH, although they do assist their university groups financially in campaigns for FECH posts. By all accounts, no great sums are involved—just enough to print ballots, make posters and streamers, and run off handbills. There was no outward evidence during 1956 and 1957 that any party was pouring great sums of money into efforts to win adepts within the university.

A truly decisive factor which lent a new stability to the FECH was the regular subsidy received from the university. This subsidy allowed the FECH to finance its day-to-day activities and, perhaps most importantly, to rent permanent quarters. In 1956 the FECH had been housed for some years in the lower story of a building fronting on Santiago's main thoroughfare, the Alameda Bernardo O'Higgins, about two blocks from the administrative headquarters of the university. The student meeting place was gloomy, unattractive, and poorly furnished. *Directorio* and other large meetings were held in a skylighted inner courtyard around which were grouped several offices and smaller meeting rooms. The FECH house had no reading rooms, lounges, or facilities for serving refreshments of any kind. It offered nothing except to those who were highly motivated politically.

Financial support for special projects continued to come from the rector's office. In 1956–1957 the FECH received about three million Chilean pesos (about $5,000) in subsidy. Additional monies were given by the rector to finance a visit to northern mining camps by a group of students who sought to bring the university's work to the attention of workers and others in isolated parts of the republic. Additional funds were given to help pay travel expenses for student delegates traveling to the Moscow Youth Festival.

Foreign embassies and the cultural institutes that several countries maintain in Chile (for example, the United States, France, and Great Britain) made occasional gifts to students. These commonly took the form of scholarships for language courses given by these institutes. Also, student leaders were not infrequently offered opportunities to travel in exchange of persons programs for short visits or longer periods of study abroad. Although Chile officially had no diplomatic relations with

Russia, large numbers of students and others travel to youth conclaves in socialist nations. Nonpolitical students sometimes accused student leaders, and leaders sometimes accused each other, of being chiefly motivated by a desire to cash in on these opportunities for subsidized tourism.

Like everything else in the FECH, plums such as these tended to be apportioned on a political basis. Once it was agreed to accept an offer, each political group expected to share in proportion to its representation in the Executive Committee. Decisions about accepting donations and other assistance, as well as the use or distribution of what was received, were thus inevitably colored and confused by political considerations.

The ideal of the university as a republic in microcosm, central to student ideology in Latin America since the days of the Córdoba University Reform movement, has not been perfectly achieved in Chile. However, the student is used to exercising a much greater role in the conduct of university affairs than would be dreamed of on a United States campus.

Some would like to see the right of student delegates to a vote in the University Council put explicitly into the university statute. Delegates occasionally complained that they were not accorded due consideration in council meetings. Technically, the council could at any time declare itself in secret session and request student delegates to withdraw. However, despite a permanent preoccupation with reforms, particularly at the school level, there was no urgent feeling that student rights were overlooked or that desired changes could not be won under the existing framework. The close contact of the FECH president and council delegates with the rector and other university officials gave them an "inside" perspective on university problems that led them often to act more like council delegates *to the student body* than the reverse. Council delegates reported at length in FECH sessions on the reasons for decisions by the rector's office, often acting to placate the demands of particular schools or groups of students.

Strikes in particular schools are sometimes directed not at local authorities but at the rector. Local school authorities may in fact be working hand in glove with student leaders to win some change desired by both students and professors. The extent of decentralization of university establishments is such that some of the small schools (particularly the few that are attached to no faculty) can bring pressure to bear on the rector most effectively through their students and the FECH. The competition among schools for exclusive domain over particular subject matters also produces disputes between schools in which the FECH is reluctant to take sides. There is thus an added byplay of intramural politics and intrigue in which the FECH and its federated schools are also involved. An unfriendly FECH can bring a great deal of grief to the life of a rector; the traditional cordiality that rectors have shown federation representatives is not unrelated to this fact of university life.

In a way, the FECH in 1956 and 1957 was living on its past. The measure of its power could be taken simply from the state of its inner resources and capabilities. The cumulative experience of the past—the weight of custom, practice, and usage—served to create an image of potency that had little basis in fact at the time but was a persuasive influence on the behavior of students themselves, as well as outside groups dealing with students. By 1956, the FECH had built up a certain momentum, a tradition and myth that seemed capable of carrying it through despite its many internal strains. If its political role was still tenuous and subject to great fluctuations, within the university it was firmly entrenched as part of the routine administrative apparatus.

Protest and Pressure

When students in Latin America break into international headlines, it is usually as a result of some mass demonstration or rioting. The image put before the world is that of a horde of wild-eyed and threadbare fanatics who alternate fitful class attendance with assaults on the palaces of dictators, insults to visiting dignitaries, and the practice of arson on municipal transport. Even in Latin America the press is likely to give student activities only passing notice, except in periods of unusual agitation. The fact that most newspapers are linked to specific political parties, of course, affects the local handling of such news.

The conservative Santiago dailies, *El Mercurio, La Nación* and *El Diario Ilustrado,* generally ignore FECH activities, or when forced to take notice of them assume a fatherly, monitorial tone. In January and February of 1957, when FRAP and Radical student whips were leading almost nightly demonstrations against price increases, *El Mercurio* gave no space whatever to these repeated skirmishes between police and student-led crowds. At the same time, it was carrying extensive reports on student demonstrations in Spain and other countries. The Communist *El Siglo* and the Radical *La Tercera,* as well as other opposition papers, by contrast, sought to magnify the scope of the demonstrations by inflating the number of participants and exaggerating the number of casualties and arrests. Thus, the picture of FECH action that the public received through the press, even in Chile itself, was selective and distorted.

In April of 1957 the FECH added one more item to the hemisphere's roster of violent episodes involving students. How do these facts square with the import of what has been said about the prevailing mood and orientation of student politics in this final period? How does an organization with an indifferent constituency and a divided leadership set in motion a protest movement that threatens to topple a duly-elected national government? How does an organization that has no organic links with labor appear in the vanguard of a mass movement in defense of the interests of the working class? If the prevailing concern is for student welfare and university problems, why does the organization seem to consume its major energies in political maneuvering and agitation? Some of the answers to these questions lie in the number and characteristics of the individuals involved in FECH action at different levels, in the relative power of the political forces that cross-cut the organization, and in the actual mechanics of day-to-day operations.

About 13,000 students enrolled in university-dependent establishments in Santiago in 1956; approximately 11,000 of these were in federated schools. The difference was made up largely of some 1,500 secondary-school students in a university-run experimental *lycée.* Nearly two out of five of the 11,000 federated students were women, but, beyond exercising their right to vote, women still played an insignificant role in FECH affairs. Outside of the schools with wholly female enrollment, only a few sent women as delegates to the FECH assembly. With only one or two exceptions, the few women delegates or members who attended were largely passive spectators. The FECH meetings tended to run late into the night. While Chilean young women seem accustomed to somewhat more freedom and independence than women in other Latin American countries, they are still restricted in their activities.

Women in the university, it was often said, did not vote as regularly as men in FECH elections, and when they did vote made their choices on religious rather than political lines. There is some evidence that negates this simple picture of feminine voting habits. There are eleven schools in the university whose enrollment is at least 50 per cent feminine. In four of these schools the proportion of all students voting in the 1956 FECH election was about the average for federated schools as a whole; in four it was below average, and in three above the average. The two schools with the largest turnout (89 and 83 per cent) and the two schools with the lowest turnout (36 and 39 per cent) were all schools where women are in the majority. The four schools in which Communists and Socialists won a majority of the votes are all schools with more women than men enrolled—these include the Schools of Theater Arts, Fine Arts, and the Conservatory of Music, all traditionally leftist strongholds. Three of the schools with a large female enrollment went to the Christian Democrats or guildsmen; the remaining three split their votes approximately evenly among the three major groups in the race. In short, there seems to be little basis for the contention that the voting patterns of women differ from those of men in the university.

Although the university remained a middle-class establishment, there was some variation in the social and economic level of the average student from school to school. In general, the small schools offering training for "short careers" *(carreras cortas)* attracted the more financially hard-pressed students. The dropout rate at all levels of Chilean education has long been a problem of grave concern to Chilean educators.[27] Even within the ranks of the select few who reach the university there is a constant attrition, stemming to an important extent from economic difficulties. Class schedules often do not permit the student to consider self-help through outside work. There are in any case few opportunities for employment, and the reluctance of university students to accept demeaning manual labor, such as waiting on tables, complicates the situation further. When students make common cause with workers on an issue such as uncontrolled price increases, they are moved by more than an altruistic concern for the popular welfare.

About 62 per cent of the federated students voted in the 1956 FECH elections. By all accounts, the proportion in each school who took any interest in FECH affairs beyond voting was considerably smaller. The average estimate by school delegates was that some 15 to 20 per cent of the students in their schools could be counted on to support FECH decisions and projects. This was approximately the proportion that turned out for demonstrations on the April morning in 1957 after the student nurse, Alicia Ramírez, was killed by police bullets as she walked away from a FECH mass meeting. Attendance at FECH assembly meetings, which are open to the public, at their peak drew no more than fifty or sixty actual delegates or school presidents in the year between mid-1956 and mid-1957. More often the quorum of thirty-four was barely reached if at all. Another fifty to one hundred university students might drift in and out of these *directorio* sessions in the course of an evening.

The real work of the FECH was carried on by the seven-man Executive Committee, the delegates to the University Council, and the captains of the political party groups who worked closely with the party representatives in the Executive Committee. Altogether, this group numbered no more than twenty-five individuals. With respect to the actual numbers of students directly engaged in organizational work, the FECH had changed but little down the years.

There were, in this third period, six parties with organized strength within the university. As noted earlier, Communists and Socialists, along with a few splinter leftist groups, constituted a voting bloc called the Popular Action Front, with its counterpart at the national level. The FRAP polled about 1,800 votes out of some 6,500 ballots cast in the elections for executive officers in 1956, and about the same number in 1957 when about 6,900 students voted. The FRAP had two representatives in the 1956–1957 FECH Executive Committee.

The Radical party is often referred to as the party of the middle class in Chile, but it is probably one of the most heterogeneous in composition. In its long history in Chile it has collaborated both with the parties of the extreme right and the revolutionary left. The leftist current within the party has usually been dominant in the university. The university Radical Group (GUR) polled 1,820 votes in 1956 and 2,210 in 1957. This gave them also two positions in the seven-man Executive Committee. With the two positions controlled by the FRAP, the working alliance of Radicals, Communists, and Socialists tended to dominate federation affairs.

The main voting strength of the shifting coalition of student guildsmen that forms the opposition to the FRAP and GUR lay in the National *Falange*. The *Falange* was a youthful, energetic, Social Christian movement that had been germinating within the university for about three decades and was only beginning to figure importantly in the national scene. In its economic doctrines it was much closer to the Marxist parties, with which it had often collaborated, both within the university and without, than to its liberal allies of the moment. However, its strong identification with the church was a stumbling block to more effective working relations with Chile's traditionally secularist left. From 1956 to 1957, and again from 1957 to 1958, FECH presidents were members of the *Falange*. In 1956 the *Falange* allied with the Liberals and, with support from independent Catholics in the university, polled nearly 2,600 votes. In 1957, after fusion of the *Falange* with the United Conservatives into a Christian Democratic party, the group won 2,970 votes.

The university Liberals ran independently in the 1957 elections and won 550 votes. The United Conservatives had run on their own the year before, polling 370 votes. In the framework of university politics these two groups are on the extreme right. The Liberals nationally are thought of as representative of well-to-do industrialists and the more progressive landowners. The United Conservative party is more closely associated with the landholding aristocracy and agricultural interests. Such facile labeling is belied by voting statistics and by the bizarre electoral combinations that are commonplace in Chile, but these remain the popular images of the interests that the several parties represent.

Within the FRAP it was the Communists rather than the Socialists who provided the chief strength within the university. Less than a quarter of the 1,800 votes that could be mustered by the FRAP were considered to be Socialist votes. As with other groups, the vast majority of these votes came from sympathizers rather than from enrolled party militants. The Communist party was still officially illegal in Chile, although an electoral reform passed in August, 1958, was to restore the voting rights of

Chilean Communists. But even when the Law for .he Defense of Democracy, which outlawed the Communist party, was being applied most stringently, Communists operated openly within the university. The rectors and all the student political groups defended the right of Marxist students and professors to express freely their ideas within the university. In 1956, when a number of law students gave testimony against a fellow student who was accused of disseminating Communist propaganda, the witnesses were expelled from the FECH and repudiated even by the Catholic political groups.

Even the highest ranks of the Communist and Socialist leadership in the university were not heavily indoctrinated; that is, there were few serious students of Marxism among them. Their Marxism seemed to stem from the direct experience or observation of inequality and economic deprivation, rather than from any purely intellectual impulse. While the top leaders were indistinguishable from the other middle-class student leaders in appearance and background, the rank and file seemed clearly to come primarily from the more economically hard-pressed students of lower-middle-class families.

The Communist party's avowed desire to work with all elements that sincerely desired "national liberation" encouraged participation by many who would be reluctant to formally enroll in an illegal movement. In the university, party functions were ostensibly open to all friendly comers. Whatever secrecy was maintained was defended as the only means of protecting the membership from political persecution.

The University Radical Group, in 1956, was probably the most numerous of the political groups in the university. If the number among their leaders in the university who had been Radicals since their secondary school days was any indicator, the Radicals were also doing a good job of recruiting in the secondary schools. In fact, at least one of the highly rated state-run *liceos* in Chile is known as "the cradle of Radicalism." The Radical party in Chile goes back to the last century when it led the fight for separation of church and state and for state control of education. Some of the most prominent educators in Chile have been Radicals, and the most cogent statements in support of state control over education come from Radical mentors.

As a group, Radical student leaders gave the impression of

being the most pragmatic, canny, and self-conscious tacticians at work in the university. More of them seemed to have their eye on the main chance; they seemed more alert to personal opportunities within their party and more sensitive to the significance for later political endeavors of their activities as student leaders.

University Radicals worked closely with the Communists and Socialists within the FECH, but were constantly engaged in an effort to outshine them. As one Radical leader aptly phrased it, "our present tactic is to run beside them but run faster." The main thing that distinguished left-wing Radicals from FRAP supporters was that the Radicals rejected Marxism and avowedly repudiated the totalitarian aspects of the Soviet system. Radical students thought of themselves as Socialists but could offer only vague notions of how collectivistic ideas would be applied in practice in Chile.

The great mass of those who gave their votes to the Radical party in the university had only the vaguest notions of what party doctrine is beyond the hallowed Radical principles of secularism, rationalism, and evolution. The party accommodated many who sought only a harbor from the political extremes. Said one girl, a Radical sympathizer and delegate to the *directorio,* "It is the political group that is closest to what has economic power and represents capitalism. Then, socialism represents the working class, closer to communism. Radicalism is between the Left and the Right."

The *Falange* had existed as an independent party for some twenty years in Chile before it fused with the United Conservatives to form the Democratic Christian party in 1957. The party had grown directly from the university as a rebellious offshoot of the Conservative party. In this final period it was captained in the university by a small and dedicated group that seemed to lack the political skills of the Marxists and Radicals. There were probably no more than fifty militant and working Falangists in the university. The avowed aim of this group for several years had been to concentrate student energies on questions of student welfare and eliminate the political intrigue and bickering that had been for so long characteristic of FECH activities. It had had little success in this direction, and by the middle of 1957 there was talk of a mass withdrawal from the FECH. The university *Falange* did not encourage this movement in part because of the upcoming national election for president. At that time, a year before the national presidential election, to be held in September, 1958, the *Falange* candidate, Eduardo Frei, was given fair odds of winning the presidency.

In an extremely class-conscious country, the United Conservatives and the Liberals both symbolize the entrenched oligarchy. They are known as the parties of the *apellidos vinosos,* the surnames that appear on the nation's wine labels. The Conservative position in the university was very close to that of the *Falange.* Student Liberals championed the principle of free enterprise and took a firm stand against protectionism. They were anxious to disavow the aristocratic identification given their party and to affirm the group's sensitiveness to social problems in Chile. In practice, Liberal spokesmen, debating in FECH sessions, seemed to swing from extreme defensiveness to arrogant aggressiveness under the goading of their leftist rivals. Even more than other groups, they felt keenly the lack of some moving and persuasive statement of their position that could have some meaning, not only for themselves, but for the broad mass of Chileans who saw themselves as caught in a hopeless economic cul-de-sac.

Party loyalties did not altogether impede some collaborative efforts. Within the Executive Committee, for example, conflicting party identifications produced in practice little open disagreement, insofar as the conduct of day-to-day committee business was concerned. This was only in part a reflection of resignation and a feeling of powerlessness in the president and vice-president, who were the two minority members of the committee. The fact is that on most issues that came before the committee there seemed to be unanimity of purpose and sentiment. By and large this was true of all problems related to the internal functioning of the university. It was also true with respect to the major student campaign of the year, the series of demonstrations against the rise in bus fares which culminated in the afternoon of rioting and looting in downtown Santiago.

The undercurrent of political rivalry came through in what were often contrived and tiresome attempts to give a political cast to issues that had no relation to party position. Thus, an atmosphere of tension and stalemate crept into much of the discussion even at this level. Executive Committee meetings are theoretically open to all visitors, but generally there were few in attendance outside of committee members. Nevertheless, much of the discourse seemed addressed to a phantom audience. Like practiced politicians everywhere, those present would withdraw into glassy-eyed meditation or proceed to carry on other business with their neighbors during these lengthy harangues.

Still, it was in these executive sessions that the native Chilean talent for compromise and evasion was most in evidence. Rival resolutions were almost always fused into single statements acceptable to all. Verbal commitments of agreement and collaboration were freely given. On occasion, a deceptive camaraderie seemed to unite political opponents. A particularly telling quip by a speaker would be celebrated with equal good humor on all sides. Yet these flashes of warmth only served to emphasize the almost ritualistic character of the political attacks routinely exchanged by these same individuals on the floor of the *directorio*.

From 1956 to 1957, the *directorio* held weekly sessions during the academic period. As has been noted, on few occasions were more than half of the 127 delegates and school presidents who have voice and vote in the *directorio* present for a session. Frequently it was not possible to hold meetings because of failure to raise the required quorum of 34 delegates.

However, *directorio* meetings are open to all comers. Large contingents from particular schools were likely to show up on evenings when a problem affecting their interests was up for discussion.[28] At the height of the agitation against the rise in bus fares, there were several meetings at which an overflow crowd of several hundred persons jammed FECH headquarters. This included no more than 50 or 60 actual delegates, perhaps 150 other university students, a sprinkling of secondary-school students, claques from the youth contingents of the several parties, curious drifters off the street, reporters, and no doubt a small representation from the political police.

The *directorio* met in a large enclosed courtyard. This courtyard opened directly onto one of the main avenues of the city. The heavy traffic of passers-by was often drawn by the tumult in the FECH; the temptation to run out into the street to stage demonstrations after a particularly rousing speech seemed ever present.

A feeble semblance of parliamentary procedure was maintained, at least during the early part of the sessions. The true political moguls seldom deigned to occupy the benches. Each one gathered on the sidelines surrounded by his small coterie. There was a constant hum of activity from these ambient cells, each of which functioned as a sort of open caucus. Discussion was monopolized by the Executive Committee members and a few other party stalwarts. As a rule, university problems, chiefly questions of supporting the petitions of one school or another, were placed first on the agenda. Although even here the political groups vied with one another to win the favor of the petitioning school, these discussions generally displayed a degree of sanity. However, near the end of the sessions, as the discussion turned to purely political items, there was a general exodus of those in attendance that left only the most dedicated party regulars on hand. Not uncommonly, the session ended in disorder, with each side climbing up on the benches and shouting insults at their opponents, until whoever was chairing the session finally declared the meeting closed.

The prize pursued in this burlesque of democratic discussion was to push some resolution through the *directorio*. There was little effort to persuade fellow students of anything. Many resolutions were, in fact, passed with practically no discussion or explanation of the thinking behind them at all. The language of these *votos* was so cliché-ridden that it took considerable concentration, not often forthcoming from the student audience, to tell what any one of them was really about.

The demonstrations against fare increases had the same unthinking and improvised character. After a brief harangue by one of the more practiced agitators among student leftists, the mixed crowd of students, workers, and idlers that joined in these protests would pour out of FECH headquarters. The university cheer and other slogans would be used as rallying cries. The police, who would be stationed expectantly in the side streets, would presently charge swinging nightsticks, while the demonstrators fled into the passing crowds. Shortly, the demonstrators would regroup, only to break ranks again under another onslaught from the police. As things became more heated, stones would begin to fly, both at the police and the buses. Each evening brought its small toll of broken heads and arrests. Party spokesmen, usually FRAP or Radical deputies (members of Chile's lower House), were called on to forestall police abuse of those arrested and to arrange for their release.

Within the university the formal position of student representatives, of course, had been strengthened since 1940. A certain
deference was routinely shown FECH officers, especially the
president, the delegates to the university council, and the
presidents of the various school centers. All current student
leaders interviewed reported fair and courteous treatment from
university officials, but few, if any, reported privileges. On the
whole, student leaders did not seem to get any special consideration with respect to meeting academic requirements. The higher
the FECH office, the more likely it was to conflict with academic
achievement. The federation president almost automatically
accepted the fact that he would fall behind academically during
his year in office. It is not uncommon for other FECH leaders and
politically minded students to repeat part or all of a year's work
more than once in the course of their university careers.

Within the parties, the position of student cadres similarly was
not one of great privilege or onerous or compromising duties. Of
all the political groups active in the university, the Communists
were by reputation the most disciplined. There is no question that
Communists, like those of every other political group in the
university, by and large followed the line set down by their party
on most political issues. Every political group was quick to charge
that their rivals "took orders" from the party hierarchy outside
the university, while asserting in the same breath that in their
own party the situation was different. However, outside of the
Communist party, which at the time was illegal, all of the other
political parties in Chile were operating in the glare of intense
publicity. In the university, as has been remarked, the Communists were practicing an "open-door" policy reminiscent of the
popular-front period. In a country like Chile, where no event of
possible political significance is too minor to escape comment, it
may not always be possible to discover the truth about what is
going on within a given party, but it is difficult to be taken in by
any single version of political reality.

Not surprisingly, the truth in this case did lie at either
extreme—neither the projected image of total submission to party
dictates on the part of rivals nor the assertation of almost
complete personal autonomy was accurate. Fundamentally, there
was sufficient flexibility in the relationship of the party militant
in the university to his party to give him a feeling of "spontane-

ity" and independence; there was enough commitment and identification to cushion minor discrepancies of viewpoint and to sustain the conviction that the party had not only the interests of the nation but those of youth and the university at heart.

Guildsman and Activist

In earlier chapters an attempt was made to document, within the limits of the data at hand, the hypothesis that as organizational forms changed within the FECH there were accompanying changes in the personality characteristics of the young men rising to leadership. However, the comparison between "the agitators" of the 1920 period and "the party faithful" of the popular front days revealed more points of uniformity than divergence between the two groups; the similarities proved far more striking than the differences. The material bearing on personality for this final group confirms the arresting persistence of a certain constellation of social characteristics and personal attitudes in the FECH leadership from generation to generation. Whatever the differences in the setting of student action or the direction given that action by student leaders of the three periods, each generation seems to be linked by a common and enduring core of values and experiences.

In shifting attention to some common characteristics of all three generations, it is important not to lose sight of one of the basic hypotheses that guided this inquiry. The major quest was for distinctive aspects of outlook and experience that might explain the particular style and flavor that each generation gave to FECH leadership. The guildsmen and activists were all party men, even as the "party militants" of the popular front epoch. But the men of the late 1930's were primarily militants of parties that had come to life in Chile as the young leaders approached maturity. They became Communists, Socialists, Nazis, and Falangists. These men accepted organizational discipline, but they were at odds with the society in which they lived. As shall be seen, the overwhelming majority of today's leaders were not just party men—they were party men who are in fairly close accord with the political views of their own fathers. In fact, about half belonged to the same party as their fathers. Within the framework of the uniformities to be documented in this chapter, there remain key differences such as this.

The careful probability sample of 1957 student leaders turned out to be remarkably similar in social backgrounds to the informants from earlier periods that have already been described.[29] Like their forerunners, the student leaders came overwhelmingly from middle-class families. More than three out of five had fathers in small businesses or in white-collar occupations. Professionals and farmers with small or medium-sized holdings made up most of the remainder. About one in ten of the current crop of student leaders came from working-class families, but this is probably as much a reflection of the broadening in the last two decades of the fields and levels of training offered by the university as it is of any powerful upward surge from the working-class sector. Whatever their origins, however, these student leaders as a group did not come from any kind of social or economic elite; that is, few had any strong claim to status that is independent of their roles in the university. In addition to those elements fresh from the working class, a large proportion of those with fathers in white-collar jobs or with "small businesses" led an extremely precarious existence economically and had only a tenuous hold on middle-class status.

About one out of three of these leaders was born outside the capital, Santiago. The presence of provincials in such numbers in the universtiy points up one facet of the tremendous movement of population within Chile from provincial cities and from rural areas to the capital.[30] Their prominence in the ranks of student leaders is suggestive of the continuing usefulness of student activity as a means of broadening social contacts and achieving status for the unknown from the provinces. The greater freedom of action of students from the provinces, many of whom escape strict parental control for the first time on coming to the university, also helps to explain the prominence of provincials in leader ranks.

Though Chile has had a negligible flow of immigration from abroad, the sons of foreign-born parents also stand out in the ranks of student leaders. The 1952 census reported that only 3.2 per cent of residents in the capital were foreign born (the figure for the nation was 1.6 per cent).[31] Still, in the sample of student leaders, 12 per cent had two foreign-born parents, and an additional 19 per cent came from families in which one of the parents (almost always the father) was born outside Chile.

Important segments of student leadership thus came from lower-middle- and working-class families, from the provinces, and from among first-generation Chileans. In an extremely class-conscious country, all of these were groups with a felt status disadvantage. They were the groups bearing the brunt of existing inequities, the ones with the most to gain from social and political reforms, and the individuals most likely to be caught up in the competition for status.

This small sample included individuals representing multiple fronts of upward status pressure in Chilean society. Respondent student leaders represented twenty-one different schools in the University of Chile. Included were young men and women preparing for careers in medicine, law, education, engineering, dentistry, pharmacy, veterinary science, nursing, music, and the theater. The group included students of administration, apprentice midwives, agriculturalists, commercial artists, and young men in the building trades. Despite the heterogeneity of professional choices, vocational interests, and aptitudes present within the group, almost all spoke of their chosen fields with great earnestness and conveyed a strong sense of commitment to their vocations.

Not all of these young men and women were in the fields of their first choice, but few expressed any lasting regrets or doubts about their actual choice at this stage. Many could have been helped by professional counseling, but hardly any felt themselves the victims of parental or other pressures. On the contrary, there was almost total unanimity in asserting that parental influences, while present, were not decisive in vocational choices. Conflict with parents over choice of profession occurred only rarely within this group, yet only two of these respondents were preparing to work in their fathers' fields.

This lack of conflict is explained in part by the great social mobility shown by this group. Of the current student leaders sampled, 80 per cent were preparing for careers in fields with higher social status than their fathers' occupations. Another 13 per cent had occupational goals of equal status with their fathers.

Only two respondents, both orphans (one a girl), seemed to have slipped backward on the status ladder.

The serious attitudes of these students toward their chosen occupations and their sense of loyalty and commitment to the professional "guild" or *gremio* flow naturally from the structure of the university itself and from student tradition. For a long time, the university has been charged with excessive professionalization, with unnecessarily compartmentalizing study and research in related fields. Whatever the case may be, the physical separation of the several schools and the relative autonomy that each enjoys promote the development of a sometimes narrow and exclusivist professional solidarity. The extensive participation that has been won by students in curriculum planning and other details of university administration, particularly at the school level, also requires that student leaders address themselves in a responsible way to the problems of their profession.

Thus, almost immediately upon entering the university, the student acquires the self-image of himself as one within an occupational fraternity; he becomes attentive, not only to the problem of his own place and his own advancement in his craft, but seeks as well to find the place of his occupation as such within society.[32] The interprofessional struggle to establish the overriding import of each field of activity for the nation's destiny is intensified by the fact that so much of the professional training and activity is centered within the university and in other institutions that are financially dependent on the government. Since all of these chronically operate with extremely limited resources, there is a constant need to justify the priority sought for each discipline.

Two basic notions—the desire for self-improvement and the ideal of serving within a field that has a strategic function to perform for the whole society—cropped up repeatedly in discussions of vocational choice. Still, by and large, respondents provided detached and critical self-appraisals. Some displayed keener insight and frankness, but almost all reported failings and weaknesses along with accomplishments and positive qualities. This is a mobile group on the way up. Only a few among those in the top echelons of the FECH or the party university groups saw professional politics as a permanent future activity. Most expected to do their best work and make their contribution to society within their occupational fields.

Nevertheless, they were able to state convincingly the reasons for their present political involvement. The following excerpts from interviews are not intended to give the substance of each party's position, but rather to convey the quality of student thinking on national issues irrespective of ideological inclination. A young Communist leader put the problem in these words:

> As far as my organization is concerned, it is our fundamental preoccupation to reach an agreement with those national sectors that are not in touch with monopolist sectors—that part of the national bourgeoisie that still has a national interest to defend, that part that is independent to the extent that it can be so. We must join with those people with whom we are in agreement at least on small, national objectives. . . . It is evident that the sector of our middle class that could be more or less independent is being favored by imperialism in Chile. They get their share and they help to suppress the striving for social rights of the popular groups.

The methodical search for a satisfying middle ground is reflected in this comment by a young Radical:

> We are never going to stop being Leftists. Almost surely we are going to crash head on within a few years with the high command of the Party. The Party is necessarily of a middle-class tendency that is difficult to break. . . but we have a carefully studied concept of what the University is. We believe that it is the organism that creates the national culture. In that way both the University and the Party carry us to the same objective, which is a popular emancipation from imperialist pressures and a kind of cultural imperialism that we have been suffering for a long time.
>
> . . . The young University Radicals are men with a clear leftist viewpoint. . . . We are neither pro-Communist nor pro-conservative. And on the international level we are neither pro-Yankee nor pro-Russian. We are simply Americans. We aspire to have our country and all America have the same authority as the U.S. and Russia in the family of nations. . . . Once the problems of extreme poverty and hunger are solved in Chile, I believe that Communism will disappear almost entirely. First of all, we need a planned agriculture. A planned agriculture means first of all agrarian reform and the division of land. Not into tiny plots but in such a way that each area is used to best

advantage. . . . I believe without knowing too much about the U.S. that they are not Marxists but that they have planned these things—the economy, education. The individual who works without organizing anything surely goes down; the one who plans and organizes everything rises. That's why I am always in agreement with economic planning for the nation.

The Christian group, a fusion of Falangists and United Conservatives looked to the family and individual moral rehabilitation as the mainsprings of a regeneration of Chilean nationhood:

In the social field, we give a central place to the family and its protection by the indissolubility of the marriage tie. With respect to education, we stand for freedom of education—that is, that it be not only a State concern. The State, of course, has the obligation to teach, but education should not be an attribute exclusively of the State. . . . In economic affairs we take a conciliatory position between capitalism and Marxism. We propose, for example, that workers share in profits. In that way they are no longer just parts of a machine producing wealth for a small nucleus of persons. Finally, we seek to eliminate the class struggle, which, for all Christians, is absurd and inhuman.

Chile is an immensely wealthy country. It has all kinds of possibilities that have never been developed. Inflation in Chile is attributable to a mistaken policy of industrialization since 1938. They forgot about the agricultural part, they forgot to mechanize agriculture, and that is the reason for inflation. . . . We believe that the basis of society is the family. In a family it should be enough for the man alone to work. That is, a man's earnings should be enough to support him and his family. Naturally, in this we try to bring about some reform in business enterprises, in agriculture, but our main objective is the family. . . . If you go to the South of Chile you will find that people live in shacks without any conveniences, without any possibility for their children to get any schooling. That's what we have to achieve. . . something on the Yankee style—that the agricultural worker should have his car, his books, his television at home.

The Conservatives and the Liberals are the lone voices in the university that profess a dedication to free enterprise approximately on the United States model. Liberals are eager to shake off the aristocratic identification that the party still retains and to prove that the group is truly sensitive to social problems:

The position of present-day Liberalism cannot be that of an Adam Smith or a Ricardo. The position of the Liberal (we also criticize this) cannot be that cold ʾopposition and indifference before social problems. We recognize that our Liberalism must be different from that of the last century. . . . Right now there have entered the party fresh elements including some from popular parties because they realize that the myth that the Liberal Party is a great aristocratic center is no longer true. . . . Unfortunately, we have the problem that our group. . . in contrast to the new Marxist groups which are always expounding their ideologies. . . . that for us that stage has passed and we young people have nothing to look to. We have to read the classical liberals but they are out of touch with the present. We have no intellectual guides, no team that can give direction to young liberals.

Many of these remarks are bound in the formalism of the convention resolution and the party manifesto. All of these respondents, of course, are devoted party militants. The remarks of some of the lesser leaders showed ignorance, confusion, and some oversimplification. Still, the general level of awareness, information, and thoughtfulness on social, economic, and political issues was impressive. True, only a handful of those in the sample had any solid background of study or reading in political philosophy or economic analysis. Nevertheless, the number who were evidently making a serious effort to think their way through to a coherent point of view on broad social problems was startlingly high. This was true of all the Executive Committee members and the two delegates to the University Council. About two out of three of the delegates to the FECH assembly and the school presidents were able to give fairly well-organized accounts of their present political viewpoints and how they had arrived at them.

These materials were searched for evidences of displaced aggression, for signs that political thought and action were serving as a means of discharging emotional pressures built up in other spheres. Considering that this is a group of intense young people who are highly opinionated, all of them experiencing some frustration and deprivation as individuals and as citizens of a nation on the downgrade, that many of them are continually involved in partisan contention at many levels, and that the future holds promise of even more hardship and frustration for all of them—taking all these things together, it was expected that their political discussions would show a great amount of free-floating indignation, a readiness to single out some specific group to bear the guilt for the individual and collective misfortunes of Chileans.

This, in fact, happened but only to a small extent. While student leftists ranted and raved against the "entrenched oligarchy" and against "United States imperialists" in flyleafs, political harangues, and street demonstrations, in the interviews their attacks were measured and meditative. There was no hesitation about pointing to evils, but there was a reasonable disposition to apportion blame severally. Communists and Socialists spoke with equanimity about failures in their own leadership as well as about the natural impulse of those benefiting from the present economic arrangement to defend it as best they can. There were no tirades against the cruel capitalist oppressors at home or in Wall Street.

A few in every political camp denounced the corruption and inefficiency of the government bureaucracy, but it should be mentioned that in 1957 there were several major scandals concerning shady deals in government agencies. Even without these evidences of malfeasance, there is enough palpably wrong with the government administration in Chile to give some foundation to the belief that a great part of the nation's problems could be solved by cleaning up this single sore spot. Unquestionably, there is some element of projection in the comments that follow. The surprising thing is that remarks such as these were so infrequent.

To face the crude reality, there are people here occupying posts that they have no business holding. There are ministers and heads of departments who simply do not have the qualifications for the job. And for that reason, things have to go badly. That inefficient administrator, in order to shine, brings in a secretary even more stupid than himself. The secretary engages a sub-secretary, and on we go. Now, speaking of why Chile is so badly off. This is due perhaps to a lack of morality in the leaders. I am going to tell you that everyone steals. Not only do they steal, they all accept bribes. What Chile needs is a government with great morality. This lack of principles is seen not only in the higher levels, it exists at all levels of the bureaucracy. The small employee is just as ready to take a bribe as the big one.

After realizing how little was coming through in the interview materials that was revealing of political vindictiveness or scape-goating, respondents were pressed more closely on this point. They were asked why, when most of Chile's basic problems were decades old and the solutions had been indicated repeatedly, nothing had happened. Who was to blame for the failure of all efforts to put the economy on a saner footing? These are some typical answers:

> It is difficult to name a guilty person, since I find that we have all been guilty, even if it is in a very small way, each one of us has added his share, just as a glass fills drop by drop. We are ourselves to blame for our situation—just as there are countries that have had much greater problems than ours—take England and France for example who suffered the terror of war on their own ground and are today carrying forward an amply satisfactory plan of rehabilitation. We unfortunately do not have the same spirit. They know what it means to sacrifice. They say, "On such a day no meat will be bought," and they do not buy it. We on the other hand say, "Why shouldn't I buy it? I am free and I'll buy it."

> Many previous governments. . . tried [to halt the inflationary spiral], but the enormous pressure of labor and other pressure groups at that time (now they are entirely disorganized) impeded them from succeed-ing. The people themselves, I don't know if it was because they lacked proper orientation, failed to see the importance of the measures.

> On the economic side I would lay the blame from my point of view, but from the point of view of the group that I would hold responsible, this blame does not exist, because they see things in a different way. I am speaking of the economic Right in Chile.

These student leaders are not philosophers or statesmen. However, considering the international headlines made by the Chilean student movement in the year under study, their remarks displayed a notably level-headed tone. There was little evidence of blind prejudice, hatred, fear, feelings of victimization, petu-lance, or rancor in these interviews. These accounts were focused on problems rather than on persons; they explained events in social and psychological terms rather than as outcomes of manipulation by sinister forces in control of power. Even in the two areas that seemed to be most affect-laden and in which prejudice is most often seen at work (that is, class prejudice and anti-United States feelings), the irrational overtones cropped up only in the minority of cases. Such fear and prejudice may be exploited for political purposes by student leaders, but on the basis of interview materials it must be said that few student leaders seemed to be importantly motivated to political action by negative, destructive impulses.[33]

With respect to religion, also, a pattern that was observed among the small groups of informants in earlier generations is given statistical confirmation. Although almost all of these young leaders received Catholic training as children, only about one in ten were practicing Catholics. Another one in ten remained nominally true to Catholicism; they did not observe details of Catholic practice and manifested only sketchy knowledge of Catholic doctrine.

The most common pattern (for better than three out of five respondents) was one of early religious training, often with a period of intense faith and devotion in early adolescence, followed by a gradual turning away from the church. Most often, the break came around the age of seventeen or eighteen, just before entering the university. Informants reported little family conflict over this loss of faith or abandonment of religious observance. These desertions provoked almost no family reaction beyond feeble efforts on the part of the mother or other devout female kin to enforce attendance at Sunday Mass. The fathers, even when nominally Catholic, seemed to have been indifferent to the whole affair. A good number of the fathers were themselves Radical freethinkers and secularists, who largely welcomed the change as a coming of age for their sons.

There were only two Catholics among leftist student leaders, both young girls who were only token Catholics. Some of the young Communists, Socialists, and Radicals forthrightly rejected the existence of God and a life after death.

> At present my feeling about whether or not God exists, is that I am not interested in whether He exists or does not exist. That is not going to provoke any change in what I am going to do. I can proceed perfectly well whether at the end of life there will be a reward or a punishment. One should rely entirely on what one does, according to one's conscience, to one's way of being, as long as one respects the rights of others so that he may be respected in turn.

I have never believed that there is a superior being who cares anything about what I do and who is going to judge me at some future time. All I believe is that man is in this world, let us say, just passing through. We should try to leave some good things behind, to make sure that our stay on earth should not be sterile. . . .

Human knowledge no matter how far it advances always arrives at problems that for the moment are insoluble. . . . I have always felt a certain modesty, for I believe that man is not the most perfect nor the best being that can exist in the universe, that leads me to think of a power greater than man that you can call God, as most people do. . . . But I do not believe in a life after death. And I have faith that all religions will end with the advance of science, that we will realize that none of the world's religions really grapples realistically with the problems of powers greater than men.

I am entirely convinced that there is something superior, and I could call that force that created the world and created us God. But I do not agree with the Catholic church that this God thinks and watches over us. I believe that the proof of divinity is in man. . . man is in all creation the most divine of things. But as far as a personal God, calling a person God, some force that thinks, that directs, that grants favors on request, I do not believe. . . .

The interviews with the small number who are steadfast Catholics today reveal one or two interesting points. In the first place, those who are militant Catholics today do not come from markedly religious families. Except for one young man from a farm family, the parents of Catholic student leaders are Catholics of the conventional lukewarm variety, no different from those whose sons have abandoned the faith. The religious inspiration of their sons came from outside the family. Second, there seems to be a subtle interplay of religious and political motivation at work among them. It is difficult to tell whether their religious views moved them to political action or whether they were won for the faith by their political activities. Witness the following comment by an outstanding young Catholic student leader:

I believe that the greatest turning point came apropos of my political activities within the University. When I saw that our Marxist and secularist fellow students hated us so intensely because of our religious views, there was aroused in me the desire to become a fervent Catholic.

But not to be one of these breast-beating Catholics, but taking the orientation of the young Catholic, a practical Catholicism, with deeds as well as words.

In short, today's leftist leaders in the university, as well as those of earlier days, showed little personal tension concerning questions of faith, the existence of God, or life after death. This pattern is probably typical for many middle-class Chileans. At least within the ranks of student leaders, the youth whose faith survives adolescence seemed to be the exception. Still, religiosity and secularism remained intimately linked to political attitudes, with some feedback from the political sphere giving new meaning to religious faith.

Yet another linkage of religion to politics and politics to early childhood comes to light in this material. A striking fact to be recorded about this last generation of student leaders is the large proportion among them who came from homes broken by the death or separation of parents. Three out of ten of the leader group questioned had lost one or both parents by death, and an additional one in ten came from divided families. Almost all of these deaths had occurred very early in the childhood of the respondents. In some cases the early death of parents had made a profound impression on the individual and was linked consciously by him to his present religious and political outlook. One student, a young Radical party leader, said:

My secularist sentiments have not been influenced by anyone. I became a Radical and a secularist because it was my desire. . . . As I matured and became fully cognizant of my problems—that is, having both parents dead and living in an economically limited situation—these were all the factors that led me to conclude that there could not exist a powerful, just, and tolerant being, if I, without having done anything, could find myself in such a situation.

Without venturing into a detailed analysis of the divergencies in present political behavior among orphaned respondents, it may be noted that this finding points to an additional area of social disablement for a sizeable proportion of the leader group. To be without parents can be a crippling disadvantage in any society. It can be especially onerous in a setting in which status, economic security, and career possibilities remain rooted in the family and strongly dependent on family resources and connections.

The majority of these respondents (about 60 per cent), who have both parents alive and living together, showed the same tone of detachment and objectivity in discussing their parents that was displayed by the more mature leaders of earlier student generations. While some did not go very much beyond a fairly conventional description of the mother and father, many revealed an unusual degree of understanding of the parents. Their reports, by and large, provided a very appealing image of Chilean family life.

The flavor of these remarks will again be best illustrated by quotations from the interviews themselves. These selections have been made with a view to demonstrating the variety (rather than the favorable majority) of attitudes toward parents, as well as the generally dispassionate and analytical tone of the discussions of parental figures.

I believe that I felt and will always feel a profound admiration for my father. I believe that his attitude toward life was exemplary in an extraordinary way. He achieved a privileged position, at least in his last years, because he was not dependent economically or spiritually on anyone. In reality, my father was at bottom a great rebel. What I most admired about my father was his dedication to serious study. Secondly, the profound knowledge of human beings that he had. . . in part attributable to his profession as a psychiatrist. . . . He had the tendency, which I also have to some extent, of laughing at the world. He was also extremely honest and disinterested. He treated many of his patients free, even in his last days when he was tired and ill himself. He was able to win the affection of people even though they ran the risk of becoming victims of the barbs he habitually cast at those around him. In my opinion, he had only one defect and that was his skeptical attitude about the possibility of solving major social problems. I think that for that reason my father never belonged to any political party. I believe that was a reflection of his individualism which did not express itself as personal egotism but rather in a distrust of the solutions of social problems by the mass or by mass movements. . . .

With regard to my parents, I should say that when one is young one often shows little understanding. Happily, for various reasons I have recently been thinking over and reviewing my parents' behavior. I have been very lucky because they have given us (together with my brother) a home in which we found a mother who was preoccupied about her sons, with great understanding and generosity (sometimes exaggerated) to satisfy our desires. She always tried to listen to us and understand us. I believe that we, that I, have erred in being somewhat indifferent to my mother. She has felt that deeply, in that she has not been able to know me as well as my brother, who is closer to her. My father also has been very generous with us and has always wanted the best for us, without regard for the sacrifices entailed. However, because of his work he has sometimes been not too close to us. Still, we have always found a great affection from them. I may even say that led by an excessive devotion for us they have, without we or they realizing it, done us harm. Now looking back and talking things over with them, we and they have all realized this. As to defects in my mother I can only point to outbursts of bad temper, attributable chiefly to her desire to absorb everything that had anything to do with us. My father was quite the opposite, always serene and unruffled. What I did notice sometimes as a child was that my father had a great many social activities and left us to ourselves.

I have said that I have always been very independent, and this is true of my family relations too. My father, in brief, is a very egotistical being, very much preoccupied about himself alone. He has indestructible principles about the world. He believes that one must work and that everyone has to fight tooth and nail for his own. He is somewhat removed from the household, because he is still a very young man. Although he is 58, you would look at him and say he is no older than 35. That is to say, he is still very much alive and my mother is fairly old. He goes out and has his fun independently of everyone else. This is a defect in any well-established home. Ours is rather strange. That is why I say it would be a defect in a well-set-up home; in ours it passes unnoticed. My mother is very different. She feels these things very keenly. She has been preoccupied for a long time. And perhaps for a long time she has sought to win him back, to recover the man—a very human thing. Lately she has become more independent; she is studying and thinking more about herself. . . . Relations between them are very bad, purely formal. The thin thread that can firmly bind one human being to another has long ceased to link them.

In the previous chapter the hypothesis was tentatively put forward that resolution of the dominance conflict between father and son by a submission on the part of the son might be linked to the later acceptance by the son of the role of disciplined party militant. By contrast, rejection of the father as an authority figure was related to political behavior fitting the pattern of the agitators of the 1920 generation. The last quotation represents one of the very few cases found among the current generation of student leaders in which there was a live and intense conflict between father and son. Discounting student leaders without fathers and those whose fathers have no political affiliation, the overwhelming majority (85 per cent) of these student leaders, all of whom are party men (whether they are political activists or guildsmen) were in accord with their fathers on political matters. Fully half of the respondents belonged to the same party as their fathers. The few cases of conflict with the father were clustered in the Communist-Socialist FRAP and among the most belligerent Radicals.

These results provide some statistical support for the hypothesis stated earlier and help to explain the generally moderate tone of university politics and FECH action in this final period. Still, there is a qualitative difference in the pattern of conformity evinced by the present generation and that of earlier party militants. The 1940 party men accepted the discipline of organizations geared to revolutionary ends—they may not have challenged the principle of authority but did question its ends. Their commitment was more profound and more demanding. The powerful psychic charge of inter-generational or parental conflict does not seem to be an important motivating factor behind the political activities of most of today's student leaders.[34] Insofar as this works in favor of a more rational and unemotional attack on political problems, it supports the development of the technical, managerial approach associated with the "bargaining interest group" or the reformer, rather than the intransigence of the agitator or revolutionary.

Diminished conflict with or rejection of fathers has not led to lesser disappointment and frustration in personal relations outside the family. The preoccupation and ambivalence concerning friendships shown by earlier generations is repeated among the young student leaders in the university today. Like their forerunners, today's student leaders attach great importance to friendship. They sought in friendship above all sincerity, understanding, and companionship. Their attitudes toward friendship were a compound of generous permissiveness, a desire to give and receive love and nurture, a longing for a mutually satisfying, equalitarian relationship. Almost all reported some disappointing experience. For a great many, these disappointments have resulted in a suspicion and distruct that no doubt will prove a further barrier to achieving the kind of deep friendship they see as an ideal.

The following comments, each taken from a different interview, show the great amount of tension that existed for these young people in the area of friendship:

Well, I am a little reluctant to use the word friends. I have had a very few friends with whom, after many years, I am in perfect accord with on most things. The others have been acquaintances that do not merit the word of friend. Probably I have some defect; I am not very trusting. But I took this tack after I belonged as a founding member to a Company of Firemen. I gave my nights and days to the Company and then found that those whom I considered my friends and buddies were sawing the floor from under me. I became aware that I should not reveal my secrets and my private thoughts to any person. . . .

I haven't had a great deal of experience with respect to friendship and I've had few problems. I still have two people from the lycee that I consider friends. I don't visit them often, but I know that at any time I can consider them my friends, and they me as theirs. I don't know if it's that in the school there's a sort of competition and that people are not frank for that reason. They always try to put themselves in first place. Often, they may even be planning a dirty maneuver against their best friend.

The people who make a bad impression on me are those who make much of their social position or knowledge and deprecate the qualities of the next person. Unfortunately, that type of person abounds within the University. Almost always the student in my school tries to be number one in everything without thinking about others. This is something we have been fighting but without much success.

I believe that the importance of having friends is something that cannot be argued. A man without friends is an anti-social being. . .and possibly there is something wrong with him mentally. I think it is absolutely necessary to have friends because it puts you in contact with the milieu in which you live, it permits you to seek together new paths, and because it is gratifying to exchange confidences with others. I consider as a friend a person who has identified himself, if not with my innermost thoughts, with my manner of acting. Also the person who has no prejudice of any kind. The person who has social prejudices

cannot get along with me. Many times I have thought I had a friend
and I have found that it made a difference because I did not have the
same social situation that he had. Then again, I have had friends who
had a higher position than mine, but who behave so correctly, that they
made me their equals. I think that is fundamental.

Fear of social prejudice and personal rivalry seemed to be at
the root of tensions with respect to friendship. This finding
underscores the significance of the university and the FECH as
arenas of status competiton among individuals. It serves to
highlight the insecurity and anxiety that accompany the ascent up
the status ladder. It brings into the open some of the emotional
charge behind the class conflict that inspires so much of the
partisan political activity of university students.

Nevertheless, realism, flexibility, and tolerance were again the
keynotes encountered in interview materials. This most youthful
group of student leaders spoke of family, vocation, friendship,
religion, and politics with a reasoning, introspective, and analytical attitude that compares favorably with that of their more
mature forerunners in the FECH leadership. Today's student
leaders are not cranks. Few, if any, seem to be working out
psychological problems through their political activity. They are
reformers rather than rebels.

Few are truly in conflict with authority in any sphere. In this
respect, they differ sharply from the 1920 generation. Nor are
they political innovators in any sense. They differ also from the
popular front generation which accepted party discipline, but
largely in new, vigorous parties, captained by men who were
young enough to appear as contemporaries to the youths in the
university. A majority of today's leaders share the political views
and party affiliation of their fathers.

Despite these differences and the generation gap dividing them,
the three groups of student leaders show some distinctive uniformities in outlook and experience. On the basis of interview
materials, almost all emerge as "low scorers" on ethnocentrism in
terms of the analytical scheme elaborated in *The Authoritarian
Personality,* which has implicitly been applied here.[35] Though
focused on intergroup bias, ethnocentrism, as defined by the
authors of *The Authoritarian Personality* and explored by them in
the unstructured interviews (as well as in the scale measurements),

covers a broad range of social and political attitudes. The low scores of these Chilean student leaders indicate a commitment to democratic values that is directly linked to a particular way of looking at the world, and that is an integral part of the individual's personality organization. The discovery of this important area of similarity among these leaders does not negate the possibility that fundamental differences could coexist. Adorno and his fellow investigators encountered a great variability in personality among unprejudiced subjects.[36] However, these results do call attention to what appear to be basic elements in the process of political socialization for at least one sector of Chilean youth.

Despite some variation with respect to attitudes toward the father, men of all three generations display similar attitudes toward parents. Wholesome patterns of warm, equalitarian relationships within the middle-class family emerge. Crucial decisions, such as choice of vocation and the stand to be taken on religion, are apparently accomplished with a minimum of conflict and tension.[37] The area of major insecurity for all three groups seems to lie in the field of friendship. Personal rivalry and status competition are disturbing elements in friendship for the more socially mobile latter generations. The oldest group, whose position is by now more or less fixed, seems more preoccupied by a search for love and nurturance that may itself reflect a longing to recreate the warm relationships enjoyed earlier in the family. The ideal of self-improvement and service to society within a profession is also highly generalized among this group.

A much more ambitious study of the developmental aspects of political attitudes than could be undertaken within the compass of this research would have to be carried out to pinpoint the main sources of democratic attitudes among student leaders and others in Chile. The contribution of the elementary school and the *lycée* in this process, wholly untouched here, is a major area requiring study. That the university and the FECH play an important role in sustaining and transmitting democratic values and in providing a training ground in democratic action is palpably clear. As has been seen, that role has changed dramatically and not always for the best in the last forty years. The FECH action does not always represent the best in its leadership, nor have we any assurance that FECH leadership represents the best that is in the university.

Still, these chapters on the backgrounds and personalities of the FECH leaders hold out the assurance that the university and the FECH are not simply turning out apprentice tyrants and demagogues. The FECH was a sharply different organization in each of the three periods studied, but there were also some continuities. The most hopeful of these, in view of the persistence of the nation's social problems, was the apparent ability of the social system to produce fresh cohorts of potential leadership with a social conscience, aware and active. If this interpretation is not wholly in error, Chileans can look hopefully to the university, not just for the scientific, technical, and professional manpower that the nation requires, but for the political leadership that alone can pull the nation through coming crises which may include a social upheaval of revolutionary dimensions.

NOTES

1. Carlos Fredes Aliaga and Gonzalo Martner García, "La Federación de Estudiantes a Través de los Ultimos Diez Años," *Juventud,* II, No. 3 (1950). This is a detailed but partisan account of the life of the FECH between 1940 and 1950. It was extremely useful in establishing the sequence of events and as a check on interview material. Leaders of the time who were interviewed include Felipe Herrera, Hernán Godoy, Hernán Behm, Pedro Godoy Lagarrigue, Eduardo Hamuy, and Nestor Porcell. There is an abundance of published materials during these years. In addition to *Claridad* and *Juventud,* both FECH publications, the Instituto Pedagógico's *Vertice,* the Law School's *Mastil,* and the School of Engineering's *Torque* proved useful sources.

2. *Claridad,* Organo de la Federación de Estudiantes, XXVI, No. 137 (1945).

3. The Universidad Popular Valentín Letelier was launched with the support of the university and opened with ten sections manned by students. It offered literacy courses, a full secondary-school program, several short vocational training courses, and general self-improvement and cultural courses.

4. Oscar Bermúdez Miral, *El Drama Político de Chile* (Santiago: Editorial Tegualda, 1947).

5. Claude G. Bowers, *Misión en Chile (1939–53)* (Santiago: Editorial del Pacífico, 1957), p. 114.

6. *Ibid.,* pp. 123 ff.

7. A novel of life in the government camps for political prisoners, written by a Communist and student leader of the popular front period, is Volodia Teitelboim's *La Semilla en la Arena* (Santiago: Editorial Austral, 1957).

8. *Claridad,* Organo de la Federación de Estudiantes, XXVIII, No. 145 (1947).

9. *Claridad,* Organo de la Federación de Estudiantes, XXIX, No. 147 (1948).

10. A thorough descriptive survey of the Chilean economy of the 1950's is the Corporación de Fomento's *Geografía Económica,* 2 vols. (Santiago: Imprenta

Universitaria, 1950). The United Nation's Comisión Económica Para América Latina (CEPAL), with headquarters in Santiago, has published a number of studies. One of these traces economic development in Chile from 1925 to 1952:*Antecedentes sobre el Desarrollo de la Economía Chilena (1925–52)* (Santiago: Editorial del Pacífico, 1954). The University of Chile's Instituto Económico traces in detail economic changes in the country between 1940 and 1956: *Desarrollo Económico de Chile, 1940–1956* (Santiago: Editorial Universitaria, 1956). See also the Corporación de Fomento's *Cuentas Nacionales de Chile* (Santiago: Editorial del Pacífico, 1957).

11. Kalman Silvert, "Diagnosticians and Inflation," *American Universities Field Staff Newsletter* (November, 1956), p. 1.

12. *Desarrollo Económico de Chile, 1940–1956, op. cit.,* chap. 2.

13. Silvert, *op. cit.,* p. 2.

14. *Panorama Económico,* X, No. 165 (1957), p. 166.

15. Octavio Cabello, "The Demography of Chile," *Population Studies* II (March, 1956).

16. *Desarrollo Económico de Chile, 1940–1956, op. cit.,* chap. 1.

17. *Ibid.,* chap. 6.

18. Kalman Silvert, "The State of Chilean Agriculture," *American Universities Field Staff Newsletter* (July, 1957).

19. Robert J. Alexander, *Communism in Latin América* (New Brunswick, N.J.: Rutgers University Press, 1957).

20. See *Ercilla,* XXIII, No. 1130 (1957), for a summary of political events in Chile during 1956.

21. Kalman Silvert, "Elections, Parties, and the Law," *American Universities Field Staff Newsletter* (March, 1957).

22. *Ercilla,* XXIII, No. 1139 (1957).

23. In the September, 1958, election the winning candidate by a small plurality was Jorge Alessandri, the Liberal candidate. Alessandri received about one-third of the nearly 1,300,000 votes cast. Salvador Allende, perennial candidate of the left, was a scant 35,000 votes behind Alessandri. Just before the election, the controversial Law for the Defense of Democracy was repealed, and Communists regained their voting rights. The surprise victory of the right and the substantial showing of strength by Communists and Socialists augured a realignment of political forces in Chile in which the direction taken by the center (Radicals and Christian Democrats) would be decisive.

24. Some direct evidence on these points was obtained in a 1960 survey of professors. K. H. Silvert and F. Bonilla, *Education and the Social Meaning of Development* (New York: American Universities Field Staff, 1961).

25. *Estatutos de la Federación de Estudiantes de Chile* (as revised by the last Ordinary Convention held September 20–25, 1954).

26. In 1955, the FECH had seceded from the National Confederation of Students, although *gremialistas* insisted that the secession was illegal, having never been approved by a convention vote. The FECH withdrawal was produced over the question of affiliation with an international student organization. FECH delegates or "observers" had attended world conclaves of the Soviet-sponsored International Student Union, as well as meetings of the rival Coordinating Secretariat of National Student Unions (COSEC). When the National Confed-

eration voted to affiliate exclusively with COSEC, the FECH delegates walked out. As is the case with labor organizations, the matter of international affiliations and the nature of national confederations are critical issues for student groups.

27. An unpublished report of a study carried out by social workers of the Department of Student Welfare of the university shows that of 981 students who in 1948 entered nine major university schools, 30 per cent graduated in the standard time period for their school, 25 per cent took longer (up to eight years), 6 per cent were still in the university, and 42 per cent had definitely dropped out. The dropout rate ranged from 31 to 64 per cent in the schools surveyed; most of the dropouts occurred at the end of the first year. In another survey, covering the School of Engineering and the first- and second-year students of four other schools (Chemistry and Pharmacy, Dentistry, Veterinary Medicine, and Constructors), it was found that about a third of the 1,723 students surveyed were not living at home. The average rates being paid by those who lived in pensions or as lodgers with private families indicated that they were occupying substandard quarters. About 10 per cent of these students had some employment.

28. The fight against the fare increase eclipsed all other FECH concerns during the year, but a great deal of time in the *directorio* was also absorbed by extensive discussion of the problems of several schools. One school was fighting for its very survival (the school for medical aides, *practicantes*). Another school (contractors and builders) was fighting to expand its curriculum to include advanced courses in draftsmanship and to enlarge its professional prerogatives to include the construction of certain types of structures without the intervention of engineers or architects. A third (the normal school for secondary teachers) was engaged in efforts to get rid of a professor with full tenure who was considered incompetent.

29. The Executive Committee members and the delegates to the University Council, who have been in the university an average of five years, are between twenty-four and twenty-five years of age. The delegates to the FECH assembly and the presidents of the school centers, as a rule, have been in the university about three years and average 22.6 years of age.

30. *XII Censo General de Población y I de Vivienda, Levantado el 24 de Abril de 1952* (Resumen del País, Servicio Nacional de Estadística, Santiago: Imprenta Gutenberg, 1956), I, 119 ff.

31. *Ibid.*, p. 145.

32. This excessive professionalism has contributed to the political fractioning of the middle class. The defense of the "guild" or *gremio* takes on a political character both within and without the university. The occupational sphere is invested with a disproportionate social and political importance, as the training and prerogatives of each occupation and its sub-departments become more and more circumscribed.

33. Gabriel Almond (*The Appeals of Communism* [Princeton, N.J.: Princeton University Press, 1954]) found similar attitudes among French and Italian Communists. He speaks of the "ethical appropriateness" of party action for individuals who see themselves as "employing effective means against immediate evils intimately experienced" (p. 376). The party, asserts Almond, "fulfills

political needs for protest against an inequitable distribution of values in stalemated societies which offer no promise of future improvement" (p. 380).

34. The trend toward conformity among youth in the mid-1950's has been widely commented on in the United States and elsewhere, although the evidence is, in fact, conflicting. Possibly the high ratio of Chilean student leaders who shared the political views of their fathers was part of a broad sociological trend. Even assuming that this is so, the link between acceptance of paternal authority and the acceptance of a particular kind of political role remains of interest.

35. T. W. Adorno *et al., The Authoritarian Personality* (New York: Harper & Brothers, 1950).

36. "... the character of the extremely unprejudiced is less pronounced and clear-cut than that of the extremely prejudiced...."(*Ibid.,* p. 389). "Our prejudiced subjects ... are on the whole more alike as a group than are the unprejudiced. The latter include a great variety of personalities; many, on the surface at least, have no more extreme variants in common than the absence of a particular brand of hostility" (p. 972).

37. The important area of sexual relations and choice of mate was not systematically explored in the interviews. In a few cases, respondents spontaneously introduced the topic. The sexual life of university students, by all accounts, is extremely restricted. Since the university career, especially in the major professional schools, commonly extends to age twenty-five or twenty-six, a serious problem is raised. The most common sexual outlet is found in occasional group sorties to houses of prostitution. Since status considerations and fears of venereal infection move students to visit only the more "reputable," and therefore more expensive, of these establishments, this solution is barred to many and only serves to compound the frustration of others. University women and other eligible marriage partners for students know that they must remain virgins or seriously damage their marriage chances. Heterosexual contacts within the university are relaxed and free but rarely advance sexually beyond adolescent petting. The fear that a premature marriage may cut off a budding career seems to be a live one, not only for parents, but for students as well. These remarks, of course, refer to a period antedating the easy availability of the contraceptive pill.

Part II

Myron Glazer

THE CHILEAN UNIVERSITY STUDENT DURING THE 1964 PRESIDENTIAL CAMPAIGN

Chapter 4

The Educational Pyramid

The research on which Part I of this volume was based was completed before the second study was undertaken. The direction of this latter work was markedly influenced by the results of the first project. It was apparent that research on the rank-and-file students could clarify the extent to which observations made about the FECH leaders could be generalized to their peers. The year prior to the presidential election of September, 1964 provided an excellent opportunity in which to study student attitudes during a period of greatly heightened national tension. A brief description of that campaign is in order.

Background to the Study

With the withdrawal of the candidate of the incumbent conservative coalition, the Democratic Front *(Frente Democrático)*, in the aftermath of a defeat in a local election, the center-left Christian Democrats and far left, largely Socialist-Communist Popular Action Front (FRAP) alone remained as potential victors. The two competing forces differed less in policy than in style and reputation. Their programs were strikingly similar, especially in their general emphasis on the need for sweeping social change. Both, as opposition parties, could freely attack the incumbent regime.

The basic program of the Christian Democratic party had been spelled out by its president, Renan Fuentealba, the previous year. Attacking the FRAP and charging it with proposing "revolution with dictatorship," he characterized the Christian Democratic program as a "revolution in liberty." The party's platform, as he presented it, stressed the need to democratize and modernize state and nation through extensive reform in all areas: economic, legislative, administrative, judicial, agrarian, educational, urban, and diplomatic. Under economic reform, for example, the Christian Democrats proposed participation by workers in industrial ownership and management, the fullest use and control of Chile's natural resources for the sole benefit of her people, and "an end to the power and privileges of accumulated money."[1] Christian Democratic leaders declared, in a manner characteristic of their whole campaign, that theirs would not be a government of a single man or party, but a collectivity, responsible in its action to all the people, who would themselves lead in the struggle for their own liberation and betterment. Their program, however, did not advocate the nationalization of American-owned copper mines.

The program of the FRAP was set forth almost a full year before the election.[2] It too focused on the need for agrarian reform, economic controls, industrialization, democratization, and an independent foreign policy. The major divergence between the FRAP and the Christian Democrats lay in the former's stated intention to nationalize Chile's major extractive industries.[3] The FRAP urged this as a vital step to prevent the exodus of millions of dollars in foreign profits and to permit their reinvestment in the national economy. The FRAP claimed that Chile had too long been bled by North American copper companies, whose operations were blatantly imperialistic. Chileans, warned the FRAP, could no longer ignore the fact that parent companies in the United States set the prices for the raw copper mined by their Chilean subsidiaries or that the highly profitable refining process still took place thousands of miles from Chile. So long as foreign capitalists controlled her most vital resource, the leftist coalition bitterly predicted that Chile was doomed to remain a servant nation.

This situation was intensified as the presidential campaign became a widening spiral of claim and counter-claim, charge and counter-charge. Under the pressure of such exchanges and because of the similarity of the two programs, partisan allegiances were personalized. Both candidates—Eduardo Frei of the Christian Democrats, Salvador Allende of the FRAP—had developed substantial personal followings over the years. Increasingly, FRAP supporters defined themselves as Allendistas, and many Freistas also appeared.

Although there were some instances of personal attacks on the candidates themselves, much more energy was devoted to vilifying the supposed "real powers behind the thrones." There was a powerful attempt to associate the FRAP coalition with Communist domination and to depict the Socialist Allende as a pawn whom the Communists would soon dispose of, were he elected, in order to set up their own dictatorship.[4]

Guilt by association also became a major FRAP weapon, particularly after the right-wing parties gave their support to Frei. A flood of headlines in the Communist press linked various *latifundistas* (large landowners) and "exploiters" with Frei and his party. Attempts were even made to associate the Christian Democratic candidate with fascism and with a small Nazi group that supported him as the lesser of two evils.[5]

In addition to making drastic attempts to discredit the opposition, each group also worked to widen the base of its own support. Ideological consistency became far less important than victory. After the demise of the right-wing coalition in the provincial election in Curico, the Christian Democrats were greatly strengthened by an infusion of conservative support. The party accepted this backing, notwithstanding its vehement attacks on these same groups only a short time before. After March, 1964, Frei stated his readiness to accept the endorsement of any group willing to support his program, but said he would not be compromised in any manner. Sarcastically attacking this position, Allende derided those who believed that support would be given "with no strings attached." Yet it was Allende himself who made an impassioned, but unsuccessful, plea to the middle-of-the-road Radical party immediately after the breakup of the conservative coalition.[6] Each national coalition, then, attempted to build its own positive image, with which a vast cross section of the population could identify, and to portray its opposition as representing only narrow and alien interests. The opposition, in turn, was at once engaged in projecting its own image, creating a negative image of its political competitors, and rejecting the negative image of itself.

Major Questions

In designing the research, a wide variety of questions were considered. It is readily apparent that all of them are of current interest to social scientists concerned with the university in developing areas, and that many of them are derived from the first three chapters of this volume. The remaining three chapters in Part II will be directed toward shedding further light on the following challenging problems:

1. How professionally committed are Chilean university students? How is position on an index of professional commitment influenced, for example, by the nature of the career, by the year of study, and by the students' political involvement?
2. What professional goals do students in the various careers pursue? What means do they posit as essential for realization of these goals? How do these responses shed light on the discrepancy between ideal and actual patterns of evaluation and opportunity in transitional society?
3. What is the "fit" between the output of educational institutions and the marketplace? What role strains derive from the disparity between the students' desire to implement professional knowledge and the inability of the current Chilean economy to employ all professionals?
4. What acceptance and resistance patterns exist among students in relation to their willingness to pioneer new areas of employment? Specifically, what attitudes exist among the youthful educated elite toward servicing urban workers and rural peasants?
5. What differences emerge in the concentration of politically involved students among the various schools? How do these differences affect professional concerns of the students in these schools? How are boundaries maintained or disrupted between these two activities?
6. Does a dearth of employment opportunities after graduation act as a major contributing factor to student political agitation? Are the nature and demands of the school's curriculum key intervening variables in student political involvement?
7. Is there a relationship between student political attitudes and

their willingness to service marginal consumers? Are we able to isolate a group of students whom we may characterize as "revolutionary" in their willingness to "pioneer new professional services?"

The primary purpose of the following chapters is to describe professional training in one nation in Latin America. This aspect of the students' role has been neglected too long. The impact of political factors will be discussed within this perspective.

Methodology

To gather data, several approaches were utilized. Contemporary Chilean newspaper and journal articles, as well as scholarly and government sources, were used to secure a picture of the official and popular thinking on educational problems, in general, and the student role, in particular. Persons well acquainted with Chilean education, including social scientists, university professors, professional practitioners, and current university students were relied on as informants. Finally, a lengthy interview schedule, completed and tested during the first few months after this author's arrival in Chile in September, 1963, was utilized to obtain the attitudes of a representative sample of university students.

The twenty-four-page interview schedule (Appendix B) included several major sections: family and educational background, professional training experiences and attitudes, political background and experiences, and political attitudes. The professional section of the schedule was strongly influenced by the approaches utilized in recent studies of United States graduate education.[7] The political questions were constructed almost entirely on the basis of observations of Chilean national life and of the intense political struggles which characterized the country in late 1963–1964. The schedule was pre-tested and discussed at great length with Chileans from different professions and of all political persuasions to ensure that our queries focused on those matters that were held to be most relevant by local observers.

The actual interviews were conducted with students in four schools of the University of Chile in Santiago, the largest and most important university in the country. The schools from which the sample was drawn are training students in fields which are essential for national development, including Medicine, Engineering, secondary school teaching, and Science.[8]

The aim was to interview approximately a hundred students in each of the schools,[9] and thirty-five names were drawn at random from those enrolled in each of the first, middle, and final years of their course of study.[10] However, the pressure of time and the great difficulty in locating some of the students required that a minimum of thirty be accepted in each of the years selected.[11]

The Chilean Education System in the Early 1960's

The most traditional element of Chilean higher education was its recruitment process. Ascribed class characteristics played an overwhelming part in eliminating the great majority of possible candidates, and the complicated university admissions procedure was limited in its applicability to less than 5 per cent of the school-age population. This limitation was not an isolated phenomenon peculiar to the Chilean university, but rather a more all-encompassing problem rooted in the entire elementary and secondary school system.

Figures officially accepted by the Chilean government in the early 1960's show that of the children who began the first grade, only 66.4 per cent reached the second grade, 21.5 per cent began a secondary school (seventh grade), and 4.5 per cent reached the last year (twelfth grade). Table 4-1 indicates in greater detail the pyramidal nature of ascendency of the educational ladder.[12]

Although no official statistics are available, it is obvious that educational progress in Chile was directly related to economic background. Furthermore, the dropout rate, resulting from economic hardship and lack of schools, was even higher in the rural areas than among urban dwellers. The small minority of large landowners could send their children to good secondary schools and on to the university. It is a notorious fact, however, that not one son of a peasant was enrolled in the University of Chile, and it was a rare exception to find anyone of this socioeconomic background in any institution of higher learning.[13]

These statements can be documented by the extremely high dropout rates in rural provinces. Table 4-2 compares educational

TABLE 4-1

Pyramid of Education: Percentage of
School-Age Population in School

Age	Grade	Per Cent
	University	
24	18	0.2
23	17	0.7
21	15	1.2
19	13	2.3
	Secondary	
18	12	4.5
16	10	9.2
14	8	15.2
	Primary	
12	6	29.4
10	4	48.9
8	2	66.4
7	1	100.0

achievement in three of the most rural provinces with three of the most urban ones.

Although these figures were indicative of a highly traditional society, an analysis of other factors pointed to the markedly transitional nature of contemporary Chile. Breaks in the traditional pattern were manifested by the publicity given to differential opportunity and to the general definition of the educational situation as a major social problem. Governmental remedial activity had been undertaken on a moderate level through school construction and the sponsorship of investigation and planning for rapid educational change. Finally, the dramatic 1964 presidential campaign stimulated radical programs for solution of the educational problems in the platforms of both major coalitions and in the speeches of all the candidates.[14]

TABLE 4-2

Comparison of Rural and Urban School Populations, 1962

Province	Per Cent Rural Population	Per Cent in Sixth Grade	Per Cent in Twelfth Grade
Chiloe	80.3	14.8	2.7
Colchagua	71.5	15.4	2.0
Linares	67.3	18.5	2.0
Antofagasta	11.1	44.1	7.0
Santiago	11.5	39.2	8.1
Valparaiso	13.2	43.7	7.7
National Average	**36.5**	**29.0**	**4.7**

*Comision De Planeamiento Integral De La Educación, *Algunos Antecedentes Para El Planeamiento Integral De La Educación Chilena* (Santiago: Ministerio De Educación Publica, 1964), pp. 252-253.

The clash between the still traditional actuality and the modern educational goals had been a major aspect of Chilean society for a number of years.[15] Notwithstanding the discussions, congresses, and seminars about educational reform held in Chile for the past thirty years, there had been substantial success only in increasing the percentage of students completing the primary school, moderate success on the secondary level, and almost no change in higher education (Table 4-3).

Preparation for University Admissions

The highly pyramidal nature of the primary and secondary school system did not automatically create an abundance of vacancies on the university level. There was a shortage of space, and a keen competition for admission ensued among secondary school students. Those who did successfully compete had to first terminate six years of primary school and six years of *humanidades,* the secondary program designed for preparation to enter the university. The *humanidades,* created to give the student elite a general cultural education, had long been under attack.

TABLE 4-3

Percentage Changes in Student Population*

Year	Sixth Grade	Twelfth Grade	First Year Higher Education
1953	17.4	2.8	2.0
1957	22.0	3.7	2.2
1962	29.4	4.5	2.3

*Comision De Planeamiento Integral De La Educación, *Algunos Antecedentes Para El Planeamiento Integral De La Educación Chilena* (Santiago: Ministerio De Educación Publica, 1964), p. 265.

One Chilean educator had noted the basic conflict that had plagued the educational system from the time of national independence. Should education be for the people or for the elite? Basically, he asserted, this had been reconciled through two educational systems. One had been directed toward the middle and upper classes and had been composed of a private preparatory school, a private or public academy on the intermediate level, which had been directed exclusively toward those who held professional goals. The second system had been for the lower classes and had consisted of inadequate public elementary schools and a few, limited possibilities for vocational and technical education on the intermediate level.[16]

The highly stratified nature of the educational system continued to characterize Chile. In many ways, most observers agreed, the secondary school still pursued the "eighteenth-century ideal." It wanted to "produce persons trained in languages, metaphysics, and the arts, rather than in handicrafts, nutrition, or social and economic planning."[17] Critics continually pointed out that the program was superficial and not designed to meet the needs of a modern industrial nation. Emphasis on memory, poor training in mathematics and science, and premature division of students into special programs in preparation for a career in letters, biology, or mathematics were among the major weaknesses.

These defects were not peculiar to Chile. A report on education in all Latin America had noted that the primary problem affecting secondary education was the lack of correlation to both elementary and higher educational programs. The report summarized the problems of intermediate education in that region:

> . . . verbalism, learning by rote, absence of student orientation and guidance services, predominance of rigid, undifferentiated, uncorrelated and encyclopedic curricula, defective science teaching, little personal use of the scientific method, and virtual inexistence of laboratory work, use of unsuitable systems for measuring academic performance, lack of communication between teachers, and lack of means for exchanging experiences and documentation. In addition, there is the inadequacy of premises and lack of supplies and equipment for facilitating teaching. Textbooks are also defective and out of date. Needless to say, there are honorable exceptions in this generally dark picture.[18]

Much work in the latter years of the *humanidades* program was geared toward the *bachillerato,* the national examination, which was a fundamental part of the admissions program to the University of Chile. Students usually decided in the fourth year of high school which examination they would prepare for. In order to enter engineering or economics, for example, a student had to attain a certain score in the mathematics *bachillerato.* Those who wished to pursue medicine studied for the biology test; others interested in law took their *bachillerato* in letters. Critics had indicated that the examination was almost entirely dependent on the ability to cram and memorize and had not been a good indicator of future success in the university. Others pointed out that the extremely high failure rate was a further indictment of the entire secondary system. About one-half of the students failed the examination each year, despite the claims that the test had been continually simplified. At that point, even success did not indicate a high level of competence.[19] Demands for changing the system of examinations had been rejected on the basis that reform had to be related to a general change in the entire secondary system.[20]

Since entrance to the university was based on passing the *bachillerato,* and entrance to the school of one's choice depended on scoring the minimum number of points required on the test for that particular career, the examination was a great source of

tension among college preparatory youth. It was a national event
publicized in the newspapers before and after the examination
day, and it precipitated great discussion and fear.[21]

The figures in Table 4-4 indicate that there was a highly
realistic basis for anxiety among Chilean candidates.

TABLE 4-4

Percentage of Successful Candidates in
Bachillerato Examination*

Examination Area	Number Successful	Percentage of Number Presented
Letters	3,114	66.7
Biology	2,287	42.4
Mathematics	1,629	53.9
Total	7,030	53.7

*Universidad de Chile, Instituto de Investicaciones Estadisticas,
"Estadistica del Bachillerato de 1963," *Boletin Estadistico De La
Universidad De Chile,* VII, 11.

In some schools a passing score on the *bachillerato* was sufficient for entrance; in others, additional tests were given as a
second elimination process. Those who did not pass the examination could retake it in six months if they wanted to enter the
University of Chile (and, in some cases, other universities). It was
not uncommon to lose a year of study because of failure or a
score too low to enter the faculty of one's choice. Others who
passed but did not score high enough frequently studied one year
in a school of low admissions standards until they again tried to
enter medicine, engineering, or other very competitive schools.

In Chile, despite all the tests and requirements, there were
many complaints that students entering the university were ill-
prepared. The dropout and repeat (failure) rate was very high.[22]
Much time and money were lost in students transferring from
one field to another in a university and in a country where

resources were scarce and the need for professionals and high-talent manpower urgent.

We now turn to a discussion of the schools in our sample.

The Traditional Elite Schools

The School of Medicine at the University of Chile was academically excellent. The entrance requirements were extremely high, and only a small percentage of the applicants gained admission to the first-year class. It was not at all unusual for students to enroll in other medical schools or related fields for one or two years in preparation for a desired transfer. The unusually small attrition rate was a source of pride and a guarantee to students that every effort would be made by the staff to facilitate their completion of the degree requirements.[23] Our responses revealed that students were generally drawn from a high socio-economic background (Table 4-5), and 23 per cent of the fathers of medical students in our sample were themselves doctors. Early orientation toward this career seemed to serve as a marked advantage toward obtaining the necessary educational and motivational background.[24] Since entrance requirements were so high, excellent previous education was most important. Furthermore, medical training represented the necessity of deferred gratification for many students. The seven-year career was longer than any other; young physicians generally spent the first three years of practice in rural areas, and the starting salary was low. This necessitated a strong commitment to the career and appreciation of its less tangible, immediate rewards.

The School of Engineering enjoyed equal prestige in the general community. Its course of study was reputed to be very difficult and resulted in a very high attrition rate among entering students. For those who did manage to complete the six-year program, the future held promise of abundant and highly paid professional positions.

Engineering was interesting because of its middle position between the Schools of Medicine and History. In addition to a small percentage from upper-class families (5 per cent), students in our sample spanned the spectrum in approximately equal numbers from the upper-, middle-, and lower-middle-income groups. As an important avenue of social mobility, engineering

TABLE 4-5
Socio-economic Background by School*

	Engineering	History	Science	Medicine
Upper	5	3	17	5
Upper-middle	25	12	17	31
Middle-middle	36	27	40	44
Lower-middle	24	45	13	15
Lower	7	13	10	3
Unknown	1	1	3	1
Total‡	99 †	101	100	99
	(94)§	(94)	(30)	(99)

*The socio-economic index was primarily derived from the responses to questions on the fathers' education and salary. Those who stated earnings of E° 1,000 (*escudos*) or more per month were assigned 10 points; E° 500-999 = 7 points; E° 200-499 = 4 points; and 1 point was assigned to those who indicated income of less than E° 200. Father's education was scored by the following: 3 points for a complete or incomplete university education: 2 points for a complete or incomplete secondary education; 1 point for elementary school attendance.

The mothers' education and salary were given minor weight, except where there was no father in the household, on the assumption that class is largely determined by the position of the father. If the mother worked, 1/2 point was added. If the mother had a job of high prestige or salary which could significantly change the family status, 1 point was added.

Students' families were then divided into five major categories. Thirteen points was the minimum for the upper class (high income plus high education); 10 points for the upper-middle group (high income plus middle education, or middle income plus high education); 9 points for middle-middle (middle income plus middle education); 6 points for lower-middle class (low income plus middle education, or middle income plus low education). Five points or less was designated as the lowest category. These results were roughly verified by checking them against the parents' occupations, a further indicator of social-class position.

The greatest difficulty arose where the student did not know, or would not state, the father's income. Moreover, in a few cases some who did indicate salaries were obviously misinformed. (Lack of accurate information on income was complicated by continual wage readjustments due to the spiraling inflation.) Where knowledge of salary was unavailable or obviously incorrect, we asked for as detailed information as possible about the father's job. From this, an average income was approximated on the basis of discussion with Chileans familiar with the occupational and class structure. Such approximation was most difficult in a minority of cases where the student's father was self-employed in a small business or was a small landowner. On the other hand, salaries of white-collar workers, including public and private clerks, low-level executives, teachers, and other professionals are more standardized and therefore easier to estimate.

†Percentages do not always equal 100 because of rounding.
‡Only percentages appear.
§Totals upon which percentages are based.

attracted, not only the sons of professionals, but also those of middle-class businessmen seeking to secure their status within Chilean society, as well as those of hard-pressed public and private bureaucrats. The small group of children from working-class families (7 per cent) was more than proportional to representation in the university as a whole. Their presence was a dramatic indication of the mobility aspirations which many students brought to this school.

The New School

An interesting point of comparison can be made with the Institute of Science. This school attracted students from backgrounds similar to engineering. Because it was new and insecure in Chile, it still had little of the prestige and high reputation which accrued to engineering. The Institute of Science, which prepared students for careers in the basic sciences, was still suffering birth pangs. It had been able to recruit and, what was much more important, to support only a handful of students in the last few years. There was little prospect of increased employment opportunities for graduates of the program because of the current controversy about the usefulness of advanced physical or mathematical research. Therefore, students faced not only the challenging requirements established by a highly competent staff, but also the great uncertainty about employment possibilities.

The Traditional Low-Prestige School

The Pedagogico was the single largest school within the university. Its program was primarily directed toward the training of teachers for secondary schools. Of the many specializations in the Pedagogico, we focused on the School of History. Its entrance requirements were much lower than those of Medicine, Engineering, or most of the other prestigious schools. Although the actual course work was not reputed to be too difficult, the school did have a high dropout rate. Our sample was divided almost equally between men (45 per cent) and women (55 per cent) who were training for a career which offered relatively low prestige and pay and for which there was a scarcity of positions in the urban areas of the country. Finally, the School of History had fewer students from secure middle-class families than did the other schools studied, and the concentration of its students' backgrounds skewed sharply downward.

Career Choice

The dynamic of individual career choice is a rather complicated phenomenon. Most students shared the need to indicate the adequacy of their present choice, even in cases where they might have been willing to drop out or transfer schools had an attractive alternative opportunity arose. History students frequently wanted to study law but could not be admitted; others were accepted and then had to leave because of academic difficulties. Yet more of these students (86 per cent) claimed to have entered the teaching career because of "preference for the material" than in any of the other schools. This may have been a combination of overcompensation and the lesser ability to speak of "prestige" or "possibility of getting a good job" as realistic motivations. A discrepancy was often observed between these statements and others made in the same interview about future plans and possibilities. One third-year student probably expressed the feelings of many of his peers when he said, "I liked both law and history—but I would have preferred law and I am still thinking of continuing in it afterward." The desire to study law was frequently not based on good opportunities.[25] As in many traditional societies the number of lawyers far exceeded the need. The prestige of the field, nevertheless, continued to draw large numbers of students.

One other possible motivating factor was the desire to use law as an entrance to politics. One fifth-year history student explained, "I wanted to study law in order to begin a political career, but I did not do well in the law school. In order to advance more rapidly, I transferred to history, since a knowledge of history is also important in politics." Even the figures showing how many applied to other schools must be viewed skeptically. Many who reported only their current school probably did apply to one or two others. The longer the students had been in the school, the less they seemed willing to speak of this. Our informants were able to point to many disparities between response and actuality among students in these later years.

In the School of Medicine there was exactly the opposite phenomenon. Students freely stated that they first studied in another school usually in order to meet medicine's high admission requirements. The number who first enrolled in the Pedagogico pointed up the problem indicated by an administrator of scientific subjects there. Many of the best students left biology teaching preparation in the first, second, or even third year to enter medicine or other related fields. Paradoxically, strengthening the program in secondary-school preparation led to a greater loss of the most capable students, who then were prepared to transfer to the more prestigious and competitive careers.

A large majority of the medical students also indicated, of course, that the "nature of the material" was the major factor involved in choice of a career. Yet another important first factor was "the influence of parents," which was higher here than in any other school (21 per cent). This was no doubt a result of both the large number of fathers who were themselves doctors and the desire of many parents to have their children study in a high-prestige school.

Many of the history students (34 per cent), it can be noted, mentioned the importance of a *liceo* (secondary school) teacher as a second factor in career choice. In the School of Medicine the influence of a role model also played an important part. In addition to parents, many medical students were influenced by "someone they knew practicing the profession" (21 per cent). This response was far more frequent among them than among engineering students (13 per cent), where the actual work of an engineer was less observable to most recruits.

Among neophyte doctors, the "prestige of the career" also figured largely (25 per cent) as a second choice. This became markedly more pronounced in the later years. At that point in their training, students were working in hospitals and were actually closer to enjoying some of the prestige bestowed on the doctor.[26]

Engineering students were generally characterized by their direct entrance to the school. They had been rejected from few other schools, had rarely studied in another faculty, and had frequently never considered any other possibility. The high prestige and employment opportunities of this field had a magnetic effect in recruiting those students who had a strong mathematics background. Their answers to why they chose the career showed the combination of ability to do the work, reinforcement and encouragement from significant others, and a realistic recognition of the rewards offered in this profession. Where there did exist some doubt about career choice, students clearly recognized and honestly stated the advantages of income and prestige of an engineering career.

Personal decisions such as these had social implications and costs. In a series of lead articles, a major newspaper discussed the necessity of adopting measures to avoid a crisis in the teaching of mathematics. *El Mercurio* pointed out that there was a marked deficiency in the number of mathematics teachers available and emphasized the differential recruitment ability of the teaching and engineering professions.

Little noted, but of related importance, were the great problems facing the Institute of Science. The precarious state of this new school in Chile not only affected the morale and ability of its practicing members but also diminished the attractiveness of the field to highly competent students. Teachers were constantly impressing upon students the basically insecure nature of the professional future they faced. The gravity of the situation was so extreme that the professors themselves were often loathe to encourage promising students to enter the Institute.[27] Motivation and reward had to be founded on individual commitment and support from a very limited professional reference group.

Who, then, were the students in this school? Why had they rejected the natural and well-formed paths of career choice? The most obvious were those who were immigrants or sons of immigrants—primarily German refugees and Italian emigres. Especially among the German (often Jewish) families it was possible to find strong support for a scientific career. A second and frequently overlapping group was composed of students who were critical of the traditional alternatives. They defined engineering, architecture, and other prestigious careers as "in" the system and, therefore, unfit for them. They especially associated engineering with business administration and management. These students frequently had found a reference group in the international scientific community through the fame of an Einstein and the world-wide publicity given to nuclear physics in their lifetime. International influences and reference groups supported student identification with those nationals pioneering these new fields. Yet a major source of role strain resulted from the disparity between the "international"-and "local" evaluation of the profession. This diminished the career's attractiveness to those students who were unwilling or unable to reject the standards currently prevalent in their society.

The challenges to the Institute of Science may be summarized and generalized as follows: Since modernization was stated as a major Chilean goal, new careers, central to its attainment, claimed assistance. The scarcity of resources, however, limited the degree to which entrenched schools supported the demands of new ones. Obviously, the less active the encouragement that the latter received from important government and university officials, the more difficult became the task to secure their share of scarce allocations. Progress in the modernization of educational institutions represented a prime indicator of the seriousness with which responsible officials were determined to press for basic changes in the over-all society. The discrepancy between ideal and actual patterns of behavior was well illustrated by the challenges faced by the Institute of Science. A close view indicated the difficulty it faced in competition with the traditional schools for both financial support and for the most qualified students. The absence of a liberal arts program, furthermore, precluded student exposure to new and less-established careers. Early decision-making in regard to career choice favored the traditional fields.

In summary, an analysis of the educational system indicated the extent to which students were members of a tiny elite Chilean youth. Recruitment was limited to that 2 per cent of the university-age group who had survived the educational pyramid. The children of the peasantry and urban workers were virtually excluded from institutions of higher education. This situation had not gone unrecognized by governmental, educational, and newspaper personnel. It was defined as a major social problem.

Significant differences, furthermore, arose among university students recruited to different careers. Medicine attracted students primarily from professional families and other secure middle-class backgrounds. Neophyte engineers came from more varied families into a career offering both prestige and financial rewards. The future teachers were more often from lower-middle-class homes. These students could expect far less substantial rewards and faced a continuing future struggle to maintain their standing in Chilean society. The would-be scientists had entered into a most challenging and unchartered career. Many had gambled although they had the necessary academic backgrounds to have been accepted into the School of Engineering.

NOTES

1. *El Mercurio* (Santiago), October 20, 1963. All translations are the author's. For a discussion of Chilean politics during the election, see Ernest Halperin, *Nationalism and Communism in Chile* (Cambridge, Mass.: MIT Press, 1965).

2. See *El Siglo* (Santiago), October 27, 1963. The election took place in September, 1964.

3. See, for example, Nilo Rosenberg, "Nacionalización de Cobre Es un Imperativo," *El Siglo,* June 28, 1964.

4. The Communist daily *El Siglo,* for example, ran a series of articles in June, 1964 entitled "Explotación en Libertad" ("Exploitation in Liberty"), deriding the Christian Democrats' slogan, "Revolution in Liberty," and identifying members of the landed aristocracy who supported Frei.

5. In the press and at mass rallies, Frei was often portrayed as a cross between Uncle Sam and Hitler.

6. The election in the province of Curico in March, 1964 resulted in the collapse of the conservative incumbent *Frente Democrático.* Its candidate, Julio Duran, had gambled heavily on the victory of the right-wing candidate for deputy from Curico, promising to withdraw if he were defeated. Duran's withdrawal gave the Conservative and Liberal parties the freedom to realign themselves. Within the month, they announced their support for Frei, while Duran was subsequently renominated by his own Radical party and ran as a third candidate.

7. The questionnaire of James A. Davis and his colleagues was especially important. Also see R. K. Merton, G. G. Reader, P. L. Kendall, *The Student Physician* (Cambridge: Harvard University Press, 1957); H. S. Becker, and J. Carper, "The Elements of Identification with an Occupation," *American Sociological Review,* XXIII (February, 1958), 50–56; I. H. Simpson, "Patterns of Socialization into Professions: The Case of Student Nurses" (Paper presented at the Meetings of the American Sociological Association, New York; August 30, 1960). The questionnaire appears in Appendix B.

8. The goal was to choose schools in traditional fields (Medicine, Engineering, and Teaching) and in a new one (Science). Another basis of selection was to compare schools of high prestige (Medicine, Engineering) and those of lower prestige (Teaching, Science) in the general society. A third aim was to include schools that are oriented toward working with people and thus concerned with social issues (Medicine, Teaching), and ones that are oriented toward technical and scientific achievements (Engineering, Science). A final goal was to select

schools that were reputed to be very politicized and left wing (Teaching, Medicine), a school that was somewhat more conservative (Engineering), and one that was apolitical (Science). The plan to interview in a fifth school, which is training students for a new career in public administration, had to be abandoned due to illness.

9 This number, of course, represented a different percentage of the total student body because of the variation in enrollment in the different schools. Thus, in Engineering, with almost 1,500 students, our sample represented about 6 per cent of the students. In Medicine, which had 1,225 students, it represented about 8 per cent. History had approximately 250 students and the number interviewed there was somewhat less than 40 per cent. In Science 75 per cent were sampled. The high dropout rate in History resulted in a total population of less than 35 students in certain years. To insure an adequate sample, the decision was made to combine the second and third years for the mid-point, and the fourth and fifth years for the final point. In Engineering and Medicine the problem of sufficient numbers did not arise. However, the six-year curriculum in both cases led to the decision to combine the final two years in order to reduce the gap between the mid- and final points. This, we felt, would have been too great had we simply sampled from the first, third, and sixth years.

10. This was true in all cases, except the final years in Medicine. There, the students are divided and assigned to different teaching hospitals throughout the city, and our random sample was drawn from only one hospital. From conversations with informants we could not determine any differences among the students assigned to the different hospitals.

11. In general, excellent co-operation in both Engineering and Medicine resulted in our completing over 90 per cent of our stratified random sample in those schools. Far greater difficulty arose in the School of History. Not only was it an extremely challenging task to track down respective respondents because many did not regularly attend class, but also lists of students, up-to-date and easy to acquire in the other schools, did not accurately reflect actual enrollment in History. The greatest modification of the sampling design occurred in the Institute of Science. Since total enrollment consisted of only 40 students, we had planned to interview them all. Serious political difficulty, however, necessitated an end to our work after 30 students had been interviewed. It was the author's impression, however, derived from informal discussions with students and professors at the school, that there were not outstanding differences among the ten students whom we had not interviewed. This observation was confirmed when we reported our initial findings to our informants in the school. For a full discussion of the problems encountered, see Myron Glazer, "Field Work in a Hostile Environment: A Chapter in the Sociology of Social Research in Chile," Appendix A, this volume.'

12. Comision De Planeamiento Integral De La Educacion, *Algunos Antecedentes Para El Planeamiento Integral De La Educacion Chilena* (Santiago, Chile: Ministerio De Educacion Publica, 1964), p. 258.

L. Ronald Scheman's survey of Brazilian law students supports our own findings and throws further doubt on the extent to which the lower classes have been gaining admission to Latin American universities. The Brazilian law student clearly is no longer being drawn preponderantly from the upper classes, especially in regard to the economic structure of the society. The system of free public education is having a visible impact, and the university law-school population, well established in the middle classes, is beginning to draw substantial numbers from the lower elements of those middle groups. The survey confirms, however, that very few members of the student body are being recruited from the great masses of the lower class. Even more revealing than the economic statistics in this respect is the education of students' fathers. Less than 1 per cent (8 out of 1,250 students polled) stated that their fathers had no education. Since 46 per cent out of the total number of adult males of Brazil are illiterate, clearly the lower classes were not present. R. Scheman, "The Brazilian Law Student: Background, Habits, Attitudes," *Journal of Inter-American Studies*, V (1963), 355.

13. E. Hamuy, in *Educacion Elemental, Analfabetismo y Desarollo Economico* (Santiago: Editorial Universitaria, 1960), asserts that literacy in Chilean urban areas approaches that of developed countries, while illiteracy in rural areas is equivalent to underdeveloped areas (p. 53). His over-all discussion focuses on the relation between urban and rural education. For another discussion of this problem see M. Tumin, "Competing Status Systems," in W. E. Moore and A. S. Feldman, eds, *Labor and Commitment and Social Change in Developing Areas* (New York: Social Science Research Council, 1960).

14. The campaign literature is extensive. *El Siglo* published the program of the Socialist-Communist Coalition (FRAP) on October 27, 1963. Illiteracy was especially discussed in the issue of June 21, 1964. The Christian Democrat program, calling for "Revolution in Liberty," was published in *El Mercurio,* April 20, 1964.

15. See introduction, by Alejandro Garreton Silva, to Comisión De Planeamiento Integral De La Educación, *op. cit.*

16. Oscar Vera L., "Los Principales Problemas de la Situacion Educacional Chilena y el Planeamiento de la Educacion," in Comision De Planeamiento Integral De La Educación, *op. cit.*, pp. 67-69.

17. F. Pike, *Chile and the United States, 1880-1962* (Notre Dame: University of Notre Dame, 1963), p. 289.

18. "Final Report of the Special Commission for the Programming and Development of Education, Science and Culture in Latin America," mimeographed (Washington, D.C.: Pan American Union, 1963), p. 40.

19. Vera, *op cit.*, p. 69.

20. *El Mercurio,* July 21, 1964, p. 3, had an incisive editorial-article, "El Bachilerato, Indice Educacional."

21. Michiya Shimbori's description of Japan, where the opportunities are more abundant, is, nevertheless, reminiscent of Chile: "Since there are so many higher institutions with so many varieties of standard and prestige, and since there is in action a nepotism which promises the graduates of leading institutions a brilliant career, there are too many applicants for these institutions. Hence the severe competition in the entrance examinations, which consist almost exclusively of achievement tests in a few academic subjects and is given once a year, in March. It is not an exaggeration to say that the whole three years of senior high school are devoted to preparation for the entrance

examination and the main concern of high school students, their teachers, and their parents is with it." M. Shimbori, "Zengakuren: A Japanese Case Study of a Student Political Movement," *Sociology of Education,* XXXVIII (Spring, 1964), p. 237.

Robert O. Myhr's description of Brazil reveals similar characteristics of the process of recruitment to higher education. "Entrance to the university requires a difficult special examination, the *vestibular.* Each faculty holds its own *vestibular* every year. This examination is a critical point in the career of the young Brazilian, for he must not only choose his professional faculty but also pass the *vestibular* to enter that faculty. If he fails, however, he must attempt the examination repeatedly until he passes or becomes discouraged." Robert O. Myhr, "Brazil" in D. K. Emmerson, ed., *Students and Politics in Developing Nations* (New York: Frederick A. Praeger, 1968), p. 251.

22. "Supervivencia y Perdida Del Alumnado De La Ensenanza Superior En Chile," *Informativo Estadistico,* No. 5 (December, 1962).

23. *Ibid.*

24. For comparable findings for United States medical students see, N. Rogoff, "The Decision to Study Medicine" in R. K. Merton, G. G. Reader, and P. L. Kendall, eds., *The Student Physician* (Cambridge: Harvard University Press, 1957), p. 112.

25. For a discussion and statistics focusing on this imbalance see "Organization of American States." *Development of Education In Latin America—Prospects for the Future* (Washington, D.C., 1963), p. 47.

26. I am suggesting here that current experiences influence perception of the factors important in past decisions.

27. This was reported to us by professors in the school.

Chapter 5

Professional Socialization
and the Impact
of Political Experiences

Introduction

The study of the process of professional socialization can be divided into several analytical categories. These include the student's involvement with learning of professional tasks, his relationship with professionally significant others, and his interaction with future clients for his services. It is through the experiences involved in this process that the neophytes develop an initial professional self-concept. They learn technical skills and attitudes associated with the implementation of their knowledge. They interact with teachers, many of whom are current practitioners, and identify with, or reject, the values and work habits of these men. Many students, moreover, have contacts with those people who at a future date will seek their professional services.[1] As a result of these relationships, the neophytes more fully appreciate the challenges associated with their work and the extent to which they and their colleagues are able to solve individual and social problems.

In the training of Chilean students, experiences in the political structure of the university had an importance beyond the formal socialization that each student underwent. Through political experiences, students moved beyond the intake of specialized knowledge and professional values to the intake of political and

229

social knowledge and values. Some students joined or sympathized with political groups which were affiliated with national parties and whose activities were often directed toward influencing both university and national events. Others, less involved, attended lectures and speeches and participated in the ubiquitous political discussions which characterized university life. In periods of political crisis, this latter group rallied to the call of the political activists and provided the mass base for strikes, demonstrations, and other manifestations of student discontent. A third group of students was alienated from any form of political activity and rejected the importance of such participation. Emphasizing nonmembership and freedom from all "deals" or compromise, some saw themselves as independent critics of the social order. Others, uninformed or disinterested, had no political-critical position that could be measured.[2]

Task Learning: The Traditional Elite Schools

The engineering program was divided into two parts of three years each. The first half was almost exclusively devoted to the study of basic mathematics and physical sciences. The purpose was to provide the students with the theoretical basis for all the work which followed and to compensate them for the deficiencies in their secondary-school preparation. A young professor in the School of Engineering told us of the tremendous gaps that had to be filled.[3] As a graduate of one of the best secondary schools in the country, with a straight A average in all mathematics courses, he was well equipped to know about the paucity of the background. His most advanced work had been with algebraic equations of two unknowns—a relatively simple concept for those preparing for careers necessitating a strong knowledge of mathematics.

In the second half of the program, students specialized in the subfields of civil, electrical, industrial, and mining engineering. During these last three years, the emphasis was on applied training. In addition to courses, students were required to spend two summers working in their field of specialization in an apprentice-style program. During the last year, or after finishing all the course work, they had to write a thesis. This was frequently the stumbling block that prevented many from actually receiving their degrees, despite their completion of the formal training.

A majority of the engineering students (67 per cent) emphasized the difficulty of their course of study, with an increasing concentration of students in this category in the upper years (Table 5-1). This reaction reflected the realistic challenge of task learning and reinforced the general image of the school as one of the most difficult in the entire university. The very high repeat and failure rate no doubt reinforced the survivors' awareness of the obstacles that eliminated so many of their classmates. The challenge of the thesis in the last year also increased student anxiety. They were cognizant of the large number who never completed this final requirement.

Many engineering students indicated that they attempted to minimize the extent to which political factors influenced task learning. Nonetheless, while less than 10 per cent of the students at the school were members of a political group, almost 50 per cent were sympathizers of one of the competing parties. The Christian Democrats had, by far, attracted the most supporters. It was readily observable, moreover, that the small number of political activists had a great impact on student life.[4] There was a strong reaction among engineering students, on the other hand, against the "politicized" environment of the school. Fully 50 per cent of the first-year engineering students cited this as a major problem. Many, in addition, said that they had been cautioned to avoid entanglement in political activity in order not to lose valuable time during the years when emphasis on the intake of basic professional knowledge was so essential.

Structurally, the medical-training program had certain similarities to that of engineering. Here, too, the first three years were devoted to a study of the basic biological sciences. In the fourth year students began to work in hospitals and emphasize clinical subjects. This continued through the sixth year, and most subfields of medicine were studied. The seventh, and last, year was somewhat comparable to an internship. Unlike United States medical training, it occurred before graduation and the conferring of the title. By this last year, almost all formal course work had been completed. Students worked full time in the hospital and prepared for the final examination administered to all candidates for medical degrees in the country. Opportunities for specialization were offered by the *Servicio Nacional de Salud,* the

TABLE 5-1

Difficulty of Course of Study in Comparison to Other Faculties in University by School and Year

	Engineering			History			Science			Medicine		
	I	II-III	V-VI	I	II-III	IV-V	I	II-III	IV-VI	I	III	V-VI
Greater	60	63	77	6	7	10	75	67	70	34	65	36
Equal	40	37	18	85	77	74	25	33	20	63	32	61
Less	—	—	3	9	16	13	—	—	—	—	3	3
Don't know	—	—	3	—	—	3	—	—	10	3	—	—
Total	100 (30)	100 (30)	101 (34)	100 (33)	100 (30)	100 (31)	100 (8)	100 (12)	100 (10)	100 (32)	100 (34)	100 (33)

public health agency that employed almost all Chilean doctors. Except under unusual circumstances, graduates had to serve three years in the provinces before they could participate in this program.

Students in the School of Medicine defined their course of study as less challenging than we would have predicted. The responses strongly indicated that the large majority (62 per cent) saw their work as no more difficult than that faced by students of other schools. Many indicated that their point of comparison was with their peers in Engineering and other highly rated schools. Their recruitment from among the best of the secondary schools and the low attrition rate characteristic of medical education were additional possible explanatory factors. Yet, the evaluation of the third-year students reflected a central fact of task learning in the School of Medicine. That year was a turning point as it marked the end of the intake of basic classroom knowledge. Students who passed this point were more assured of successfully completing the program of training. The rate of anxiety was highest among this group.[5]

In many subtle and important ways, students entering the first-year class in the School of Medicine were to have a unique experience in Chilean higher education. Most were very well aware of the social problems facing their country. This had motivated many to seek a career in medicine. Yet it was immediately obvious to the students that, as far as they cared to think into the future, their major challenge would be to learn the basic materials in the biological sciences. They sensed that they were in training and that to become good doctors had to be their immediate concern.

From their own experiences in the classroom, and from what other students had told them, they knew that there was an important difference between the School of Medicine and many of the other schools. There was a marked, and usually successful, attempt by the professors to distinguish between professional commitment and political interest. The classroom was a place where medical knowledge was imparted and learned. One's political difference had to be put aside at its door. While students at other schools might be affected by strikes, those in Medicine who were engaged in research or clinical work had to remember that their major responsibility was toward its furtherance. The tension between these two activities was, perhaps, keener here but more closely regulated.

Students, however, were not oblivious to the political activity going on around them. They listened to many discussions in the cafeteria, and they read the political posters in the halls. As in all other schools, election time gave rise to heated dialogues between those who supported FRAP and those who supported the Christian Democrats for the major offices of the FECH. They found that in recent elections their school had voted for the Christian Democrats, but that more than one class delegate or even school president had been of the opposing group.

The two major groups boasted approximately equal numbers of members. These students represented about 10 per cent of the student body. Far more substantial numbers, in addition, indicated their overt sympathies for one of the two competing groups. Among these students, Christian Democratic sympathizers numbered more than twice as many as those who supported the FRAP. Unlike the School of Engineering, nevertheless, many Christian Democratic supporters in the School of Medicine defined themselves as "leftists." Many observers, then, characterized the school as containing a majority of socially conscious and radical students.

Indeed, when we first approached the student council president of the school to seek his co-operation in interviewing medical students, he quickly cautioned us about the intense resistance we would encounter. Medical students, he said, were deeply concerned with Chilean social problems, left-wing in their orientation, and quite likely to be hostile to North Americans. It was only after assuring him that we had already secured the active support of an important FRAP student leader that he acquiesced. His general observations about the students' attitudes were later borne out by their responses to our queries.

Task Learning: The New School

The Institute of Science was so very much in its formative stages that students in the various years of the program were following different courses of study. The more advanced students began in the School of Engineering, then transferred to the new

School of Physics, which was subsequently incorporated into the Institute of Science. This institute included specialized training in mathematics, chemistry, biology, and physics. Thus far, all students had emphasized a specialization in physics or mathematics, with a small number indicating a possible interest in biophysics. Theoretically, this was a five-year program, but the difficulty of the course of study and the changes in the program frequently had made a sixth year necessary. Students followed a five-year schedule of classes and laboratories and then engaged in thesis research in the last year. During this period, students received first-hand exposure to tasks through research and teaching assistantships, under the close supervision of their professors.

The science students generally believed that their school presented a greater challenge than others in the university (70 per cent). In addition to a direct statement to this effect, they made many supporting comments throughout the interview. One student indicated, for example, that because of the strict requirements, he had been unable to develop his interests in other activities. Another felt that the high demands even resulted in a lack of time to interact with his fellow students. Our many discussions with professors strongly supported the view that task learning was extremely demanding. As in engineering, many students had insufficient preparation in mathematics and the physical sciences. The high standards were a severe challenge even to the best-prepared students. The less capable or motivated were soon discouraged. Women seemed especially vulnerable. Since a secondary-school-teaching career in science was possible, transfers to the Pedagogico were not uncommon. We readily observed this phenomenon among the female students we interviewed.[6]

Many of the science students were concerned about the constantly changing emphasis of the training program, which had resulted in a situation of flux to which they had difficulty adjusting. Their anxiety was reinforced by their recognition of the lack of university support which the Institute received. This affected them, not only as students, but also as future professionals. Their insecurity was increased by the inadequacy of salaries and research budgets. Many students also specifically indicated that the lack of laboratories and other facilities was a major difficulty. Although it was not a suggested problem area in our interview schedule, a large number of students in the last years mentioned it.

There was little political activity among students at the Institute. While there was an awareness of their future professional problems, there was no tendency to solve them via direct action geared toward changing the social order. The imposing work demands seemed to undermine any propensity toward active involvement. Membership in university political groups was almost nonexistent. Similarly, well over 50 per cent of the students indicated that they were nonsympathizers. Nonetheless, when asked to define their political self-identification, a larger percentage than in any other school except history selected a "leftist" designation. Those who voiced a preference were almost equally divided between FRAP and Christian Democratic supporters.

Our experiences in conducting the research further revealed the depth of political concern among the students. After the Brazilian military overthrew Goulart in April, 1964, and as anti-United States suspicions rose sharply in Chile, many science students vigorously challenged our integrity and accused us of being CIA agents. They exhibited a marked degree of anxiety that at some future date their political views might be used to disqualify them for overseas graduate study. The insecurity they felt about their professional future helped create an atmosphere of near hysteria. This was quite inconsistent with the tone of the training they were receiving but highly reflective of the precarious nature of a science career in Chile. In our public confrontation with the students, one future scientist expressed the anxiety of many of his peers. He charged that while their names were never solicited, it would be a simple matter to piece their identity together. In a poignant statement filled with reproach he said, "I helped you, and answered your questions, and now you don't know how sorry I am. You have my life in your hands."

Task Learning: The Traditional Low Prestige School

There was a five-year program for the training of history school teachers. In the first three years students were officially matriculated in the School of History of the Faculty of Philosophy and Education. During this time, they studied history, geography, and related liberal arts courses. In the fourth and fifth years they enrolled in the Instituto Pedagogico, where they took a variety of education courses, continued in advanced history and/or geography classes, completed a requirement for practice teaching, and wrote a final thesis. In this program, as in engineering, many students did not receive their degrees. Again, the thesis requirement was a major hurdle. In response to this grave problem a series of curriculum reforms had recently been instituted. Group theses were now the rule. Research was to be conducted in conjunction with a two-year seminar program, which would hopefully facilitate speedier completion of these projects.[7]

In the School of History, the students overwhelmingly judged their course of study to be as difficult as those in other schools (78 per cent). The small number of students who saw the work as more challenging was more than balanced out by those who defined it as being relatively easier. The reference group for these students seemed to be composed of their peers studying in other schools in the Pedagogico. The physical proximity of all schools in the Faculty of Philosophy and Education facilitated interaction and comparison. There was also some common course work during the first years of study. This aided students in more closely viewing the demands on, and time input of, their peers who were preparing in such diverse schools as Journalism, Spanish, and Philosophy. Transferring among these schools was not uncommon and furthered the basis of comparison within the faculty.

Unlike most of the other schools, which consisted of old buildings and new annexes, and which were spread out all over the city of Santiago, the Pedagogico boasted a large and lovely campus. New students were impressed by the spirited atmosphere. They were immediately beset by partisans of various political groups, who handed out literature presenting their points of view or called attention to articles in the national press. It was obvious that the divergent ideas were taken very seriously by the students in the school. The groups, student miniatures of the national parties, violently attacked one another and attempted to impress on everyone the importance of supporting their positions.

Members of these groups tried to contact each student personally. All the first-year students were approached by members of the Christian Democrats. New students were much impressed by their organization and by their offers to help them become accustomed to the routine of the school work and to assist them with any registration problems. Students supporting the coalition called Movemiento Universitario Izquerdista (MUI) also approached them. They explained that their group was primarily made up of Communists and Socialists but that it was an independent leftist movement. While they seemed to be less efficient in contacting all the incoming students, they had a file on every history student and his political preference.

It was extremely difficult for students to remain neutral or aloof. The intensity of political struggles was reflected in, and augmented by, the approximately equal strength possessed by the competing groups. Over one-quarter of the students were active members of a political group. The MUI and its affiliates claimed a slightly larger membership than the Christian Democrats. Party membership in the School of History far exceeded that of the other schools studied. Sympathizers, who included well over one-third of the students, were equally divided between the two major parties. The Radicals, who were still an important national force, could garner only a tiny number of supporters. Parties further to the right of the political spectrum were almost completely devoid of university strength. Only one-third of the students at the school were both non-members and non-sympathizers, a figure which was far smaller than in any of the other schools.

The extent of political involvement among history students was caused by a variety of factors. Not the least of these was the extent to which secondary school teachers were relatively underprivileged among Chilean professionals. In the School of History, the students' overriding professional concern was with obtaining employment after the completion of their training. The shortage of jobs was not a consequence of too many history teachers for the population, but rather of too many teachers for the existing number of secondary schools and for the number of students presently attending them. In addition, although positions were more readily available in the provinces than in the large cities, it was difficult to recruit a professional staff to remote areas. Thus, while young teachers faced keen competition for opportunities in desirable locations, other jobs were filled by unqualified persons because of a dearth of applicants. There was, thereby, a direct link between the desire for increased professional opportunities and the expansion of the market for professional services in the large cities. Unlike medicine, there was a central relationship between a history student's future economic opportunities and basic changes in the entire educational system.

The dependence on social change may have accounted for the very high degree of politicization and reaction in the school. One student, no doubt articulating the views of many of his peers, carefully explained a prime motivation for his political interest and activity. For him, the maintenance of the status quo represented a condemnation to underemployment and lack of appreciation for his professional skills. Only with the victory of a political group advocating drastic education reforms could his future brighten.[8]

While some turned to politics as an answer to their professional problems, others were repelled by this behavior. Some critics believed that political activity quickly deteriorated into machinations, factionalism, and personal and party manipulations, rather than to serious idealistic efforts to solve professional, social, and political problems. *Politiqueria,* which sums up this "dirty" aspect of politics, was frequently mentioned as one of the major problems of the school. Many other students supported this concern when they complained that the school was too "politicized" or that many of their peers were more interested in political intrigue than in serious criticism of their society.

Task Learning: Instrumental and Symbolic Types

The actual class schedules of students in science, engineering, and medicine were quite heavy. The combination of lectures and laboratories occupied these students, not only in the morning hours, but also during many afternoons. Indeed, once student physicians began their work in the hospitals, they spent from eight in the morning to six at night there. There was a heavy emphasis in all of these programs on the instrumental aspects of task learning. Although the nature of the sanctions differed, students were expected to internalize knowledge and show their proficiency with professional tasks. Students were strongly conscious of the work demands and of the negative consequences of the failure to meet them. Success in one stage of training was an absolute prerequisite for entrance to the next. Failure resulted in either delay or exclusion from professional ranks.

History students, on the other hand, usually had classes only in the morning. By the nature of the subject they were free from the time-consuming laboratories that were prevalent in the other schools. Our own observations, strongly supported by those of informants, led us to conclude that their work demands were far less severe. Although there did not seem to be a marked difference among the reported study time input in the various schools, we found that history students spent much more time in after-class informal discussions, had a greater propensity to miss classes, and generally appeared less concerned with the difficulty of the program. These observations were reinforced by the problems we encountered in attempting to locate history students. On several occasions we went to required classes only to find many students absent.[9]

There were, of course, hard-working history students. These were largely responding to self-motivation. There was a large body of material to be mastered for those who desired to do so. Yet the school did not impose stringent work demands, nor did it use effective sanctions. Although students did repeat courses, there was apparently little dropout based on inability to master the material. This type of program is effective with mature and highly motivated students. In such cases internal demands, supported by peer group norms, reduce the importance of explicit sanctions. This approach is highly problematic among large groups of young students who have not been socialized to this type of motivation.[10]

The problems were intensified by a loss of class time resulting from a variety of strikes. It was not unusual for the Pedagogico to miss as much as one-third of its school year because of issues that ranged from the nationally vital to the locally trivial. While this also plagued other schools, some had developed mechanisms for reacting to its most destructive aspects. A national strike in the fall of 1964, for example, curtailed classes for over a week. The Institute of Science announced to its students that their inter-semester vacation would be utilized to make up for the missed classes. Similarly, medical students were required to compensate for time missed at their hospital positions. The emphasis in these situations was on the professional obligations of knowledge intake and task practice. The schools required commitment in the face of competing demands.[11]

In summary, many writings on Latin American universities have emphasized the tension between modern and traditional task involvement and the subsequent inconsistency in the socialization process, which are characteristic of the university in a transitional society. On the one end of the continuum are those students who are involved in a socialization process which is consistent with Simpson's description in her study of nurses.

> The first task of socialization is. . . the transformation of the lay conceptions of the outsider into the technical orientations of the insider . . . this transformation [is accomplished] by emphasizing the mastery of technical skills and knowledge as a prerequisite for professional status.[12]

Chilean professional socialization generally seemed to follow this pattern.

On the other end of the continuum, student training was characterized by attenuated demands to master professional knowledge and by a lack of actual practice in implementing professional skills. Instead of emphasis on the intake of knowledge and the practice of tasks, these students were exposed to a learning process that emphasized the ritualistic aspects of education. Students did not have to master much professional knowledge. They had to spend a number of years in the university, enroll in certain courses, take examinations that could be passed through last-minute rote memory, and possibly pay a small matriculation fee.[13] These extreme points on the continuum represent *instrumental* and *symbolic* types of task learning. Only a small number of students in our sample fell into the latter category.

Political activity, it must be stressed, can be supportive of either one of the end points of the continuum. Students who are deeply involved in political activity may define intake and practice of knowledge as a relatively unimportant concern. This symbolic position would allow them to invest the bulk of their time and energy in political action. On another extreme are those who maintain that instrumental concerns are essential for the development of the society. It is precisely to further such norms and to break the social power of symbolically oriented groups that such students may also engage in political-critical activities. It is essential to emphasize, therefore, the possibility that politically concerned students may also be among those who are most instrumental in their professional attitudes. Similarly, their peers who reject the significance of the political role may not necessarily emphasize the importance of these professional values. On the contrary, they may define task learning in symbolic terms and see their professional role as one which primarily permits them access to social rewards through the attainment of a university title. This issue will be discussed in greater detail in the next chapter.

Significant Others

The second analytical stage in the process of professional socialization is the degree, character, and result of students' involvement with professionally significant others. These are primarily, though not exclusively, the people who make up the teaching staff of the various schools. The most obvious form of interaction between teacher and student takes place as the former attempts to impart knowledge to the latter.

Evaluation of Professors

In contrast to the general statements that are made about the poor quality of teaching in Latin American universities, we found an extremely high incidence (59 per cent) of positive evaluation by the students.[14] There were important differences within each of, and among, the various schools. In Engineering (70 per cent), Physics (100 per cent), and History (76 per cent), the first-year students were the most positive in their evaluation of their teachers. This approval, although still high, decreased somewhat after the student had been in the school for two or three years. The lowest point was at the final phase of training (Table 5-2).

The least positive evaluation occurred in the last years of engineering (29 per cent). Here, by the time they reached the fifth or sixth year, students had engaged in field work and/or had had

TABLE 5-2

Evaluation of Professor's Teaching Ability by School and Year

	Engineering			History			Science			Medicine		
	I	III	V-VI	I	II-III	IV-V	I	II-III	IV-VI	I	III	V-VI
Good	70	67	29	76	56	36	100	58	50	63	62	70
Average	30	30	62	21	33	58	—	42	50	37	32	30
Poor	—	3	6	3	10	7	—	—	—	—	6	—
Total	100 (30)	100 (30)	100 (34)	100 (33)	99 (30)	101 (33)	100 (8)	100 (12)	100 (10)	100 (32)	100 (34)	100 (33)

paid experience as neophyte engineers. This practical experience brought them in close contact with practicing members of the profession. They quickly learned that the most prestigious and respected engineers frequently did not teach in the university. This exposure, reinforced by the apparently low level of engineering teaching, further reduced the evaluation of instructional efforts. This negative reaction was consistent with the response to several other questions and focused on an important component of engineering education; that is, sufficient emphasis had not been placed on the importance of teaching.

The final years of history teacher education focused on courses in pedagogy. Students' previously high evaluations of their professors' ability dropped sharply during this time. Several students expressed the criticism that the pedagogy courses concentrate almost exclusively on theory. There was not a secondary school in Chile, the critics stated, where this material would be useful.

The situation among science students was very difficult to evaluate. The changing nature of the school had meant that every class had had a different experience. First- and second-year students had been in the school only since the young Ph.D. physicists assumed teaching responsibility. These students were generally impressed by their professors' efforts. Fourth-year students, who were repeating an entire year because of previous poor training, could not possibly have a similar evaluation. The positive reaction rose sharply in the sixth year, where students were having a special seminar with their highly respected advisor, in which they were being carefully counseled on their thesis research.

Medical students were most notable for their high evaluation of the teaching at all levels of the program (62 to 70 per cent). Unlike those in the other schools, students were most positive during the last years (70 per cent). This reaction was directly attributable to the character of clinical training. The most highly respected specialists in the country were professors in the university and section heads in the university-affiliated hospital. As part of their training, students interacted with the most knowledgeable and prestigious men of their profession, who approached their instructional duties seriously.

Interaction with Professors

A second type of contact with professors occurred in less structured situations. Beyond evaluation of teaching ability, we were interested in determining whether students felt that they had had enough opportunity to consult with professors about their current work or about future plans. Student responses indicated a far less satisfactory situation (Table 5-3). In almost no class did a majority of students feel that they had had sufficient opportunity to talk to their teachers.

This problem was especially acute in the first and third years of engineering, where student discontent was further documented by their statements about the actual number of times that they had spoken to their professors. Even in the fifth and sixth years, when students took more advanced courses, there were large numbers who stated that they had had little contact with their teachers outside of the classroom (62 per cent). Part-time teaching appointments and the aura that surrounds the professor, in combination with large classes, inhibited this type of interaction.

This situation had not gone unnoticed in the School of Engineering. The extremely high failure rate had been attributed in part to the lack of guidance that was available to incoming students.[15] There had been discussions and plans to institute an advisor system. Under this program, each fifty students in the first-year class would be assigned to a professor, with whom they could discuss their problems.

Identification with a Role Model

The vast majority of students (75 per cent) had some person or combination of persons whom they identified as models for their future professional work. As could be predicted, there was generally a greater incidence of identification in the upper years of each program, with history students as the only exception. It is highly interesting to note the large percentage of students who indicated that they had a professor as a role model. Although there were some increases through the years, the incidence among the first-year students was almost as prevalent as among their more advanced peers (Table 5-4). The nature of the identification,

TABLE 5-3

Sufficiency of Opportunity to Discuss Professional Plans with Professors by School and Year

	Engineering			History			Science			Medicine		
	I	III	V-VI	I	II-III	IV-V	I	II-III	IV-V	I	III	V-VI
Sufficient	13	13	44	36	27	36	38	33	70	41	32	49
Insufficient	83	87	56	64	73	65	63	67	30	59	68	52
Reject	3	—	—	—	—	—	—	—	—	—	—	—
Total	99 (30)	100 (30)	100 (34)	100 (33)	100 (30)	101 (31)	101 (8)	100 (12)	100 (10)	100 (32)	100 (34)	101 (33)

TABLE 5-4
Presence and Type of Professional Role Model by School and Year

	Engineering			History			Science			Medicine		
	I	III	V-VI	I	II-III	IV-V	I	II-III	IV-VI	I	III	V-VI
None	33	37	27	27	10	29	50	33	10	31	21	9
Friend	13	13	9	3	3	—	—	8	—	—	3	6
Relative	7	7	—	9	3	7	—	—	—	6	15	6
Professor	40	33	50	52	67	61	25	42	80	38	27	46
Acquaintance	—	3	9	3	—	—	—	—	—	9	12	6
Combination of people	7	7	6	6	7	3	25	17	10	16	21	27
Secondary-school teacher	—	—	—	—	10	—	—	—	—	—	3	—
Total	100 (30)	100 (30)	101 (34)	100 (33)	100 (30)	100 (31)	100 (8)	100 (12)	100 (10)	100 (32)	102 (34)	100 (33)

however, was markedly different. First-year students in engineering, for example, attended large lectures. Most had indicated that they had spoken to professors "few" or "no" times outside of class. Their affirmation of a role model then was of a somewhat romantic nature, based upon the glamour of a *catedratico* giving lectures on subjects that are so different from work in the secondary school. This early experience, associated with the very important step of entering the university, was most significant in all schools, but probably especially so in fields such as engineering or science where most students had had little contact with the work of such professionals in their pre-university lives.

There was a very high degree of identification in the last years of medicine and science. Not only were professors significant in their present status as teachers, but also they were the men who will be the future professional reference groups. The medical *catedraticos* were the most respected specialists, and students were constantly in contact with them in hospitals, clinics, and other professional work situations. Many of the neophyte physicians aspired to be exactly what the professors are—teachers, specialists in the hospital, and men with large private practices. In science the same phenomenon was in effect. The professors were among the most important scientists in the country. Students hoped to join them as junior colleagues immediately after completing their training.[16] Lipset's observations on the importance of professors seems most applicable to the science students:

> The eminence of teachers in the world of science and scholarship, their interest in their own subjects and their academic self-esteem based on their belief in the worthiness of their calling and accomplishment are additional factors which determine whether students become integrated into the structure of the university as an intellectual community connected with the centre of its society or whether they will become attached to an autonomous and more or less alienated student community.[17]

In all the faculties studied professors seemed meaningful to their students. The ability to attract the best of professionals to university instruction, then, was of the utmost importance. No less so than in other countries, Chilean students entering professional training were susceptible to a variety of influences from their teachers. The character and ability of professors seemed especially significant in professional socialization.

It is notable, moreover, that apparently there was no conflict between identifying with a professor and engaging in political activities. On the contrary, political activists were more likely than their peers to indicate that they had a role model for their future professional activities (Table 5-5). Almost one-half of them identified with a professor. This seemed to be equally true among Frapists and Christian Democrats. It is, of course, quite likely that the professors selected were themselves highly political and, indeed, may have partially exerted their influence over students for reasons external to their instructor role. Nonetheless, the qualities that even the most active students listed as especially admirable in their professors were those directly linked to the professional role. These included dedication to work, professional knowledge, teaching ability, and interest in students.

Most notable throughout the entire student body was the strong emphasis on those characteristics which were directly related to fundamental, modern professional qualities—skills, knowledge, dedication, and love of work. These characteristics, rounded out by admiration for a pleasant personality, gave a picture of the total person emulated by the neophyte professionals.[18] One fifth-year engineering student spoke admiringly of his professor's "personal order; he works with great consistency and regularity and really enjoys and loves his work." A history student spoke of his desire to emulate "the spirit of work and broadmindedness. He has the capacity to see many problems from all points of view—without partiality."

In summary, the students' responses indicated that task orientations were strongly influenced by the nature of the training personnel. In modern situations professors are often extremely important as role models, not only because they are the ones who are able to grant full professional status, but also because they influence students' attitudes and beliefs in emotionally oriented interactions. In the traditional situation, characterized by part-time, poorly trained, and unmotivated professors, opportunity for strong professional identification is minimized. Teacher-student interaction is limited, and the professor's responsibility often does not include a concern with the professional values internalized by the students.

In transitional societies, professor-student interaction differs

TABLE 5-5

Presence and Type of Professional Role Model by
Position on Political-Critical Index

	Active Partisan	Critical Sympathizer	Non-involved
No	19	32	26
Friend	5	4	6
Relative	10	3	6
Professor	48	42	46
Acquaintance	3	3	6
Combination of people	14	17	8
Secondary-school teacher	1	—	1
Reject	—	—	1
Total	100 (88)	100 (78)	100 (151)

markedly. Our data show that some schools, such as the Institute of Science, were able to attract a core of professors, committed to scholarly work, who derived, not only prestige, but also income and satisfaction, from their university association. For them, teaching and research were central concerns. Imparting of technical knowledge and meaningful interaction with their students were important professional activities and strongly competed with nonteaching and nonresearch interests. In other instances, such as the School of Engineering, it was extremely difficult to recruit a staff of full-time professionals committed to their university positions. Students registered concern about this situation, and steps have been contemplated to facilitate its alleviation.

Politically involved students in all schools, moreover, admired those characteristics in their professors that were indicators of professional competence. Like their nonpolitically involved or less involved peers, they expressed little interest in the importance of a professor's political activities or the range of his personal contacts. Students seemed to identify with instrumental values and to reject those associated with a symbolic orientation.

Interaction with Clients for Professional Services

The third component of the socialization process concerns the amount and degree of student interaction with persons who will be the clients for their future professional services. Contacts may occur in unpaid or paid apprentice-like situations, or in related part-time work. Some of these relationships are an integral part of the actual training experience of all students, while others involve only a handful in special training or volunteer work.

Apprenticeship

Largely because of the nature of the work, medical and history students had the most direct interaction with their future clients as part of their training programs. The student physicians spent the majority of their time during the last four years working in the hospitals. They had intensive contact with patients, as well as instruction from their future reference group of doctors and hospital staff. Similarly, fifth-year history students had to complete a practice-teaching requirement in a secondary school to qualify for their degrees. This was less time-consuming and intense than the medical program, but, nevertheless, it provided direct involvement with clients (pupils) in an apprentice situation.

The training of engineers was somewhat different. The clients for their services were not so clearly defined. An engineer could do technical calculations in an office and never directly consult with his ultimate clients. Apprenticeship for engineers did not concentrate so much on this aspect of the training as it did on contact with professional reference groups. All engineering students were required to work two summers in a job directly related to their field of study. They worked with practicing engineers, who could indeed be the clients for their services, as well as their future reference group.

The situation in science was even more complicated. Professionals in the new Institute of Science had not clearly defined who would be the clients of scientific services in Chile. In part, the professors, many of whom had recently returned from graduate training and work in the United States and England, defined the international scientific community as their clients. Contact with these scientists was made through publications and attendance of international meetings. Since this definition was highly disputed in Chile, professors verbally acknowledged that the training would also be valuable in teaching situations and in industry. The students had no contact with industry, but did have teaching or research assistantships in their later years of study. These appointments were geared to give them training for graduate study abroad, practice in teaching university students, and familiarity with the international scientific community.

This was a major area of strain in the development of this new professional school. There was the great imbalance between the well-defined and well-supported role of the scientist in the developed world and the very unclear and precarious nature of this role in Chile. The problems were much more than philosophical. Who would appreciate their work? Who would support it? Could high-level and expensive research be justified where resources were unavailable for the solution of fundamental social problems?[19]

The underdeveloped position of science in Chile was similar to that in other transitional societies. The gap between these countries and those that were far advanced in their industrialization process was enormous.

Today between 15 and 30 of the 120 countries of the world, with less than one-third of its population, possess practically all of its science. They spend more than 95 per cent of the world's research and development funds in order to produce, first, practically all of the world's research output in the form of research papers, technical reports, discoveries, patents, and prototypes of new products and processes, and second, most of the new generation of trained research workers in science and technology.[20]

Paid Employment

Only a small percentage of the total number of students were actually engaged in part-time remunerative work. Involvement grew as the students passed through the program and reached a climax during the last years of study (15 per cent).

This finding was especially interesting when compared to a survey of Brazilian law students:

> In Brazil, it is well known that most university students, and law students in particular, work in addition to attending class. The survey held no surprises in this realm, indicating that, overall, 75 per cent of law students held some type of extra-curricular employment.[21]

In Chile the highest number of students who worked were in engineering (33 per cent). This supported the general impression that after the first three years of intensive basic work, engineers could and did seek employment either within the university or with private engineering firms. It was reported to be a significant source of support, and thus enabled students from a wide variety of backgrounds to finance their studies. Several of the students indicated, in addition, that some of the most important training they had received was acquired on the job. One sixth-year student stated that since the school is so large the staff does not have time to counsel students on their work plans and professional thinking. In the small engineering firm it was possible to receive this kind of guidance from practicing professionals. Paid employment was also functional as an entrance to the labor market. Contacts made at this time frequently assisted young engineers in getting their first jobs after graduation.

Fewer history students (23 per cent) had part-time employment. For those who did, it had often proved to be an equally important experience. Several future teachers gave classes in private secondary schools, while others had tutoring jobs. Two of the students who had the strongest professional self-images were a boy and girl who were engaged in serious research projects. The former was intensely involved in a study sponsored by an international agency, in which he had the opportunity to work with leading experts in his field. He was receiving a first-hand and deeply gratifying exposure to research. The girl worked as an assistant in one of the research institutes of the School of History itself. She, too, had a strong sense of the meaning of research, of the graduate work she wanted to do, of her concept of the function of history and historical research in Chilean society. This type of work experience, however, may have had some dysfunctional consequences. While it served to increase a certain aspect of professionalization, it simultaneously increased the desire to leave the classroom. This "pull" is similar to that exerted in many parts of the world. The greater the differential rewards between classroom and nonclassroom activity, the more potent will be the "pull" exerted.

Volunteer Work

A third type of contact with clients occurred with marginal groups. In Chile there was an active concern with extending professional services to the urban slum dweller and to the rural poor. Two major areas of emphasis focused on the attempt to reduce illiteracy and to increase the primitive health standards. The national *alfabetizacion* (literacy) campaign was one of the major projects of the FECH, and it had involved students from many of the schools. Most significant for professional development, perhaps, was the participation of students from the Pedagogico who were brought into first-hand contact with many of the nation's educational problems.

Medical students had also been involved in bridging the gap between the "two countries." In a variety of programs instituted during their summer vacations, the future physicians had traveled to remote sections of the country. They had faced the problems inherent in providing basic health services. Students had experienced the challenge of practicing where sophisticated equipment was absent and where people had to be convinced of the utility of modern medical knowledge. The impact of these experiences will be discussed in greater detail in the next chapter.

These programs had been growing in scope, in the number of students involved, and in respectability. Both professionals and nonprofessionals could readily remember times when such ideas were neither thought of nor implemented. A professional in his late twenties recounted his participation in the first group of student engineers to work on a voluntary construction program. At that time many parents raised their eyebrows about the meaningfulness of this kind of practice. There were now severe cracks in the traditional concept of professional services for a limited few by a limited few. It could more accurately be characterized as service by a limited few for a growing number. The concept of a professional elite serving a closed market was being challenged.

The process of professional response may be outlined in the following manner. First, a few pioneer students and others may voluntarily extend their services to marginal social groups. Idealism, supported by strong social and political consciousness, and often financed by political and religious groups, is a major propelling factor. This was dramatically illustrated during the 1964 presidential campaign, when students were recruited by the major competing parties to provide health and educational assistance. These activities received greater publicity and general recognition as the vocabulary of economic development became widespread. "Progress" in implementing programs of local assistance may be defined by the success of student task forces working in rural areas and urban slums. Vacation periods became times of increased student involvement. Professors, as part of their professional activity, assumed leadership posts. Reaching out to new clients became a concern of the schools themselves. Informal activities thus became institutionalized. Formal internship programs and commitment to work in given areas after graduation were made part of an explicit obligation of young professionals.

NOTES

1. This, in a slightly revised form, is taken from I. H. Simpson, "Patterns of Socialization into Professions: The Case of Student Nurses" (paper presented at the Meetings of the American Sociological Association, New York, August 30, 1960).

2. Alignment with any of these polar positions does not in any way presuppose a radical or conservative political outlook. Communists in Chile, for example, are

regarded as working within the system as political activists who are willing to accept the traditional methods of the system to gain power. In other countries, groups with similar political philosophies may have rejected all methods imposed by the system and may be working as an underground group or as guerrillas in the hills. In such a case, they would fall into the critical group seeking to form new groups based on new methods and assumptions.

Variables influencing degree of student involvement and political beliefs are discussed in the author's doctoral dissertation. We found that membership in political groups in secondary school strongly influenced the student's propensity to join when he arrived in the university. Moreover, students with a strong Catholic orientation were more likely to affiliate themselves with the Christian Democrats. Marked consistency was noted, furthermore, between the students' political beliefs and those which they said their fathers held. Our data strongly supported Bonilla's findings that there is little inter-generational political rebellion among Chilean university students. For a further discussion of these points see Myron Glazer, "Chile," in Donald K. Emmerson, Ed., *Students and Politics in Developing Nations* (New York: Frederick A. Praeger, 1968), pp. 286–314.

3. Our close friendship with several engineering professors gave us many insights into the functioning of the school.

4. To measure political involvement, students were divided into three categories. In the first, or "active partisan" group, are those who stated that they were leaders, members, or sympathizers completely in accord with a particular university political group. In the second, or "critical sympathizer" category, are those students who sympathized with one group but who had strong reservations either about that group or about the usefulness of any type of political involvement. Also in this category are those who did not state that they sympathized with any group, but who voiced a distinct preference for one of the national parties and who voted for its affiliate in the university election. Members of the "non-involved" category include those who claimed no political affiliation, who defined themselves as having no interest in politics, and who showed no consistent voting pattern.

5. For a discussion of similar turning points in professional education see Myron Glazer, "Graduate Education for a Career in Science: A Case Study of Student Physicists" (Master's thesis, Rutgers University, 1961), p. 81. Also see R. Fox, "The Autopsy," mimeographed (Bureau of Applied Social Research, Columbia University, Publication A-262), p. 3.

6. Many of our insights into the Institute of Science derived from conversations with its faculty. One of our closest friends in Chile was a teacher at the school who described to us the great difficulty his students had in mastering basic mathematical concepts. He felt that the time had not yet come when the Institute could recruit the best of the secondary school graduates.

7. Juan F. Marsal has observed that these difficulties may result from the passive attitude which most Latin American students bring to their studies. To complete a major research project, therefore, becomes a difficult challenge.

Concern with curriculum problems has been evinced by some of the Latin American governments. In Central America, five small nations have established the Consejo Superior Universitario Centroamericano (CSUCA), the High

Council of Central American Universities. These countries have set up CSUCA in an attempt to liberalize their curricula and to minimize the duplication of resources. They have attempted to modify the rigid program of study and reduce the overlapping of courses in the individual faculties of the same university by offering a two-year general studies program before specialization. Enerson believes that "the general studies program can be expected to develop a vitality of its own. Electives will be permitted. Almost certainly there will be greater emphasis on the humanities and the social sciences." H. E. Enerson, "University Education in Central America," *Journal of Higher Education* (April, 1963), p. 202. For further discussion of this point see G. R. Waggoner, "Problems in the Professionalization of the University Teaching Career in Central America," *Journal of Inter-America Studies,* VIII (April, 1966), 193–213.

Student demands for such reforms date back to the beginning of the century. In 1908 there was a congress of Latin American students from several countries. At that time the oral examination system was attacked. Students also spoke out against the dry lectures, asking that they be replaced by seminars.

8. Much valuable information about student life and attitudes was elicited through informal conversations with history students on the school grounds or in the cafeteria. The relationship between career opportunities and political activity is also posited by Bakke. He especially emphasizes future lawyers, but includes other students who are also dependent on government positions. See E. W. Bakke, "Students on the March: The Cases of Mexico and Colombia," *Sociology of Education,* XXXVII (Spring, 1964), p. 219.

While many observers may decry the politicization of what are initially academic issues, many Latin American educators apparently place a heavy burden on students to initiate necessary reforms. This is a task which falls hard on the ordinary student who is burdened by family or work responsibilities. Often his secondary school experience has not prepared him to seek high standards of academic excellence in himself or his professors.

The professional character of the schools mediates against students having an over-all concern with the total development of the university. Students become quickly dedicated to securing scarce resources for their own *facultad* or school. As was noted above, the role of the rank and file student in most Latin American universities makes it unlikely that he can be the far-sighted advocate of university reforms. This task most often falls to the politically dedicated students who have the time and assistance to agitate for new curriculum or more adequate facilities. And politically astute student leaders will use political weapons both to secure programs favored by their professors as well as those which these men might define as detrimental to university development.

For a useful summary of the views of Latin American educators see Russell G. Davis, "Prototypes and Stereotypes in Latin American Universities," *Comparative Education Review* (October, 1965), 275–281.

9. We experienced a contradictory situation in the School of Engineering. We often found it extremely difficult to convince first-year students to give up the hour or two required for the interview. Their concern with mastering the basic knowledge was especially evident prior to examinations.

Empirical material available dealing with students' study and work habits is extremely limited. Williamson, reporting on his study of Colombian students, presents a critical picture: "A visit to most Latin American universities finds a limited repertory of study techniques, if any at all, with libraries frequently devoid of users and with only partially filled shelves. Highly socialized approaches to study are found in the 'study seminars' visible on the prado (grounds) of the university, and its neighboring cafés. An even more traditional vignette is the audible recitation of the student as he paces the length of a colonnade memorizing critical or not so critical sentences or paragraphs." R. C. Williamson, "University Students in a World of Change: A Colombian Sample," *Sociology and Social Research,* XLVIII (July, 1964), p. 400.

10. For the effects of the structure of graduate education on student motivation, see Glazer, "Graduate Education for a Career in Science," pp. 63–67.

11. This is in contrast to the "typical" Latin American university, described by R. P. Atcon, "The Latin American University," *Die Deutsche Universitäts Zeitung* (February, 1962), pp. 7–49.

12. Simpson, *op. cit.,* pp. 2–3.

13. For a discussion of such patterns in Colombian education, see: R. Morse, R. Wickham, and A. Wolf, "Education in Colombia," mimeographed (Ford Foundation Mission to Colombia, June, 1960). Similar findings in Mexico and Colombia are reported by E. W. Bakke, *op. cit.,* pp. 220–228.

14. Bakke's description is the sharpest indictment: "The symbolic word as to the inadequacy of instructors is 'taxi professor.' The content of this concept suggests a lecturer who is a professor in name only, carrying on jobs outside the university, who seeks a bit of additional income and the prestige of a university connection by teaching one or more courses. In the midst of his preoccupation with many concerns he suddenly remembers it is time for his lecture, hops into a taxi, rushes to the university, delivers his lecture, and rushes back to his 'real' job. Or he may not, and frequently does not, show up at all. Of course he is delighted when the students go on strike, for then he has a good excuse for not coming to class. When he does come, he is poorly prepared." Bakke, *op cit.,* p. 216.

15. For figures on the dropout rates in the University of Chile, see the report of the Universidad de Chile, Instituto de Investigaciones Estadisticas, "Supervivencia y Perdida del Alumnado de la Ensenanza Superior en Chile," *Informative Estadistico,* No. 5 (December, 1962).

16. For a comparable discussion of American medical students, see E. C. Hughes, "Stress and Strain in Professional Education," *Harvard Educational Review,* XXIX (Fall, 1959), 319–329.

17. S. M. Lipset, "University Students and Politics in Underdeveloped Countries," *Minerva,* III (Autumn, 1964), 44.

18. R. C. Williamson's findings indicate that Colombian university students also rank knowledge of the material and effective lecturing as the most important characteristics in their teachers. Unlike their Chilean counterparts, they seem to de-emphasize the importance of research interests. Williamson, *op. cit.,* p. 400.

19. For just the opposite problem which faces much of contemporary American research see T. Roszak, "Seduction of the Scientist," *The Nation,* CXCII (June

3, 1961), 478; H. A. Shepard, "Basic Research and the Social System of Pure Science," *Philosophy of Science,* XXIII (January, 1956), 52.

20. S. Dedijer, "Underdeveloped Science in Underdeveloped Countries," *Minerva,* II (Autumn, 1963), 61.

21. R. Scheman, "The Brazilian Law Student: Backgrounds, Habits, Attitudes," *Journal of Inter-American Studies,* V (1963), 344–345.

Chapter 6

The Professional Role
and the Impact
of Political Involvement

Introduction

In this chapter we turn to a closer analysis of the professional attitudes of Chilean students and the relationship of political involvement to these attitudes. The discussion begins with a statement on the nature of professional concern voiced by the students, and terminates with a brief exposition of the implications of student attitudes for the modernization of their country.

Quality of Professional Commitment

Among those questions bearing on professional attitudes, there were several which attempted to elicit (1) the means students would employ to achieve professional success, (2) the types of job characteristics most important to them, and (3) their desire to implement their professional knowledge.

The Means

In determining the means which students regarded as necessary for the attainment of their goals, we focused on several aspects: how the students defined the realities of advancement in Chilean professional life, what they believed this situation ought to be, and finally, how students would choose for themselves in a conflict situation.

We first listed six characteristics on an ascription-achievement continuum, ranging from social position of family to professional ability. The students were asked to rate, in order of importance, the three characteristics which, in their opinion, were currently most important in obtaining a desirable position in their professions.

Their responses indicated that students were very much aware of the great contemporary significance of such features as family background, personal contacts, and political affiliations in influencing career opportunities. Although there were important variations by school, a very substantial number of the total group rated these as more potent than achievement-oriented criteria of professional ability, grades, and recommendations of one's professors (Table 6-1).

TABLE 6-1

Actual Factors Necessary to Obtain a Good Position by School

	Engineering	History	Science	Medicine
All achievement	5	6	43	19
Primarily achievement	39	27	40	48
Primarily ascriptive	48	38	10	29
All ascriptive	7	29	—	1
Doesn't know	—	—	7	2
Total	99 (94)	100 (94)	100 (30)	99 (99)

After the students indicated which factors they felt were actually important in obtaining a good position, they were asked what they thought such factors ought to be (Table 6-2). Their responses readily demonstrated that there was a marked difference between the students' conception of what is and of what should be. In every school the vast majority of the students stated that the achievement-oriented characteristics should be the determining, or at least predominating, factors in influencing students' future career opportunities. The students, then, strongly rejected the ascriptive factors so characteristic of a traditional society in favor of more universalistic norms of evaluation.

TABLE 6-2

Factors That Should Be Necessary to Obtain a Good Position by School

	Engineering	History	Science	Medicine
All achievement	54	60	87	79
Primarily achievement	36	34	10	18
Primarily ascriptive	10	5	3	2
All ascriptive	—	—	—	—
Reject	—	—	—	1
Total	100 (94)	99 (94)	100 (30)	100 (99)

The respondents were subsequently asked how they would choose in the following situation in order to test more fully their attitudes in this area:

Two professors have asked you to serve as an assistant and you can only accept one of these positions.

Professor A is very highly thought of as an expert in his field and you are certain that you will be able to learn a great deal from him. However, he has very few contacts which would be of help to you in getting a job after graduation.

Professor B is also a competent professional. Even though you do not have as high regard for his ability, you know that he has many contacts that will be of great help to you when you begin to look for a job.

Which position would you choose?

The overwhelming majority of the students in every school and every year responded that they would like to work with Professor A (Table 6-3). Thus, when asked to project themselves into a future conflict situation, their responses again were consistently away from the customary paths of interaction in the society and indicative of a high degree of professional commitment.

TABLE 6-3

Professor Preferred to Work with by School

	Engineering	History	Science	Medicine
Definitely A	48	68	70	59
Probably A	33	21	20	33
Definitely B	3	4	—	—
Probably B	16	6	7	8
Other	—	—	3	—
Total	100 (94)	100 (94)	100 (30)	100 (99)

Symbolic vs. Instrumental Orientations

Students were also asked to select the two characteristics of a future job that were most important to them. The factors listed ranged from good income and high prestige to the opportunity to serve the community (Table 6-4). The responses in all the schools focused most heavily on the opportunity for "professional growth" (56 to 77 per cent). Strong emphasis was also given to

TABLE 6-4

Two Most Important Characteristics of a Job by School

	Engineering	History	Science	Medicine
Political liberty	37	32	43	26
Social prestige	17	5	10	10
Income	38	21	23	11
Gain professional recognition	11	15	7	11
Perfect skills	56	77	70	74
Help people	40	49	37	63
Other	—	—	10	4
Reject	—	—	—	1
Total	100 (2) (94)(2)	100 (2) (94)(2)	100 (2) (30)(2)	100 (2) (99)(2)

the importance of service to the community, especially by student doctors (63 per cent) and teachers (49 per cent). Furthermore, little significance was given by the students to income or prestige, with the exception of the engineers who placed strong emphasis on the former (38 per cent).

To test more specifically the range of attitudes to the symbolic vs. instrumental orientation to task performances, we ask the students to choose between the following positions:

You have just graduated and have been offered two jobs.

Job A is a very distinguished position, especially for a person of your age. However, there will be very little opportunity to apply the most modern methods you have learned in your education.

Job B is a job of much less prestige, but you will have the opportunity to use directly your professional knowledge and the opportunity to improve your skills.

Which would you choose?

Although some engineers (19 per cent) and teachers (13 per cent) showed a preference for the more symbolic position, the overwhelming majority of the students selected the more instrumental path[1] (Table 6-5).

TABLE 6-5

Job That Has More Prestige vs. Job That Allows Use of Training by School

	Engineering	History	Science	Medicine
Definitely prestige	5	5	3	3
Probably prestige	14	8	3	2
Definitely training	44	65	67	72
Probably training	39	20	23	21
Reject	—	1	3	1
Total	102 (94)	99 (94)	99 (30)	99 (99)

To specify consistency of response and possible explanatory variables influencing degree of professional concern among the Chilean students, we have constructed an index combining the three last questions utilized above.[2] The results emphasize the heavy concentration of students in the high-concern category (Table 6-6). In attempting to specify the students who were high, mid, or low on the index of professional commitment, we found that background variables of sex, socio-economic status, religion, and secondary school did not offer any explanation. In all schools

TABLE 6-6

Position on Professional Index by School

	Engineering	History	Science	Medicine
High-professional	33	57	67	63
Mid-professional	22	24	10	21
Low-professional	45	19	23	16
Total	100	100	100	100
	(94)	(94)	(30)	(99)

the quality of professional attitudes seemed to be most correlated with the important variable of degree of political involvement.

The Relationship between Professional Commitment and Political Involvement

Table 6-7 indicates the high correlation between degree of professionalism and degree of political involvement. Thus, 64 per cent of the active partisans were to be found in the high-professional category, and only 13 per cent were in the low-professional group. In contrast, while 41 per cent of the nonpolitically active students were also highly professional, fully 33 per cent were in the low-professional category.

These results challenge the widely asserted view that political activism is a direct impediment to professional modernization.[3] The implication of this position is that were Latin American university students less politically active, they would almost inevitably devote their energies to professional concerns, which, in turn, would accelerate development of their countries. The Chilean evidence strongly questions the existence of the polarization. Rather, political and social ideology seemed to give strong impetus to the rejection of the remnants of traditional society and increased the desire for change and modernization. Among these students there was often a direct marriage between their political and professional goals.

TABLE 6-7
Position on Professional Index by Position on
Political-Critical Index

	Active Partisan	Critical Sympathizer	Noninvolved
High-professional	64	52	41
Mid-professional	22	18	26
Low-professional	13	30	33
Total	99 (88)	100 (151)	100 (78)

Nevertheless, important areas of role conflict do exist. One frequent source of such tension involved strikes within the university. How did students who were both highly political and highly professional resolve the conflict over the strike situation? Were they more or less likely to support the strike, even when it meant interference with the intake of important professional knowledge?[4]

Table 6-8 clearly shows that in all professional categories the political activists were most "definitely" in favor of the strike and least numerous in the "no" category. It is especially notable that among the high professionals, the percentage of "definite" responses among the activists (68 per cent) was more than double the combined percentage of students in the other two groupings (30 and 31 per cent). Degree of political activism, therefore, appeared to be a vital intervening variable influencing students' attitudes in favor of the relative significance of the strike.

The strike is a key mechanism used by Latin American students attempting to influence university and national policy. Their concerns were crystallized in, and given direct impetus by, the University Reform movement of 1918. Beginning in Argentina, it spread to all Latin American countries with varying degrees of intensity. As discussed in Part I of this volume, historical circumstances limited the effectiveness of the Reform

TABLE 6-8
Vote to Strike by Position on Professional and Political-Critical Indexes

	High-Professional			Mid-Professional			Low-Professional		
	Active Partisan	Critical Sympathizer	Non-involved	Active Partisan	Critical Sympathizer	Non-involved	Active Partisan	Critical Sympathizer	Non-involved
Definitely Yes	68	30	31	50	30	25	42	29	23
Probably Yes	20	46	38	35	56	50	42	33	50
No	11	23	31	15	15	20	17	36	27
Other	2	1	–	–	–	5	–	2	–
Total	101 (56)	100 (79)	100 (32)	100 (20)	101 (27)	100 (20)	101 (12)	100 (45)	100 (26)

movement. Nevertheless, Chilean students in 1964 were still very much influenced by the Reformist tradition, and the strike could be best understood as their most effective weapon, both facilitating and inhibiting legitimate improvement of the university.

The above comments are not intended to indicate that the student strike is always necessarily detrimental to the educational process. We know that in the Chilean university this mechanism has been used in an attempt to uplift professional standards. In one significant instance, students threatened to strike in order to prevent the appointment of a professor who was deemed poorly qualified. It was considered by many that this individual was using his personal contacts in the administration of the school in order to obtain a highly desirable post. Students pressured for the appointment of a far more competent rival. Their protest was directed toward the institutionalization of more objective criteria for the appointment of professional personnel. In conjunction with the faculty, they were successful in establishing explicit standards.

The negative implications of student action can be seen in the indiscriminate use of the strike mechanism. Within the same school, students boycotted a final examination because of the professor's unwillingness to change the examination date to meet their wishes. Despite previous good teacher-student relations, the students were determined that the professor should capitulate to their customary prerogative of postponing examinations after they have once been announced. The call to strike was almost an automatic response and minimized possibilities of peaceful reconciliation.[5]

Although our earlier findings indicated that the two student roles tend to be complementary, the response to the question of a strike demonstrated that there were important areas of potential role conflict. This often extended beyond the strike issue and had consequences for the student's concept of the primary purpose of his entire university education, especially in times of heightened national political tensions. To test students' attitudes further, the following problem was posed:

A says that the most important factor for the development of Chile is to have well-trained and prepared people. Therefore, the major responsibility of the student is to devote the majority of his time to learning the materials in his field and only a minimum of time to other activities.

B says that Chile needs basic social changes before it can bring about any other changes effectively. He believes that the student has a responsibility to devote a good part of his time to political activities, even if this reduces somewhat the amount of time he can spend on his studies.

With whom do you agree?

Our results strongly supported our previous findings. Chilean students, generally, saw the intake of technical knowledge as the primary rationale of university study. Yet differences, again, arose among those with varying degrees of political involvement (Table 6-9). Although a majority of active partisans in all schools (56 per cent) chose the central importance of professional concerns, this group was still less committed to the professional choice than the critical sympathizers (67 per cent) or noninvolved (79 per cent) groups. Conversely, the active partisans were most convinced of the need for basic social change (38 per cent).

These responses confirmed our previous findings in regard to the strike. Although we found a high correlation between high professional commitment and political activism, and while both orientations were toward the central importance of modernization of the social system, significant conflict did at times arise over the most effective means for the attainment of social and economic change and how students could best affect this change.

Implications for Economic Development

The burden of the discussion in this section will be upon an exploration of the following questions:

1. Which students were willing to engage in pioneering activities with the urban poor and in rural areas?
2. Which students were willing to accept positions that would increase the stature and teaching level in the university?
3. Were students susceptible to foreign employment?

The Medical Student

There was an active concern in Chile with extending professional services to the urban slum dweller and to the rural poor.

TABLE 6-9

Technical Competence (A) vs. Basic Social Changes (B) by
Position on Political-Critical Index

	Active Partisan	Critical Sympathizer	Noninvolved
Competence: Definitely A	23	33	41
Competence: More A than B	33	34	38
Changes: Definitely B	14	7	3
Changes: More B than A	24	20	9
Neither	2	4	3
Other	5	3	6
Total	101 (88)	101 (151)	100 (78)

One attempt to develop such services occurred during our stay. This was a major summer program involving eighty-two fourth-, fifth-, and sixth-year students from the School of Medicine. The site was Chiloe, one of the most primitive and rural provinces. The thirty-day trip was sponsored jointly by the School of Medicine and the National Health Service, in order to give the students "an integrated vision of the medical reality that they would have to face upon the completion of their studies." [6]

In this environment students experienced a completely different set of circumstances from those in the medical school. In addition to the vaccination program carried out, students were exposed to one of the major causes of mortality, infant diarrhea. The neophyte physicians introduced basic concepts about the necessity of washing hands with soap and water, gave lessons on what to do in areas where soap was not available, and generally supplied very fundamental information.

In servicing these consumers, medical students encountered a whole new set of problems. In addition to the stark medical needs, they learned that providing service often involves the ability to justify treatment and educate prospective patients about their needs. Students had discussions with community leaders, public meetings, and showings of films to indicate the importance of vaccinations, which are, of course, taken for granted in the more metropolitan and developed areas of the country.[7] This kind of experience well pointed up some of the concerns of the medical students. One of our keenest informants said:

> In hospital training we are given careful instruction on how to speak to patients, to instruct them on medicinal, psychological and diet remedies. We might well tell them to take their blender and make a banana and milk combination, etc. What good does this type of instruction do for people who never heard of a blender and have neither bananas nor milk?

As a result of their involvement with the realities of contemporary Chilean society, many other medical students also indicated to us that their training did not sufficiently emphasize or prepare them to face and solve their country's major medical problems. Excessive emphasis on specialization had the contrary impact. Thus, amid new exposure and changing concepts of what a medical education is all about, the whole training program was called into serious question. For example, a medical school delegate to the FECH, summarized the results of three conferences involving medical students. The underlying theme of his statement was the necessity for an integrated and dynamic approach to medical education. What was needed, he argued, was a thorough realization of what Chile is—a rejection of the wisdom of the past and of overzealous borrowing from the practices of the medical professions in highly developed countries.[8]

This significant stream of criticism and social consciousness among the students was by no means the total picture. Our data reveal that most future physicians resisted positions in small towns with primitive medical facilities, or in large cities with marginal consumers, as they projected themselves into the future.[9] Youthful idealism was not sufficient in a social structure in which the highest rewards still lay in specialization, work in large Santiago hospitals, and a private practice geared to middle- and upper-class urban dwellers. Thus, a great tension existed between the road to high prestige and professional success and what was idealistically recognized as an important social problem which had been given only sporadic attention. In essence, the combination of high specialization and the distribution of social and economic rewards produced a situation in which the excellence of medical training did not result in the alleviation of basic national health problems.

The History Students

Student decisions as to future professional tasks, institutional positions, and locations were central, not only to personal, but also to national development. To gain further insight, we asked the history (teaching) students about a variety of future employment situations. The student teachers placed the highest positive evaluation on public secondary-school positions in a middle-class urban area. The next most desirable position was in the university, although it was well known that such jobs were very difficult to obtain.

Although there were no secondary schools in the *callampa* slums, these prospective teachers were asked how they would evaluate such a position were it available to them. There was no greater contrast in Chilean society than that between the *callampa* and the solid middle-class neighborhood. As in most centers of rapid population growth, there were extraordinary differences between those who were well-to-do and relatively secure and the newcomers who arrived from the countryside without wealth, education, or personal contacts and who lived on the edge of the community in tumbledown dwellings made from scraps of wood, cardboard, and other readily available material.

In view of the contrasts, it was very impressive that a large number of students considered working in such depressed areas (56 per cent). Variation in decision-making was somewhat clarified when the students were divided by their degree of professionalism and political activism (Table 6-10). Not only were the activists in every professional group the most willing to work in a *callampa,* but also the activists within the high-professional group (78 per cent) were the most affirmative, and those in the low-professional category (50 per cent) were least so. It is also important to stress that the other students in the high-professional group were more willing to accept such employment (63 per cent) than were students in almost any category. High professionalism, therefore, was a key characteristic among those willing to pioneer in new and difficult types of urban employment and became even more potent when combined with high political involvement.

When our focus shifted to attitudes toward working in the countryside, we found that degree of political activity became an inhibiting variable. Now the most active were among the least willing to accept rural employment among all the professional categories. High professionalism was therefore neutralized by high political involvement (Table 6-11). The most politically active students were most willing to accept difficult employment if it permitted them to remain close to the hub of national events but least willing to accept it when it entailed living in rural areas.

The Engineering Students

The engineering students, who more often emphasized their interest in prestige and financial rewards than did their peers in the other schools, were also less unwilling to accept rural positions. For them, these activities did not involve great sacrifice. Financial rewards upon graduation were more abundant outside the large cities, as were more challenging opportunities for professional growth. The ambitious engineering graduate had less fear of rural "exile" than his teaching or medical school peers. Many engineers saw this type of employment as an initiation into highly desired entrepreneurial or administrative positions in the major cities, which they hoped to obtain at the peak of their careers. In this sense, there was less conflict between the engineering students' goal of professional advancement and the needs of national development.

This entrepreneurial and managerial orientation was highly indicative of, and may be highly functional in, the transitional

TABLE 6-10

History Students' Willingness to Work in a Public School in a *Callampa* by Position on Political-Critical and Professional Indexes

	Non-Professional			Mid-Professional			Low-Professional		
	Active Partisan	Critical Sympathizer	Non-involved	Active Partisan	Critical Sympathizer	Non-involved	Active Partisan	Critical Sympathizer	Non-involved
Yes	78	63	63	70	38	50	50	33	17
No	22	32	38	30	63	50	50	67	83
Reject		5							
Total	100 (27)	99 (19)	101 (8)	100 (10)	101 (8)	100 (4)	100 (6)	100 (6)	100 (6)

TABLE 6-11

History Students' Willingness to Work in a Public School in a Rural Area by Position on Political-Critical and Professional Indexes

	High-Professional			Mid-Professional			Low-Professional		
	Active Partisan	Critical Sympathizer	Non-involved	Active Partisan	Critical Sympathizer	Non-involved	Active Partisan	Critical Sympathizer	Non-involved
Yes	52	68	75	40	75	50	50	50	33
No	48	26	25	60	25	50	50	50	67
Reject		5							
Total	100 (27)	99 (19)	100 (8)	100 (10)	100 (8)	100 (4)	100 (6)	100 (6)	100 (6)

stage of industrialization. Engineers believed that their skills enabled them to move into a great variety of positions, instead of merely preparing them for highly specialized work. Though this is also true, to some extent, of industrialized nations, the overwhelming emphasis on entrepreneurial and managerial goals is much more characteristic of a society which has not yet reached the point where specially trained administrators capture high-level business and government positions. This entrepreneurial and management-oriented spirit can be functional in a society where large sectors of the country are still vastly untapped by business enterprise or controlled by backward and monopolistic firms.[10]

Another significant difference between engineering and all other students was the pronounced lack of enthusiasm for university positions by the former. Pay and prestige differentials, of greater importance to engineering students than others, distinguished industrial and government opportunities from university opportunities and placed the university in a poor competitive position. However, we did have very extensive contacts with one planning center in the University of Chile. This group was staffed by highly competent young engineers, who emphasized the central role of economic factors in influencing the attainment of technical goals. The great significance of this group lay in its ability to recruit some of the most able graduating students. Although the impact had not yet been sufficient to affect general student evaluation on university positions, some change was under way. The cycle of the best engineers going only to better paying industrial and government positions, reinforcing the low prestige of full-time university positions and undermining the quality of teaching, was slowly being challenged.

The Science Students

In contrast to the responses of the engineers were those of the science students. For them, a university position was the only one consistently rated very highly. No other institution commanded a comparable degree of loyalty, and even the prestigious international organizations were only mildly attractive. In Chile, however, the situation for scientists was extremely difficult. The profession was not old and established like teaching, but it also suffered from low prestige and salaries. It was unformed and disadvantaged in the competition for good students and jobs, and in appreciation of its contribution. While there was superficial recognition of the need for training people in the basic sciences, there was at the same time a strong feeling in powerful quarters that Chile could not yet afford to support scientists working, for example, in experimental or theoretical physics. When the time comes that the country is ready to use such skills, it was argued, it will be able to acquire the necessary researchers.

Dedijer's discussion on the difficulties facing science in certain types of developing countries is pertinent here. Where there is little effort to modify industrial products because of near-monopolistic practices, innovative contributions are little solicited.[11] Research is then almost always "pure," simply because its results are never demanded or used by their native agriculture or industry.

Thus, on the one hand, Chilean newspaper articles discussed in laudatory terms the creation of an Institute of Science to give degrees in physics, mathematics, biology, and chemistry to fill a large gap in manpower needs.[12] At the same time, the floundering Institute had its budget cut annually, was forbidden to buy equipment needed for a recently formed research group, was limited to no more than fifteen students per year, and was in many ways discouraged by university authorities, who showed little concern that the entire Institute might be still-born.[13]

The contrast that clearly emerged between newspaper publicity and reality was reflective of many education issues. From reading the papers and following the forums, commissions, and planning sessions held, one received the distinct impression of tremendous public concern and action. A closer look at the situation revealed that enthusiasm on a surface level far exceeded the willingness to accept and carry out the structural changes necessary to achieve the stated goals. Powerful people in the university could then deplore the poor training in mathematics and science in the secondary schools, which resulted in large part from inadequate training of high school teachers. Yet, they simultaneously refused to accept fully that in order to improve teacher training, Chile had to attract scientists to the university who were well educated and deeply involved in their specialties. Chileans who had gone to the United States and England to obtain Ph.D.'s in mathematics, physical science, or biology found it difficult to remain in their country to train future professionals when they were denied the support necessary to work in their fields of specialization. Ironically, under these conditions the best-trained and most professionally committed young scientists might be precisely those who were most driven to foreign employment.[14]

Foreign Employment

Many of the science students defined foreign employment as an opportunity for gaining greater professional competence. For others, it was a guarantee of professional positions, no matter what the situation was in their own country. Indeed, this tendency to look favorably upon employment in other countries was widespread among the other students as well (Table 6-12). In this situation, the variables of political involvement and professional commitment offered no explanation, nor did any of the other variables tested.

TABLE 6-12

Willingness to Work in a Foreign Country after
Graduation by School

	Engineering	History	Science	Medicine
Yes	50	58	63	38
No	29	21	20	32
Undecided	21	20	17	29
Total	100 (94)	99 (94)	100 (30)	99 (99)

There was considerable public concern in Chile about the exodus of high-talent manpower, and criticism was severe of those who succumbed to the temptation of foreign employment. Many proposals had been put forth to counteract the trend.[15] Some students, nevertheless, considered opportunities for personal and professional advancement more important than a commitment to the solution of national problems. For them, the alternatives were simple. For others, who were more dedicated to national development, the decision was replete with conflict. It was a dilemma which young professionals faced with increasing frequency. Dedijer sums up this situation very clearly, and his discussion appears applicable in Chile even for those young professionals who have not studied abroad.

> The reluctance of the highly trained young scientist from an underdeveloped country to return to his own country upon completion of his training is not simply attributable to deficient patriotism or enslavement to the money bags and fleshpots of the advanced countries. In many cases it is motivated, at least in part, and in some cases it is entirely motivated by the knowledge that it is difficult to do good research in their own countries. Not only are equipment and financial provision incomparably poorer than they are in the advanced countries, but scientific administration is usually far more bureaucratic and antipathetic to the needs of scientists for freedom from petty controls.[16]

Consequences of Student Professional Concerns

The evidence collected from our study of students at the University of Chile in Santiago showed a high degree of professional involvement among student doctors, engineers, physicists, and history teachers. However, this should not compel an automatic assumption that such concern had only positive implications for Chilean economic and social development. For those students who were very committed to high-quality professional performance, the attractions of working conditions in the advanced countries or in international organizations were very frequently irresistible. This was particularly true in science, where jobs in Chile were scarce, where facilities for advanced research were limited, and where few opportunities existed for postgraduate specialization. Similarly, in medicine, students were well trained, ambitious to specialize, and often under-motivated to deal with the primitive health problems which beset much of rural Chile.

It became quite evident, then, that qualitative professional training in itself was not sufficient to solve the manpower shortages from which Chile was suffering. As was the case with many Latin American countries, the greatest problems existed in building new professional groups and motivating members of the traditional professions to work with low-income groups in urban and rural areas, where professional services were desperately needed but were virtually nonexistent. In such situations a special kind of professional identification was demanded. Professionals were needed who were not only technically competent but also aware of their country's problems and motivated to assist in their solution.

We maintain, furthermore, that political involvement did, at times, serve to support directly the type of professional concern that was most geared to solve the society's most urgent problems. The Chilean evidence indicated, for example, that there was a marked difference in students' willingness to pioneer by practicing their professions in remote geographical areas and among those urban groups who had hitherto been excluded from the market for professional services. Attempts to explain the divergent student orientations by the use of such variables as sex, socio-economic background, and religion were unsuccessful. Our results indicated that the most potent variable was the degree of political involvement exhibited by the student. In 1964 this type of involvement most often consisted of an identification with the reformist or revolutionary national political parties. Our evidence strongly leads to the conclusion that political ideologies which were supportive of social change, which emphasized the importance of modifying or drastically altering the social order, which rejected the current distribution of rewards, which denied the innate inferiority of the economically underprivileged, which advocated the broadening of the society's opportunity structures, and which emphasized the responsibility of youth to engage in this process as part of their student role were often highly functional in directing youthful energies into those channels most needed by the society.

On the other hand, our investigation also revealed that in certain situations political involvement did conflict with the trainee role and had negative results. Under certain conditions political activity and affiliation inhibited the propensity to pioneer professional services where there was a conflict between the needs of the political and professional roles. Moreover, in other instances it directly interfered with the intake of professional knowledge by drawing off too much of the students' time and energy into political activities.

We believe that there is an urgent need for further research on Latin American university students before broad and often questionable generalizations are made about their degree of student professional commitment, its possible contribution to national development, and its relationship to political activism.

NOTES

1. E. W. Bakke believes that the student "image" in Mexico and Colombia is still "confused." Students have not yet "digested" the two major components of a professional as a person who has prestige and contacts or as a person who is concerned with the implementation of knowledge. There is a very strong movement toward identification with the latter, however. E. W. Bakke, "Students on the March: The Cases of Mexico and Colombia," *Sociology of Education*, XXXVII (Spring, 1964), pp. 214–215.

   Other research also challenges the view that Latin American students are uninterested in implementing their professional skills. In a study of Argentine youth, David Nasatir found that almost half of the sample (43 per cent) of those enrolled at the University of Buenos Aires stated that the most important reason for seeking a higher education was to obtain professional training and to develop those abilities directly applicable to a career. This result compared quite favorably, Nasatir observed, with the responses of North American students. Among the latter 36 per cent emphasized the acquisition of a degree. Only 23 per cent of the Argentine students indicated the same motivation. D. Nasatir, "Education and Social Change: The Argentine Case," *Sociology of Education*, XXXIX (Spring, 1966), 169–173. For his comparative data for the United States Nasatir cites R. K. Goldsen *et al.*, *What College Students Think*, (Princeton, N.J.: Van Nostrand, 1960).

   An earlier study of Argentine students by Kalman Silvert also found students to be both instrumental and innovative. In medicine, for example, two-thirds of the students were concerned with the practical and vocational aspects of their education. These students also tended to be both upwardly mobile and among those who were most concerned with modernization. He reported similar findings in ". . . the Faculties of Economic Sciences and Exact Sciences as well. It is only reasonable that technological change, the necessity for a high degree of specialization, and emphasis on economic development should lead modernizing Argentines to insist upon improvement of vocational training at the university level, even at the apparent expense of some cherished notions of the popular university." K. H. Silvert, *The Conflicting Society: Reaction and Revolution in Latin America* (New Orleans: Tulane University Press, 1961). pp. 64–65.

2. A simple point index allocated 4 points to those who "definitely" chose the

more instrumental job, 2 points to those who "probably" would make this decision, and 0 points to those who "definitely" or "probably" would choose the job offering great social prestige. Similarly, students were awarded 2 points for any one or 4 points for choosing any two of the following: opportunity to increase professional knowledge, to gain professional recognition, or to work directly with people to improve their life situations. Zero points were given in each case where students chose social prestige, income, or political freedom as primary job characteristics. In the final question students "definitely" deciding to work with the more competent professor were given 4 points, those "probably" working with him were allocated 2 points, and those who did not want to work with him 0 points. On the basis of this scoring procedure 12 points were the maximum which any student could secure. Those with this total and their peers who achieved 10 points were rated as "high" professionals. Students with 8 points were placed in the "mid" professional category, and those with 6 or less in the "low" category.

3. See R. P. Atcon, "The Latin American University," *Die Deutsche Universitäts Zeitung* (February, 1962), pp. 7–49; J. P. Harrison, "The Role of the Intellectual in Fomenting Change: The University," in J. J. Tepaske and S. N. Fisher, eds., *Explosive Forces in Latin America* (Columbus: Ohio State University Press, 1964).

4. The question posed to the students was: There is a probability of a student strike in your faculty for what you consider to be a justifiable reason. You are an officer on the *Centro de Alumnos* and can have an important voice in the decision to strike or not. At the same time, you are involved in several interesting and important courses in which you are receiving valuable professional training. You would vote: (1) definitely to strike; (2) probably to strike; (3) probably not to strike; (4) definitely not to strike.

5. We analyzed this situation at some length with the professor actually involved in the situation. R. C. Williamson has discussed the reaction of university students in Colombia to the use of the strike: "In view of these responses some correction might be made of the stereotype of the university student as a perennial striker. While the verbalizations of students are not necessarily valid, it would seem that for most subjects the strike was justified only when focused on the welfare of the students or of the university. However, in some instances, for the student the strike becomes his sole means of communication where other conventional verbal processes fail to function, parenthetically, in a culture area where poetry enjoys a brighter halo than does logic." R. C. Williamson, "University Students in a World of Change: A Colombian Sample," *Sociology and Social Research,* XLVIII (July, 1964), 401.

6. *El Mercurio,* January 18, 1964.

7. Similar changes also seem to be occurring in other Latin American countries. E. W. Bakke reports that in Mexico and Colombia, the concept of the university "as a servant of the people" has been growing. "In both countries the medical students spend a substantial portion of their final year carrying medical service to a particular village which lacks such service." There have been attempts, supported by the medical students, to include other students in this type of program, Bakke, *op. cit.,* pp. 213–214.

Hennesey believes that this type of exposure can have a radicalizing affect on student-physicians. "In spite of, or it may be because of, its high prestige, medicine has always tended to be a sensitive faculty politically. First-hand contact with diseases caused by malnutrition or bad housing can arouse the social conscience even of upper-class students. . . . The practice which is becoming common, following Mexico's lead, of universities insisting on a year's service in a rural area before graduating, could make medical faculties still more radical." Alistair Hennesey, "University Students in National Politics," in Claudio Veliz (ed.) *The Politics of Conformity in Latin America* (New York: Oxford University Press, 1967), p. 139.

8. J. Raffo, "Problemas de la Enseñanza," *Cuadernos Médico-Sociales* (December, 1963), especially p. 38.

9. The tables supporting these observations and others in this chapter can be found in Myron Glazer, "The Professional and Political Attitudes of Chilean University Students" (Ph.D. diss., Princeton University, 1965), chap. 6.

    The allocation of doctors in Chile is an important national problem. In 1959, Santiago, with 30 per cent of the population, had 64 per cent of all the Chilean doctors. A similar situation prevailed in dentistry. In 1960 the capital city claimed 58 per cent of the nation's dentists. Since most of the doctors and dentists trained in Chile live in Santiago, they are reluctant to leave their families and friends for a position in the more primitive rural areas. The high concentration of specialists in the capital also makes it difficult to establish high-quality professional schools in the provinces. Another way to view the figures is to state that there were 12.7 doctors per 10,000 population in the capital city of Santiago and only 1.4 doctors per 10,000 population in the rural province of Malleco-Cautin.

    For further discussion, see R. C. Blitz, "The Role of High-level Manpower in the Economic Development of Chile," in F. Harbison and C. A. Myers, eds., *Manpower and Education* (New York: McGraw-Hill, 1965).

10. There are also very serious dysfunctional aspects of this attitude, which have been described by Fischer in his discussion of Asian professionals. The goal of administrative employment has not resulted in efficient bureaucracy but often has culminated in waste of much valuable talent. "For example, engineers, chemists, and economists prefer to be administrators while leaving complex technical tasks to individuals who have had little specialized training. Surveys made of activities of elites in Thailand, Burma, Indonesia, and India indicate that in some fields as many as 60 per cent of those trained are not using their skills or the specialized knowledge which university training has given them." J. Fischer, "The University Student in South and Southeast Asia," *Minerva,* II (Autumn, 1963), p. 52.

11. S. Dedijer, "Underdeveloped Science in Underdeveloped Countries," *Minerva,* II (Autumn, 1963), p. 79.

12. Within a period of only a few months in late 1963 and early 1964, a rash of articles appeared heralding the importance of basic research. These also spoke approvingly of the university's initiating study in scientific investigation and a physics course for secondary school teachers. For example, see *El Mercurio,* October 29, 1963; November 30, 1963; and January 21, 1964.

13. These observations derive from lengthy conversations with members of the Institute's staff; these scientists were an impressive group from the standpoint

of education background, commitment to their work, and desire to remain in their country. Confirmation of their statements came from enlightening discussions with persons knowledgeable of the thinking of officials in the highest university councils.

Even in the United States there are on-going controversies about the significance of basic research and the extent to which it should receive national support. It was not until the Soviet Union launched Sputnik that the lack of attention to basic research was defined as a major national problem. Scores of publications and numerous well-attended conferences then began to focus on the necessity of rejecting a short-sighted policy in favor of major investments in personnel, equipment, and buildings. The tremendous resources of the United States have allowed it to fill in major gaps in certain areas relatively quickly.

14. The problems of the new scientific professions in some Latin American countries are further aggravated by their vulnerability to political instability. In 1964 the military government of Castelo Branco issued an *Acto Institucional* which allowed dismissal or detention of all employees, subject to judgment of investigatory commissions set up by the armed forces. Among those dismissed by the more than 800 commissions on summary investigations were scientists, other research workers, authors, teachers, and professors. Many scholars were imprisoned or physically abused; others were interrogated or dismissed. The apprehension and panic which ensued resulted in a number of trained researchers and scholars seeking employment abroad. Forty-two professors or research workers in physics, chemistry, sociology, economics, medicine, and other fields left by the end of the year. Twenty who were abroad decided to remain out of the country. By December, 1964, approximately thirty university teachers had been dismissed or "retired" and about one hundred thirty intellectuals were known to be in prison. Others declared that their research was no longer free, but directed and censored by political considerations. Many of these incidents apparently were not planned by the central government. Frequently local animosities and unauthorized decisions of hard-liners resulted in local "purges." The consequences, however, are the same. Social and political instability led to fear, repression, emigration, and a serious loss in number and decline in quality of personnel in universities which could ill afford it. See "The Brazilian University under the *Castelo Branco Regime,*" *Minerva,* III (Summer, 1965), pp. 555–558.

Similarly, the military government of Juan Carlos Organía ended Argentine university autonomy on July 29, 1966. The effort to enforce this radical change resulted in police violence, and many interpreted this decision as an end to academic freedom. Indeed one of the ugliest incidents occurred at the building of the Faculty of Exact and Natural Sciences the day after the decree was promulgated which ended university autonomy. According to participants, including Professor Warren Ambrose of the MIT faculty, police entered the building in force and brutally attacked unarmed students and teachers. No quarter was given because of age, sex, or scholarly reputation. Severe wounds were inflicted as the victims were first struck at random and then forced to run a police gantlet.

By the end of the summer more than two-thirds of the professors had resigned from the faculty. This figure eventually rose to over 90 per cent. Since most of these men were holding full-time positions in the university they were in difficult economic straits and a special committee of United States professors was established to help them find jobs outside Argentina. Thus with the only center of high-level research in the country destroyed, a mass emigration of physical and natural scientists from Argentina occurred, leaving numerous students without guidance and supervision in their training. This situation intensified an already serious "brain drain" of many capable scientists to countries where resources were more readily available for research. For a full discussion of these events see Latin American Studies Association, *A Report to the American Community on the Present Argentine University Situation* (Austin, Texas, 1967).

The success or failure in building new careers and changing work attitudes in old ones can have a vital impact on government policy. The Castro government, for example, has transformed the university into an institution serving national economic development. Scholarships are provided for those entering certain careers in an attempt to produce the necessary technically trained manpower. The nation's youth are utilized as a vital resource in socio-economic change. Indeed, every attempt has been made to replace the emphasis on military heroism by one which rewards the commitment of those who use their skills and energies in a wide variety of national service projects. There has been an attempt to join youthful idealism, commitment to national goals, and an identification with an innovative work orientation.

The failure to achieve these goals, on the other hand, was a costly one for the Bolivian government after the revolution of 1952. Students who sympathized with the revolutionary government attempted to reorder the university. They were unsuccessful in spite of support from both the powerful unions and the government. As a result, the universities failed to provide either political support or the technically trained manpower so desperately needed by the country. The traditional law career continued to grow while needed engineers and agronomists were graduated in far smaller numbers. As a last measure the government set up its own technology institute which rejected co-government and imposed a severe academic regime. The institute survived only as long as did the revolutionary government itself. Two recent summary articles on the Latin American university are particularly useful. For a discussion of Bolivia see Hennessy, *op. cit.;* also see Timothy F. Harding, *The University, Politics, and Development in Contemporary Latin America,* Latin American Research Program, Research Seminar Series No. 3 (Riverside, Calif.: University of California Press, June, 1968). For a far more critical account of the Castro government and its attempt to control the university see Jaime Suchlicke, "Cuba," in Donald K. Emmerson, ed., *Students and Politics in Developing Countries* (New York: Frederick A. Praeger, 1968), pp. 315–349.

15. *El Mercurio,* October 14, 1963, October 18, 1963, and May 23, 1964. Emigration of trained professionals also plagues highly industrialized societies. See *Time,* February 21, 1964, p. 46.

16. Dedijer, *op. cit.,* p. 68.

Part III

Frank Bonilla / Myron Glazer

SUMMARY
AND CONCLUSIONS

Chapter 7

Summary and Conclusions

The University of Chile is more than a century old, and it is one of the most prestigious institutions of higher learning in Latin America. In 1957, when the study in Part I of this volume was carried out, the university enrolled nearly 13,000 students, just over half of all those in the country. The FECH, the student organization of the University of Chile, is now celebrating its sixtieth anniversary. The three periods in FECH history that have been singled out for attention here are not the most critical, nor do they necessarily merit most intensive study from a historical viewpoint. They were selected to represent disparate frameworks of student action, in order to maximize the opportunities to observe structural changes in the organization. At these three periods in the life of the FECH, the researcher could examine the organization in an early militant and semi-revolutionary epoch (1918–1922); in a period of ascendancy of the left, when the popular and official temper was extremely favorable to students (1936–1940); and finally as a fairly moderate political force with and accepted role in the university administration (1956–1957).

Three main variables were used to define the changing situation of action for the student organization. Economic, political, and ideological factors were viewed as the principal external elements fixing the framework within which student action in each period was played out. The most persistent of these elements was a permanent and increasingly acute economic crisis. Mass poverty, inflation, and grave social inequalities were ever present.

289

The frustration of hard problems, with no promise of immediate solution within the existing social framework, remained a constant. These deep-rooted social and economic problems served as a continuous focus of concern and a stimulus to action for students. It was the shifting impact of new and resurrected ideologies and of changes in the political balance of power within the nation that produced the most dramatic changes in the institutional forms of the student organization.

The changes in both the ideological sphere and the distribution of power among the contending parties in Chile during the periods studied reproduced in many ways a process that was world-wide. These changes reflect and document the sensitivity of Chilean political life to developments outside the nation. The wave of pacifism and anti-militarism, the influence of anarchists and idealistic Socialists on student thought immediately after World War I affected, not only Chilean university youths, but young intellectuals around the globe. The crystallization within the university of the struggle between Nazis and anti-fascists, as well as that between Socialists and Communists during the popular front period, also paralleled events in other nations. The mood of conservatism, the emergence of a politically moderate, technically oriented, reformist, anti-Communist leadership in the mid-1950's was also in line with broader trends throughout the hemisphere and elsewhere within the United States and Western European orbit. That is to say, the university political movement in Chile and elsewhere in Latin America has its place intellectually within the mainstream of modern political trends in thought and action. Quite often, local problems are merely confused or exacerbated by interpretations based on ill-digested, imported ideologies; nevertheless, the responsiveness of the student organization to ideological developments abroad must be underscored.

More important, perhaps, in defining the realistic limits of student action was the distribution of political power within the nation, particularly the relative power held by groups sympathetic to students. In this regard, the three generations studied differed radically. Each may be taken as illustrative of a particular type of relationship between the established political powers and the student organization. In the 1920 period there was no political group that fully expressed the ideals and aspirations of students; no political party won the allegiance of students; the student organization was not put at the service of any party. The wholesale repudiation of the past by students included the rejection of the tutelage of all existing parties; the more radical students considered all forms of organization as inevitably corrupting. Here, then, is an example of the student organization working autonomously, *of students standing more or less alone against the existing order*. This is the classic image of the student movement, but it is not the most characteristic situation of student movements in Chile or elsewhere in the hemisphere. The fact is that since the great surge of youthful revolt after World War I, the trend, with few exceptions, has been for youth organizations to grow and operate in close association with adult political organizations.

The popular front and the contemporary period show the student organization in a situation that has been more common in Latin America in the last two or three decades. The shift of student allegiances to party organizations—whether these parties are in power, are a "loyal" opposition, or illegal and clandestine groups—has created a set of problems that has frequently threatened the survival of student organizations and made them a focus of perplexed, when not hostile, adult attention. At this point, it becomes necessary to begin discriminating between the external, political role of the student organization and its functions within the university itself.

Changes in Student Organization

The differences observed in the FECH organization in the three periods studied may be viewed in at least two ways. They may be regarded as steps in a continuous process of development or as discrete examples of variant forms of a particular kind of organization produced in different environments. In the case at hand, there is some theoretical justification and profit to be had from looking at differences from both points of view. It will be argued here that the second approach is more appropriate when discussing the outward political projections of the FECH action, and that the first approach is more useful in studying organized student action within the confines of the university.

Discontinuities in the FECH life and action were most evident in the political sphere; the federation's relationships with political groups never approached the formality or permanence that was achieved in relations with the university administration. The opportunities for the cumulation of stable traditions and the routinization of transactions were simply not equally present in both spheres. Within the university the FECH developed and matured fairly steadily in a given direction; its political growth was more erratic and lacking in pattern. The secure position of the FECH within the university gave it a strong hold on life and at the same time served as a bureaucratizing and moderating force on student action. By 1957 the FECH was so well entrenched within the university that it could survive, and did function to an important extent exclusively, as a *university* organization. Full student participation in the administration of university affairs *(el co-gobierno)* had not been achieved, but students exercised *through the* FECH a significant and institutionalized influence on university affairs. The FECH was the only recognized representative for students before the rector and the University Council.

Except in periods of disorganization that affected the entire university, the FECH had never pitted itself against any university administration. Reforms achieved over the years had been won with the support of many professors as well as students; the University Council and the rector had acted as a restraining force rather than as direct opponents of student aims. The openness of university administrations to student petitions and the many and continuous instances of co-operative endeavors and mutual deference had established a body of formal and informal links between student leaders and university officials. The federation in 1957 looked entirely to the university for financial support; its prestige was rooted in the accomplishments of the university and former student generations. The FECH leaders counted on the moral support of the rector's office even when making political protests.

However, the instability of the political environment hampered the crystallization of stable patterns of interaction among student groups, parties, and governments. In other words, the discontinuities and reversals of national political life can cut off or reverse any hypothetical, built-in maturational process of organizational development. The opportunities for the charismatic star to rise in student ranks repeat themselves. When more mature political leadership fails, when the political opposition is inert or crippled by an oppressive government, students move into the foreground. The impotence or inaction of other traditional elites revitalizes the role of students as providers of political guidance to popular groups. Throughout Latin America, the repeated demonstrations of the potency of *el pueblo* with the leadership of students, intellectuals, and other civilians against the armed force of dictators serve to cement and give new life to the image of the university and the student organization as the ultimate bulwarks of freedom and the sources of trustworthy leadership in times of political crisis.

In Chile, as elsewhere in Latin America, the honeycombing of student organization with party factions has the same depressing effects. The student organization does not present a united, external front to political groups. Communication between party and the student federation is not channeled through any central authoritative body; the parties work with and through their own outposts in the university. Partisan interests become hopelessly intermeshed and confused with the objectives of the student organization proper. Manipulativeness, indifference to long-range objectives, and expedience characterize the leadership. The unpoliticized mass of students tends to grow alienated and indifferent to appeals from the student organization. The counter-appeal of a completely depoliticized and narrowly student-oriented organization takes on increasing attractiveness. If the parties that control the student group are in power, they displace students from any true leadership functions outside the university. If they are not, they try to use students to bolster their weak situations or to embarrass and harass those in power. In any case, the student organization becomes in itself a tool and an object to be won and used rather than a set of values to be served. The university becomes an arena in which the national political struggle is reproduced in microcosm. A cyclical pattern of ascent and decline in the vigor of the student organization is produced, associated in part with the natural turnover of top leadership, but more directly tied to a basic rhythm of action and reaction, of movement from extreme political activism and externally directed operations toward political moderation and a reversal of attention to university affairs. The reversal in Chile has more than once been powerful enough to produce a real schism in student organization. This pattern of attack and withdrawal may constitute an innate characteristic of this type of organization. In the Chilean case, the sixty-year process of consolidation and bureaucratization of the university functions of the FECH has been accompanied by an inner cyclical alternation in dominant orientation toward what is external and political and that which is more narrowly of interest to students and the university in its teaching functions.

This book has emphasized the usefulness of studying the structure and operations of student organizations in Latin America, with some systematic attention to the context in which they operate, both academically and nationally. Whatever its limitations, the FECH has been a vehicle for transmitting and sustaining democratic values. It has been a force for progress within the university. The readiness of students to attack injustice and resist political oppression has helped to keep the nation on the path of political moderation and legality.

The study in Part II of this volume attempts to supplement the investigation of the FECH by surveying the attitudes of a larger sample of students at the University of Chile. The research has been primarily directed toward an analysis of the role of university students preparing for a variety of careers that are essential for economic development. It has been concerned with whether, during a period of heightened political tension, students placed their major responsibility in the political arena or in the professional arena. The events surrounding the 1964 presidential campaign served as a dramatic background for the research.

The rank and file of Chilean students appeared much less volatile than their peers in far-off Asian universities, or than those just across the border in Argentina. Students in Chile generally regarded mastery and implementation of professional knowledge as primary concerns and more important than political activities. The greater the difficulty of the curriculum and the training process, the less was the likelihood of political involvement. Even where a dearth of future professional opportunities might have led to a predication of greater political action to effect social change, the challenge of a difficult training program served to reduce this type of activity.

Science students, when faced with the greatest difficulties in obtaining employment after graduation, still invested very little of their time and energy in politics. The history students, who also suffered from limited professional opportunities but whose program was least taxing, were the most politicized and most radical. The highest concentration of conservative students, on the other hand, occurred among the engineers, for whom the rewards upon graduation were immediate and abundant, and whose elite status is most easily secured. The medical students also derived high rewards upon obtaining professional status. This and their rigorous training program, however, neither vitiated their deep social concerns nor precluded a more left-wing political orientation. The very nature of medical training gave them an early and firsthand exposure to the many basic problems in Chilean society.

A recent study of student trade-unionism in several European countries has contributed to a better understanding of the Chilean situation.[1] F. A. Pinner sees "anticipatory socialization into a vocation" occurring as professional practice becomes a major avenue to social status; "ideological protest" as resulting from the absence of professional role models, unclear specification of professional tasks, inadequacy of available positions, or a social crisis which blurs the future into which the student must step; and "role-seeking" as the student's attempt to change a "malleable" social order and thus find a place for himself.

Many of the engineering students seemed to fit most directly into the category of anticipatory socialization.

> To the extent that the student, oriented toward his future occupation, strives for early acceptance into, and protection from, the profession, he is socially conservative: it is not to his interest to oppose a social order within which he seeks to achieve status.[2]

Engineering students expressed the highest degree of satisfaction with their profession's salary, prestige, and social power.[3] With a firm grasp upon reality, these students predicted that during their professional lives, their salaries would range from adequate to excellent. Of all the students, they foresaw the least difficulty in maintaining an acceptable standard of living. The degree of satisfaction even rose slightly in the upper years of study. Similarly, engineers were extremely satisfied with the prestige which the society accorded their profession. Though the response was more mixed, they were also, by far, the most satisfied with the influence which professionals in their field had in government affairs and in the ability to affect their conditions of work. Many pointed to the heights to which engineers could aspire and proudly indicated that the then president of the republic, Jorge Alessandri (1958–1964), and his entire first cabinet, were engineers.

The situation with respect to the medical students differed somewhat from that of their engineering peers. Although both professions had ready access to many of the rewards available in Chile, the involvement of the medical students with their country's social problems and their concern with basic social change made it difficult to fit many of them into the pattern suggested by Pinner's scheme. In addition, certain aspects which made medicine less attractive than engineering were emphasized by the medical students. Although there was a great deal of satisfaction with the prestige afforded to doctors, there was a marked concern with the initial salary. This was especially true of students who were closest to embarking on their careers. Although expectation increased as students projected themselves into their professional futures, the initial financial returns were inconsistent with the other aspects of their social position and were a cause of discontent among neophyte doctors. This was further reflected in their definition of the degree of influence which the profession had over its conditions of work. Their subjective definitions were far lower than those of students in engineering. Although doctors could look forward to a very successful professional future, they were faced with very challenging early years of practice. Low salaries, obligation to work in rural areas, and the pressing health problems of Chile's population were at great disparity with the generally high evaluation and rewards given the profession in the society.

History students exhibited a higher degree of dissatisfaction than their medical or engineering peers. While there were some who seemed to be satisfied with the social position of their careers, the majority were not. Marked dissatisfaction was exhibited in regard to income, power, and especially prestige. Again, students in the upper years were the least satisfied. The conflict between the achievement of university status and the paucity of comparable professional rewards strongly characterized the total group. Unlike primary school teachers, who had not studied at the university, students in the School of History had taken the giant step of university enrollment. Their five years of preparation not only equipped them with greater professional skills, but also made them members of the miniscule elite who held university degrees. This achievement, however, did not give these students the kind of social position which members of other professions had attained.

Facing a lack of desirable employment, many history students were involved with a "protest ideology." Anticipatory socialization was often precluded because of the need to reject the current distribution of professional rewards and opportunities. A basis had to be found to explain their current disadvantaged situation and to support change-directed activity. The historical facts of social injustice and relative professional deprivation made radical ideologies appealing because they proposed to solve both situations simultaneously.

The situation of the science students could best be characterized by the term "role-seeking." They had strong role models, who had stressed the need to pioneer professionally. The path of political action was not the only available one. If the science students did not see the social order as "malleable," at least they defined it as susceptible to modern influence through the diffusion of the idea of economic development. This, they hoped, would result in an expansion of desirable professional roles.

Placing the scientists on the hierarchy of professional groups was difficult. Judged by the criteria of their education and reputation in the international scientific community, the members of the profession were equal in standing to the members of any Chilean profession. Judged by acceptance and reward within their country, however, they were far lower. Although their own professors had repeatedly warned them about the problems of securing adequate employment after graduation, the evaluations of their professional futures by many students were far brighter than the reality would indicate. To be sure, there were students who expressed dissatisfaction with the income, prestige, and power which their profession commands. Yet an equal number ranked their profession highly, using these same criteria. Their appraisals seemed based, not upon what they could obtain with their university degree, but rather what their professors had obtained through advanced work in other countries. They appeared to have distorted their possibilities by neglecting to consider full the life-and-death struggle for survival in which their infant profession was engaged in Chile.

In all schools professional attitudes seem to be affected by the degree of political involvement. In general, the most active students were the most committed to implementation of professional knowledge as a form of service to the community. They seemed most concerned with working either with the underprivileged or in those jobs most directly related to modernization of the social system. The one major exception was their unwillingness, in most cases, to leave major cities for rural areas. Furthermore, this group continually emphasized achievement over ascription as the means they would employ to attain their aspirations, and it continually de-emphasized the value of income and prestige returns. Conversely, the politically noninvolved students were those whose views differed most from the activists. Among them we found the greatest stress on income and prestige, the least concern with service to the community, and the widest range in choosing between achievement and ascriptive means.

The often-affirmed antithesis between professionalism and student activism is thus challenged by these findings. If national development needs require a coupling of political commitments to technical capacity among strategic occupations, then intensive professionalizing, shorn of any political referents or motivation, seems unlikely to perform this task. Fascination and impatience with the sporadically disruptive aspects of student political action fasten attention on the impulsive and pathological features of youthful efforts at self-assertion and social criticism. The counter-impulse to pacify the university by rooting out politics by any means and making professionalization the exclusive aim of higher training can prove costly and self-defeating. The relative restraint of Chilean authorities in this respect, even under considerable provocation, is justifiably an item of national pride and palpably a source of political dividends.

NOTES

1. F. A. Pinner, "Student Trade-Unionism in France, Belgium, and Holland: Anticipatory Socialization and Role Seeking," *Sociology of Education*, XXXVII (1964), 177–199.

2. Pinner, *op. cit.*, p. 196.
3. All students were asked the extent to which they are satisfied with the initial and subsequent income they would receive as professionals, the degree of prestige afforded their profession in Chile, and the influence their professions have to affect conditions of work. The tables upon which the following discussion is based may be found in Myron Glazer, "The Professional and Political Attitudes of Chilean University Students" (Ph.D. diss., Princeton University, 1965), chap. 6.

Myron Glazer/Penina M. Glazer

Epilogue

Introductory Note

A two-month visit is scarcely enough time to become fully re-acquainted with a country and its people. Most of June and July, 1969, were spent visiting with students and professors in the four *facultades* in which the 1964 survey had been concentrated. Our questions focused on the degree of change which had occurred during the preceding five years, specifically during the eighteen months of the latest reform movement in which the entire power structure of the university had been seriously challenged. We also studied documents and traced the sequence of recent events as reported in the national press and popular journals.

The nature of Chilean academic life in the last months of this decade is reminiscent of events and attitudes in the United States. Academia is now very much in the real world. It has become a major battlefield. The words of our Chilean colleagues, their experiences, frustrations, and dreams are international in their significance as the roots and meaning of the university are profoundly questioned.

The latest Chilean university reform is basically the story of an alliance of students and younger academics to re-make their institution into a model for democratic participation and national relevancy. There could have been no reform without the determination of the younger professors to overturn a system in which they labored in the shadow of a handful of powerful *catredráticos*. In the course of this struggle colleagues and friends have severed their relationships and have modified or drastically changed earlier positions.

Background to Revolt

In the late 1960's the quality and goals of Chilean education continued to draw harsh criticism from many students, professors, and administrators, and between 1967 and 1969 the University of

301

Chile underwent a series of dramatic changes. The problems resulting from inadequate educational resources, highly specialized training, centralization of bureaucratic power and insufficient involvement in national problems produced a series of challenges to the internal structure of the university and its relationship to the rest of Chilean society. The confrontation stemmed from the continuing crisis of Chilean national life, the attempts of the reformist Christian Democratic government to meet the demands of various sectors, and the determination of student and academic leaders to transform the university itself into a more effective national institution.

In recent years traditional university structures and attitudes have been directly and severely undermined by the rhetoric and actions associated with the 1964 presidential election and the subsequent reform efforts of the victorious Christian Democratic party. Programs to expand enrollment and revise curriculum at the primary and secondary school level could not but serve as a potent catalyst for university reform. Although President Frei may have given greater emphasis to elementary and secondary education, both his supporters and opponents in the university were unwilling to postpone changes there.

Some writers on Latin American affairs have long noted the discrepancy between the efforts of university people to democratize their society and their failure to transform their own institution. The University of Chile, in its internal structure, has been one of the most conservative institutions in Chilean society. Notwithstanding FECH influence in university affairs, most decisions have been made by high-level administrators and full professors, with younger academics and students having little voice in matters affecting their work. In addition, the division of the university into autonomous facultades, with their partisan professional interests, has hindered the development of a truly intellectual community. The facultades, furthermore, have effectively resisted efforts to reduce rigid curriculum requirements or to introduce new methods of teaching.

Beginnings of Reform

The initial impetus for the latest reform movement occurred in the faculty of Philosophy and Education (the Pedagogico) during

1967. Its strong left-wing orientation and the militancy of many of its students have already been described. The election of a Communist dean in the Pedagogico as well as active reform movements in several other Chilean universities precipitated demands for student participation in facultad decision making. Young professors simultaneously sought full representation in departmental and facultad councils. The unilateral acceptance of these demands by the Pedagogico authorities was condemned by the Consejo Superior, the central university council, as illegal abuse of power. The council's demand for punitive action against the Pedagogico leadership led to the resignation of the rector of the university who criticized the Consejo Superior for its rejection of his peacemaking efforts. The university was momentarily without formal leadership, and a university-wide confrontation resulted.

Students quickly moved into the power vacuum. Marxist students seized the university radio and television station, and the Christian Democratic students occupied the university's central administration building in downtown Santiago. The pressure of events and the demands of the Marxists caused the Christian Democratic students in the FECH to assume a far more militant position. By its occupation of the key university buildings the FECH again asserted its leadership of the student body.

Although it had successfully urged rejection of co-government in a referendum which had been held only a year earlier, the FECH now criticized the inaction of the central university authorities. It demanded a total restructuring of the university, including transformation of the teaching career and implementations of new instructional methods, as well as student participation in university government. The FECH urged the university to fulfill its historic function as the true servant of the nation. All the reformers agreed that an upgrading and expansion of research as well as a greater commitment to extension work in the community were crucial. Many defined the university as a revolutionary institution itself in need of overhauling before it could attempt to restructure national life.

These events galvanized student action in a variety of facultades. Many participants in these events described the sense of excitement and exhilaration which they experienced. In Engineering, students seized the buildings and allowed access only to those professors willing to discuss reform measures. The reformers succeeded in democratizing participation at all levels of decision making. They overturned a system whereby the dean and a small coterie of advisers allocated resources and made key appointments.

In Medicine, students and younger professors successfully challenged the authority of the dean and elected in his place a popular, highly respected, and reform-minded young professor. Prior to the reform, in some of the more autocratic departments the heads not only determined the composition of the courses, but also brooked no intellectual disagreement from younger men even though some had specialized in a particular sub-area of the *cátedra*. The reformers successfully broke the power of the *catedráticos* within the school and also won greater acceptance of the view that Chilean doctors must be better prepared to meet critical national health needs.

The recently formed faculty of Science had been founded in 1965 as a reform faculty and had already excluded those professors unwilling to accept a reformist and politically activist milieu. Although little change occurred there as a direct result of the most recent university upheaval, several scientists became leading spokesmen for the reform movement and one has become a major candidate for rector.

As a result of the events of May and June, 1968, and the eventual agreement between the FECH and Consejo Superior which ended the occupation, university-wide *plenarios* (conventions) were planned for September, 1968. In preparation for these meetings various reform commissions labored over reports and proposals for further institutionalizing the reform. The *plenarios* opened with a recurring theme, a bitter critique of Chilean cultural dependence on the imperialist United States. The necessity for the university to serve as a vanguard of social change was stressed. To achieve this, the university needed far greater financial support; a more democratic internal organization; an end to the autocratic power of the *catedráticos* and the development of appropriate departments; more objective criteria for evaluating teaching and research performance; less rigid curricula; a credit system giving students greater flexibility in changing careers; and provision for more adequate library and guidance services. The reports concluded that the sweeping changes should be directed by an all-university senate in which faculty, students, and non-academics would be represented.

The Reform Evaluated

A year has elapsed since these meetings were held, and the reformers may be credited with three major accomplishments: student participation in many important decisions affecting the university; democratization of the facultades resulting in greatly increased influence by the younger academics; and the representation of non-academic personnel in all university councils. Many of the people interviewed praised the responsibility exhibited by both students and young faculty. Students in some departments in the Pedagógico and in Medicine were particularly singled out for their maturity and their commitment to upgrading the level of university life.

Those more dubious about the reform and its goals, however, question the impact of the democratization on the institution. They charge that standards of scholarship have been undermined by calls to reject all foreign support and by the power granted to less capable academics to review research proposals. This issue is a particularly sensitive one in the Pedagogico's History department. There, several senior professors perform their major research in institutes completely independent of departmental influence. One senior professor had gathered an internationally respected team of researchers through long and arduous efforts. His own work had won support from United States foundations such as Rockefeller and Ford. He and his colleagues were then able to continue their costly research into economic history, purchase essential microfilm documents, and bring well-known scholars to their institute. He charged his reform-minded colleagues with simply wanting to re-divide the scarce available resources rather than attempting to increase overall research support and urged them to pressure university and government officials to finance research more generously. He feared that his institute was doomed by the repeated, and, to him, senseless demands to cut off foreign research funds. Moreover, he rejected the contention that foreign foundations simply supported non-relevant and non-controversial research. On the contrary, they did not provide funds for research on the colonial period as some reformers claimed, but rather stressed more contemporary issues.

The reformers reject this analysis. They believe that the younger academics in the department are as competent as the select few admitted to the institute. Those who are excluded are simply unable to be as productive because inadequate resources and low salaries make second jobs essential. The reformers charge that the elite members of the institute use scarce research funds to build private fiefdoms. Only by placing these institutions under departmental jurisdiction can a unified and effective department be built. The forging of a dynamic history department, they assert, is of higher priority than building the reputations of a few privileged professors. Democratization of the facultad had put a great deal of responsibility into the hands of the younger staff members. They felt that their efforts would be undermined were the independent institutes to function outside the jurisdiction of departmental decision making.

The issue of research is central to the reform. Many reformers emphasize that the focus on teaching reflects a misconception of the function of the university. They believe that teaching is primarily dedicated to passing on existing knowledge and accepted ideas, thus supporting the status quo. Scientific research, however, supersedes these limits and is an agent of change. The demand for more research is generally coupled with a desire to make it more relevant for national development. Reformists believe that the university should develop its own intellectual resources to enable it to become independent of imperialist nations.

From our perspective, there is a paradox inherent in these goals. Independence among Chilean scholars may result from limiting foreign funds and the number of foreign scholars working in Chile. Yet it may also impede an effective and desirable internationalization of scholarly work when genuine opportunities for this arise. It may foster an academic xenophobia which is in itself ineffective as a defense against cultural penetration. Enthusiasm for work on national importance, moreover, may lead to a disregard for theoretical research, particularly in the natural sciences. Applied research is rarely sufficient to nurture a community of scholars. Without such a broad-based community it is impossible to end intellectual dependence on more advanced

nations. Many reformers at the University of Chile are sensitive
to this issue. Among some, however, the zeal for work related to
national development could result in a form of anti-intellectual-
ism. The manner in which this tension is resolved can significantly influence the direction of Chilean scholarship in the years
to come.

The issue of the distribution of resources also continues to be
debated. Critics of the reform, particularly in Engineering, decry
the process by which funds are now allocated within the school.
Before the reform, the dean and a small advisory group decided
on the distribution of resources. Today, a much larger and more
representative group is involved. The critics argue that the size is
unwieldy and hinders speedy and effective decision making. They
prefer to rely on the wisdom of the dean and, doubtless, on their
personal ability to obtain their share of available resources. This
question has created animosity among former friends who constantly argue about who the "true reformers" are and whose
programs will better serve the school.

Many engineers also deplore the attempt of reformers to
involve the university in all contemporary issues. Surely, they
argue, the university will only become more of a political target as
various national parties strive to capture its commissions to
support their positions. Illustrative of this argument is the
controversy which ensued over the nationalization of American
copper mines. Some reformers believe that the university should
have investigated the basis of the government's position as well as
the critique of the left-wing parties, in order to take a public
stand.

One young engineer spoke at great length about the course of
the reform and the possibility of his leaving the country. His
graduate work at a prestigious American institution had provided
him with the credentials for international professional mobility. It
had exposed him to the relative stability of scientific research in
the United States, and he was seriously talking about a position in
an industrial laboratory. He argued that his facultad was likely to
be overrun by those seeking to politicize the entire university and
wondered how long he could continue to work under such
pressure. He particularly condemned the proposed Academic
Senate as a ploy by political activists to seek power. Who would
run for such a position, he asserted, but the man who thought

little of his professional work and much about solidifying his future prospects through political contacts.

Foreign migration by highly talented Chileans could become a serious problem during the contemporary crisis. For the university to upgrade its standards, it must be able to secure the commitment of those possessing intellectual and scholarly skills. It is evident that in the school of Engineering, and elsewhere in the university, men of great ability are now to be found on both sides of the reform struggle. Since neither side has a monopoly of competence, a crucial question remains. Will victory for either side spell disaster for the other? At present the anti-reformers are in a strong position. In Engineering attempts to replace the dean with a more reform-minded person have failed, and the majority of professors and students have united to resist any further change which would endanger their conception of proper professional performance or undermine the privileged position of Engineering in the university. The intensity of these feelings has even led to discussion of seceding from the university and forming an independent institute of technology.

Nonetheless, a few engineers continue to strive for a more thorough reform. One such leader is a young man who was educated at the University of Chile and who later received a doctorate from M.I.T. He is firm in his own beliefs yet deeply appreciative of the opposing positions of his colleagues. Most important, he is extraordinarily honest in evaluating himself and others. He believes that Chilean engineers are usually well trained. They lack, however, a sense of confidence in themselves and commitment to the solution of national problems. He affirms that their training should continue to be at a high technical level, but argues that heavy emphasis should be placed on national service. Professionals with social and political sophistication are crucial for developing the country. The goals of achieving both academic excellence and training for national relevance can only be achieved, he believes, if the reform movement continues in the facultad. The struggle over the reform will be a long one. Patience is a crucial characteristic for those committed to fundamental changes. He anticipates that it may take as long as ten years to fulfill some of his goals.

Conflicts have also beset the facultad of Science with resultant personal antagonisms. Many scholars affiliated with the institute of Science left Chile after the institute had been transformed into a full-fledged facultad in 1965. Perhaps most tragic is the situation of a distinguished and internationally esteemed former member of the faculty of Science who has been completely rejected by many of his scientific colleagues for his "reactionary" views. He was unable to accommodate his scientific commitment to the political goals of his fellow scientists. He had insisted on the complete separation of political ideology from scientific efforts, a view which is out of step with the reformist faculty.

He has been particularly condemned for his alleged involvement in the case of the left-wing Argentine scientists who were expelled from Chile in 1969. Many of his colleagues accused him of writing a letter to the national authorities in which he charged that the Argentines had improperly engaged in political activities. The letter reminded them that as Chile's guests, welcomed after the Ongania purge, they should be restrained from attempting to influence university affairs. Although the Frei government never made its reasons public for acting against the Argentine scientists, many university people believe that the letter was used as a major rationalization by the government.

These accusations are vehemently denied by the scientist who described his futile attempts to publicize his position. He stated that he never intended to bring charges against the Argentine professors and had written a letter only for internal university use. How the letter fell into government hands he does not know. In spite of his explanation, he has been charged with naivete and with malice. An extremely prolific and productive scholar, he has not published in over a year.

Many other participants spoke sensitively and sadly of the disruption of professional and personal relationships which have occurred as a result of the reform struggle. Positions have now quickly hardened and labels have often pre-empted the necessity of debate. Most crucially, mutual trust has often been the first victim of passionate commitment.

Those who view the reform as part of a much larger struggle for social change believe that the costs are not excessive. They are willing to accept professional or personal dislocation so long as it may contribute to the creation of a university which will ultimately assume a major burden for national development. The reformers can legitimately point to the many changes which have already occurred as indicative of the gains to be won. Many students and professors are now working in an environment characterized by far more enlightened policies. These men who have remained loyal to the reform believe that Chile's national problems demand a commitment to build a relevant university.

Politics and the Reform

The problems of insufficient resources, inter-generational conflict, inter-school rivalries have all been exacerbated by an intense political competition which has come to dominate the entire reform movement. A position on every issue now has political implications. Because the Communists control many significant positions in the reform, many educational issues are defined as either pro- or anti-Communist struggles. Opposition to the reform in the press and among certain university groups has coalesced around an anti-Communist stance. There is a prevailing belief in some circles that the Communists are simply vying for power and national advantage and have little interest in modernizing the university.

Even among the reformers there is a wariness and hesitancy about the role of the Communist party. Socialists, who have supported Communist party leadership in the drive for student co-government and in the controversial strike for greater representation of non-academics, have accused the Communists of excessive interest in institutionalizing the reform commissions and in worrying more about winning the rectorship than revising curriculum or encouraging socially relevant extension work. A number of independent reformers who have credited the Communists with initiating and leading the whole movement, nevertheless, have pointed to a series of Communist party decisions which reflect party rather than university needs. They charge, for example, that the Communists recently led a month-long strike for greater representation of non-academics rather than for reasons of dedication to revolutionary ideas. One left-wing department head accused the Communists of delaying reorganization of the anachronistic faculty of Philosophy and Education because of their fear of losing majority control in subsequent elections. Communist educators and supporters defend their position with considerable evidence, on the other hand, that without them there would have been no reform.

Consequently, even seemingly innocuous issues have become part of bitter political debate in which lines have hardened considerably since the initial enthusiasm of the early reform. A decision to reorganize the system of professionally oriented facultades, for example, has been shelved because of political inability to devise a rational alternative. A number of other programs have been dropped from discussion as political parties have begun to compete for elected positions and concrete forms of power. Supporters of the reform are now so divided that many issues have not received the attention they deserve. A substantial number of academics have become totally alienated from any reform because of their distaste for political infighting.

A Tentative Conclusion

It appears that the reform of 1968–1969, like preceding efforts, will not fulfill many of its primary aims. In part, changes have been impeded by the difficulties of administration previously outlined. But frustration is also inherent in the very goals set by the reformers. It is significant when greater internal democracy, more social relevance, and widespread academic excellence are espoused as goals. It is crucial, however, to resolve problems which arise in trying to implement them. It is apparent that the dismantling of the old bureaucratic system of the rector, the highest council and the facultad has left no organized academic group available for the reorganization of the university. Party based political forces have easily filled the power vacuum and are now a vital and integral factor in further educational reform. At the same time, there is an increasing number of independent, but politically sophisticated and concerned, academics who are organizing to try to influence the reform and to take the leadership away from the political parties. Their dominant interest appears to be to upgrade and modernize the university. Whether they can unite in effective alliance remains an open question.

At this moment, then, feelings of uneasiness, frustration and waiting dominate the university. The students have returned to their classes, and many seem content with their greater influence in elections and academic councils. The struggle has largely fallen to the younger professors. This, in itself, is unique in Chilean history. Whether the lost momentum can be regained very much depends on their ability to forge a coalition of all those interested in fundamental university change. The forces of resistance are powerful, however, and the many schisms in reformist ranks serve to arrest the transformation of the university.

Appendix A

Myron Glazer

A Note on Methodology. Field Work in a Hostile Environment: A Chapter in the Sociology of Social Research in Chile

Too often, chapters dealing with methodology simply emphasize the technical aspects of sociological research. These are vital, but by no means the only problems encountered in contemporary field work. Successful research goes beyond good theory and techniques and extends into the far more sensitive areas of cultural and personal relations. This is especially true in those countries and in those situations in which strong feelings of anti-Americanism are present. There the investigator must often overcome suspicions based upon the factor of nationality before he can hope to obtain the cooperation and understanding so essential to his project.

Americans of professional status are often ill-prepared to face this evaluative criterion and expect to be judged as individuals. Although professionals are aware of the existence of anti-Americanism in Latin America, they experience a form of culture shock when ascriptive prejudice is directed against them. As "strangers," they are lightning rods, often attracting free floating suspicion and hostility. They may seek friendly relations with all individuals but because of the marked cleavages among the political groups, pressure will be exerted upon them to indicate where they stand. In times of heightened group antagonism there is little tolerance for neutrality.

This is not to assert that, at the outset, the researcher can expect to find only difficulty and resistance. On the contrary, as a foreigner, he is also the subject of curiosity and interest and his views are usually solicited on matters concerning his country and others. In addition, he is often able to obtain the cooperation which may be withheld from his local, professional colleagues as a result of the prestige which accrues from the more developed state of the social sciences in his country.

What often develops, therefore, is an attraction-repulsion relationship and the social scientist will be compelled to make several basic decisions. These include how he will present himself, how he is to react to the activities of his government and embassy, and the manner in which he will respond to the just, as well as unjust, criticisms of his country. To the extent that these decisions are properly based will he be better able to overcome resistance and obtain essential cooperation from all groups. My research on Chilean university students dramatically illustrates the many pitfalls which face the investigator, the action which he may take to overcome some of these problems, and the extent to which he is dependent on the environment created by the fluctuating evaluations of United States foreign policy.

First Days in Santiago

My wife and I arrived in Santiago in September, 1963. I had previously written a general study proposal which I had already discussed at length with sociologists and university students in the United States, Mexico, and Peru. I felt, however, that any specification of the project and the actual preparation of the questionnaire or interview schedule would have to await several weeks of direct experience with the Chilean situation.

During this initial period I spent a good part of my time speaking to Chilean and foreign social scientists. The project was generally well received by them, as well as by other Chileans knowledgeable in various aspects of their national life. There were repeated warnings, however, that my major problem would be to secure the cooperation of all student groups. Although I had found Chileans extremely friendly and hospitable, I was warned against the innate suspicions which left-wing students harbor about North Americans. I was strongly advised to seek their cooperation first. Premature contacts with students of the center or right, it was pointed out, would only confirm the belief of the left-wing students that I was hostile to their cause. An initial relationship with the left, furthermore, would not seriously prejudice me with the other students who were more disposed to be friendly toward the United States and who would, therefore, be willing to lend their assistance to my project.

In extensive conversations with members of the staff of FLACSO[1] these suggestions were carefully considered. The director, Peter Heintz, and a young Chilean sociologist, Edmundo Fuenzalida, were especially helpful by reporting their experiences with research studies involving university students. With their assistance I was able to form several basic decisions. First, I would associate myself with none of the research organizations in Santiago. Although students might ordinarily be reluctant to assist an American sociologist, they would possibly be willing to accept me were I to stress my status as a foreign university student who needed help from the Chilean peers. This independence from formal association with Chileans or foreign nationals suited my own definition of how the problem should be tackled, and was to prove a very important factor in allaying suspicions which arose later.

Two further courses of action were decided upon at the outset, in the hope of diminishing the possibility of later repercussions. Any form of contact with the American Embassy was to be excluded. Although I had been told that there were several highly qualified and informed persons on its staff, I was most anxious to avoid any later accusations that my work was sponsored by, or connected with, any official United States agency. To minimize suspicions within the university itself, I felt it would be wiser to refrain from requesting help from any of the teachers or administrative personnel except where this was absolutely essential. The assistance necessary to carry out the project was to be sought primarily from the students themselves. This decision turned out to be an extremely fortunate one. Where I neglected to follow this path I ran into the most difficult and threatening situation.

Initial Contact with the Left

Among the Chilean sociologists whom I had met soon after my arrival in Santiago were several who were active in the Socialist party. I asked one of them if it would be possible to meet some of the more important student leaders. This was arranged by a Chilean social scientist, who had been a student leader during his university days, and who continued to maintain strong contact with those influential in university affairs. In typical Chilean fashion he invited my wife and me to dine at his home so that we could meet two or three of the more important Socialist students. Our first real contact with the student left, therefore, took place under most auspicious circumstances. We did not discuss my project but talked about American politics and the currently popular folk artists in the United States. The two students whom we met that evening were most interested in these aspects of American life, and though obviously critical of American foreign policy, seemed pleased to meet students from the United States. Our own political views were not discussed, but our familiarity with such journals as *Monthly Review* and with the currently important issues on the American left indicated that we were conversant with radical culture and politics in our country. In turn these students discussed aspects of Chilean social problems, student life, as well as the folk music currently popular in the university. They also sang the latest rendition of "Yanqui go Home" and several songs of the Cuban Revolution. Pleasant conversation, accompanied by folk singing and excellent wine, made for a most enjoyable evening.

I was extremely pleased by our reception. My response was reinforced by the surprise of other sociologists when I reported how smoothly the first meeting had gone. They had been certain that I would encounter greater difficulty. Soon after that evening I invited the two student leaders to my home. The purpose of this meeting was to tell them about my research and ask if they would be willing to assist in its implementation. I was extremely concerned that, although they had been friendly on a social level, they might reject my overtures to secure their support for my work. Any doubts of their good will were immediately dispelled. They were most willing to discuss the research and offered ideas and suggestions. In addition, they promised support in the schools in which they were most influential and agreed to introduce me to important student leaders in other schools. It was not long after this evening that they invited me to attend a party to meet students from the School of Medicine. The gathering was at the home of Salvador Allende, a leading Socialist and the presidential candidate of the FRAP, the Socialist-Communist coalition. The date fell on November 22, 1963.

I can distinctly recall walking up the street to the Allende home in a state of near emotional exhaustion. The news of President Kennedy's assassination had stunned the world. My level of tolerance for anti-American quips was very low. I had almost decided not to attend the party but felt that this was an excellent opportunity to meet important students. I had resolved, however, to reply firmly and even emotionally to any verbal attacks which might be made on my country. This proved unnecessary since all the guests were as shocked and almost as upset as I by the day's events. They shared my utter disbelief, and together we pondered the implications of President Kennedy's death for world peace. Several of us sat huddled in front of the radio listening to the latest news broadcast. All were concerned by what effect his passing would have on United States–Latin American relations.

That evening I became acquainted with several of the most important student Socialists. Many, although very critical, had placed some faith in Kennedy's program, hoping that it might lead to a better understanding of events in Latin America. The result of his untimely death was a well-spring of good feeling for the United States. This, unfortunately, was dissipated about four months later with great repercussions for my work in Chile.

Although my first reception had been excellent and I had been able to form friendships with many Chileans, interactions with some other left-wing students proved to be more difficult. Among these people anti-Americanism was clear and open, and they were obviously reserved and suspicious of our motives. They questioned us very closely about our own views, especially toward Cuba, and United States policy in Latin America. My wife and I had decided that we would respond to any of these questions as honestly as we could. We criticized the United States where we felt it warranted, but at the same time insisted that the ruling groups of Latin America bear their share of the responsibility for existing problems. In addition, we continued to emphasize that these students really knew little about life and politics in the United States. We repeatedly stressed the complexity of the situation and rejected their monolithic caricature.

Our position always won a respectful hearing and, although we never gained the complete confidence of many of them, we were able to secure their cooperation where it was necessary. Unfortunately, it did not become clear until later that their suspicions were not based upon personality factors alone. Those who continued to be most reserved were not Socialists but members or strong sympathizers of the Communist party. I made a serious mistake by not taking sufficient steps to comprehend the basis of the resistance and to make sure that I had the complete support of at least one or two influential Communist students. My growing sense of confidence about the project's success lulled me into a false belief that I now had sufficient support from the Chilean left. This view was partly reinforced by our Socialist friends who were not overly encouraging when I asked about the possibility of meeting "intelligent" Communist students. My failure to press for these introductions was to haunt me later when the study came under heavy attack by the Communist who had not been sufficiently briefed.

Contact with the Christian Democrats

Because of the strong emphasis on the importance of contacting FRAP students first, it was not until several weeks later that I first met Christian Democratic student leaders. My meeting with them was accidental, and the circumstances perhaps a little unfortunate. It occurred in a cafeteria while I was having coffee with several Socialists. The president of the FECH, a Christian Democrat, passed near our table and was hailed by one of the group. I first believed that this was an excellent chance meeting. The Socialists would not only have been aware of my contact with the opposition group, but also instrumental in bringing it about. While meeting with the Christian Democrats later in the day, however, I sensed a certain reserve among them. Although they never openly indicated the basis for this, I was quite sure that my introduction to them through the Socialists had only served to prejudice my case. They may have associated me with the left, or have felt slighted because I had failed to contact the Christian Democrats first. On the other hand, this may have been an example of their sensitivity to FRAP criticism that they are too friendly to the United States. Furthermore, because Christian Democratic students tend to be more radical than those with the national party leadership, their reservations may have derived from their genuinely critical attitude toward the United States. In any case, contrary to statements made to me about the greater friendliness of the Christian Democratic students, leaders of this group were by no means easily won over. They, too, had to be convinced of my motives, and of the reasons for my interest in political questions.

After contact was made with the two major political forces in the university, it became apparent that it was going to prove difficult to gain their cooperation and yet maintain friendly relations with both groups. I decided to emphasize at once the independent policy which I was going to follow. I could not, obviously, befriend one group to the exclusion of the other. To complete my work, assistance was necessary from all major political forces. Each group must realize that I was maintaining friendly relations with the other. This I continually verbalized. Yet I also believed that it would be a wise policy to attempt to segregate interactions with members of opposing groups. Therefore, I tried to avoid holding joint conversations with members of the left and the Christian Democrats.

The Actual Data Collection Begins

During the summer months (January and February) we had asked several Chilean students and professionals to work with us as interviewers. This gave us a team of five and, more importantly, meant that Chileans were actively involved in the data collection process. We were not interested in the political views of our interviewers, asking only that their affiliations be unknown to the students whom they were going to interview. For obvious reasons, we thought that such knowledge could bias the responses.

Our pre-tests had been conducted not only with current university students, but also with several highly astute young Chilean professionals. These included sociologists but were by no means restricted to this group. On the contrary, we desired the criticisms of recent graduates of those schools which we planned to study. A fortuitous consequence of this factor was our ability to indicate at a later time that Chileans had worked on every stage of the study. Indeed, had we attempted to do all the interviewing ourselves and confined our advisors to the international sociological community, the outcome of the field research might well have been different.

Aided by the efficient services of the third-year engineering delegate,[2] and beginners' luck, we completed thirteen interviews on the first day in the School of Engineering. Just at that point, however, a strike was called by an important segment of the public employees union and the students were asked to support the demands for higher wages. The FECH decided to do this, and the university was closed for three days. This interrupted what had been a carefully planned interview schedule, and indicated to us the volatility of the factors which might intrude and make our research task more difficult.[3]

The Schools of Physics and History

When the work gained momentum after the strike, I considered the possibility of starting to interview in other schools. During the summer vacation period I had spoken to a young professor in the Institute of Science[4] and had received assurances of his full cooperation. In a follow-up conversation at the beginning of the school year he repeated his willingness to assist me. Since I had explained the nature of my project in our first meeting, I now simply showed him a copy of the interview schedule. He and a colleague perused it quickly and introduced me to the course delegate. The professor explained that I was interested in studying the institute as part of broader research on the university and because I had previously conducted an investigation of a physics department in an American university. He asked the delegate, who was also the president of the student council, to assist me in making appointments with all students.

This was the only school in which I had worked through a professor. I had broken my own rule because of the special nature of the institute. Its small size and totally unpoliticized nature led me to believe that the precautions taken elsewhere were unnecessary. The class president had posted a list of students who were to appear and had passed the word that cooperation was compulsory. When I learned of this a few days later, I jokingly discussed how simple this procedure would make our work in other schools.

The president himself was part of the first group to be interviewed. I conducted the questioning, which began late because of the necessity of discussing scheduling arrangements. We spent the remaining half hour in general conversation concerning the president's unique reasons for choosing physics as a career. Since the next group of interviewees was just arriving, I suggested that we postpone the interview until the following week. The interruption was unfortunate since I had not fully explained the project to the president. This event compounded the several errors which I had already made in the school. After two weeks of excellent success, in which we had completed thirty interviews,[5] the situation dramatically changed.

In the interim, the Brazilian Revolution had erupted, and the government of Goulart had been overthrown.[6] There had been a great discussion of this situation in the Chilean press. Many students condemned the action on the part of the United States and President Johnson in so quickly recognizing the so-called revolutionary regime. Criticism came not only from the Socialists and Communists but also from the Christian Democrats. They all strongly questioned the motives of the United States and asserted the view that the United States had actively intervened in Brazilian internal affairs. They pointed out the seriousness of the situation for Chile. Would it not be possible, and even likely, they argued, that the United States would act similarly were a leftist government to gain power in the September presidential election? American policy in all of Latin America was coming under heavy attack. The post-Kennedy good-will period was over.

There were almost immediate repercussions in the School of History. My wife was interviewing a student who identified himself as a member of the Communist executive council. He challenged our motives and demanded a questionnaire so that his colleagues could ascertain the "real" goals of our research. My wife responded that only I was able to give him a copy and suggested that he speak to me. The question which most concerned the Communist leader was: "Do you think that any group, no matter how much you are in disagreement with its policy, should be allowed to take office if it wins in the next presidential election?" He believed that this question had been designed by the United States government or its intelligence agencies to ascertain the reaction of the students. This information, he asserted, could be used by the United States in preparation for future military intervention.

It was obvious that his suspicions could have very serious consequences. The Communists were very strong in the school and could prevent, if they chose to, the successful completion of our work. I immediately asked one of our interviewers who was a friend of the suspicious student to explain to him who we were, what kind of work we were doing, and why we had included political questions. The interviewer later reported to me that he had spoken to his friend and had allayed his worst suspicions. He had pointed out that this study had not been devised by intelligence agents, but that, on the contrary, Chileans, including himself, had been involved in every stage of the research. Though this information seemed to be somewhat satisfactory, rumors persisted and circulated in the School of History. We were accused by some students of being actual C. I. A. agents. Others asserted that the United States government was secretly sponsoring the study. Still other students saw us as dupes and believed that the results of the study would ultimately be confiscated by the American authorities for their own purposes. Many rejected our explanation that we were attempting to secure a representative sample and accused us of trying to ferret out those with the most radical opinions. These attacks appeared insurmountable at the time and the life of the study was in jeopardy.

Two factors prevented the utter collapse of the project. I had many extensive conversations with my Socialist friends within the school in which I carefully retraced the purposes and goals of my study. We discussed the various accusations at length and I was able to convince them that these were completely without justification. In this instance bonds of personal friendship sufficiently outweighed the intensity of anti-American feelings generated by recent events. The Socialists, in turn, exerted enormous pressure, using the great prestige which they enjoyed to persuade the student body to continue to cooperate with me. The Communist leaders seemed to take their cue from my Socialist friends. Although they did not commit themselves to a policy of active assistance, they refrained from an official condemnation of the project. I am frank to state that I never was able to ascertain all the reasons for their neutral course of action, but it is an understatement when I say that it was most welcome. Ultimately, only two students refused to cooperate.

Far more serious difficulties began in the School of Physics on the same day that my wife spoke to the Communist student in the School of History. One of the professors informed us that several students had complained that they had been deceived by the nature of the study. They had thought that there would only be questions related to their professional views and values, so that they could see no reason why political questions, or questions related to their parents' beliefs, had been included in the questionnaire. Although only a few students had been involved in these discussions with this professor, it was clear the suspicion was spreading throughout the rest of the student body. We were quite surprised by this turn of events, since in the actual interviewing situation many of the students had indicated that they were very much interested in our study, its results, and had been most willing to cooperate.

Several days later student council officers met with several of the professors. Late in the morning I called the president to determine whether we were going to be able to continue interviewing. He informed me that the council had decided to hold a general meeting of the entire student body on the following day. At that time the officers would speak to the group and place before them the alternative paths which the school could take. These would include continuing to cooperate with the study, discontinuing such cooperation, or taking the case to the FECH.

That evening I spoke to the vice-president of the FECH, who was one of the most important Christian Democratic leaders in the university. He maintained that cooperation with the study was an individual choice "in a free country" and was not something that the FECH could vote for or against. He volunteered to call the council president to inform him of these facts and to support our request for continued cooperation. I also spoke to several student FRAP leaders and asked them if they, too, would call the president. My goal was to attempt, in every way possible, to reassure him of our motives and to indicate that we had support from students of all shades of political opinion.

A few minutes after the meeting started the following day, my wife and I were invited in to speak to the physics students. About half of the student body attended, and it soon became clear that three or four were the most active and suspicious. How do you convince someone you are not a spy? I tried to play down their concern about what we might do with the information by appealing to their feeling as scientists. I knew how difficult it was for physics to gain acceptance in Chile and how their efforts and goals were often misunderstood. Could they now impugn the motives of someone else attempting to engage in research? I sought to assure them that to accuse us of spying was nonsense. At this point one student indicated the basis of his fear. We had claimed that their names were not known to us and would not appear in the study. He charged, however, that we knew all about him, from how many brothers and sisters he had, to where his parents had been born. It would be an easy matter to piece together his identity. In a poignant statement filled with reproach he said, "I helped you, and answered your questions, and now you don't know how sorry I am. You have my life in your hands." We sought to calm him with the assurance that the information would be put on IBM cards, that the original interviews would be destroyed, and that we were in no way interested in the response of individual people. We would report only on the reactions of the group as a whole and no one's identity would ever be revealed.

At the height of the discussion, a student who had been sitting in the back arose and introduced himself as a representative of the MUI,[7] the left-wing student federation. He said that he had listened to my statements about the importance of sociological research in creating better understanding between the United States and Chile. He categorically rejected this view and from a prepared text recited the points which he felt were important before greater understanding could occur between the countries. The primary solution was an end to the policy of the United States imperialism in all of Latin America. Only when this occurred, he asserted, could there be hope of relaxed tensions.

The discussion continued until several proposals were put forth. These included the following: that those students who wanted to continue should be allowed to do so; that the student council of the school take the matter to the FECH; finally, that the question be brought directly to the rector of the university. If the students had voted to do either of the latter two, it would have been virtually impossible to continue interviewing in the other schools.

The students voted to choose the first alternative. Official sponsorship by the school of the study must end, and cooperation was to be a matter of individual choice. Since this is the way it should have been from the beginning, we were quite willing to accept the result.

The vote reflected the conflicting nature of the students' attitudes. In private conversations after the meeting several students indicated that they were ashamed by what had occurred. We must not think that they usually treated people in such a manner. Their personal fears were at variance with their customary hospitality. Moreover, it was evident that the haranguing nature of several of the speakers had antagonized many who held independent political views.

What was the cause of the hysteria in the institute? Why had it erupted in a school which is highly unpoliticized, and where our interviewing appeared to be progressing so well? It is essential to understand that in Chile there are very few jobs in the field of physics. It is highly important for a young scientist desiring to do significant research to obtain a graduate fellowship for study abroad. Many students reported to us that they knew of people who had been denied visas to travel and study in the United States. They had heard that the American Embassy had extensive files on the political attitudes and activities of many Chileans. How could they be assured that their support of the left wing, or their criticism of the incumbent Chilean regime, would not be taken as an indication of their unfitness for a United States visa? The time was ripe in Chile for this kind of fear. In this atmosphere general suspicions of United States motives, kindled by the Brazilian situation, had crystallized themselves into and had been exaggerated by fears for their future professional opportunities.

These events made further interviewing in this school impossible. We had succeeded, however, in preventing the issue from reaching an all-university level. The insights derived from this experience, moreover, enabled us to avoid many of the pitfalls when we approached the School of Medicine. I carefully cultivated the full understanding of important student leaders, and enlisted their aid in explaining the project to those whom we would interview. I drew the sample in the presence of an officer of the student council and the list of names was retained by him. Although I had been warned that it would be extremely difficult to work in the School of Medicine, the research proceeded without incident even though anti-American sentiment in Chile did not substantially diminish.

The following week, just as the storm of controversy seemed to subside, a student whom I was interviewing casually asked me whether the study was sponsored by the United States Embassy. I quickly attempted to reassure her that my project had nothing to do with any official United States agency. She remarked that her brother had been doing a good deal of interviewing for a commercial polling corporation, and that he had learned that the embassy was sponsoring a study of student political views. She had therefore assumed that this was the study to which her brother had referred.

I was very much concerned with the implications arising from a confusion of my own work with an actual operation sponsored by American authorities. Since I had had no contact with the embassy, I asked a friend, who knew several people there, if he could find out about the existence of such a project. He spoke to the appropriate embassy officer who seemed stunned. He admitted that such a study was being planned, as the embassy was now interested in conducting genuine social science research in order to perform its tasks more effectively, but its sponsorship was highly secret. My friend asked when he might be able to see the results, since as a social scientist he was also interested in student attitudes. The embassy official responded that the information was classified and that the data would not be made public for twenty-five years. The social scientist, declared that this type of activity was creating extraordinary difficulties. The whole basis of scientific research, he argued, was to make data available for others to build on. Classified studies violate this principle. How can Chileans or others, he asked, determine whether a study is legitimately sponsored by a social science organization, or clandestinely supported by the United States government for other purposes?[8]

The implications of this question are far-reaching for social science. Field research in Latin America takes place within a context of traditional anti-United States hostility and is influenced by the fluctuating evaluations of contemporary United States policy. We are powerless to change the former and have little influence to modify the latter. Yet the environment for research is also dangerously complicated by a factor over which the academic community does have far greater control. The increase in the number of studies supported by military and intelligence agencies of the federal government has served to make the investigator more vulnerable to attacks on his integrity, and has often lent credence to the charge that he is a tool, witting or unwitting, of his country's foreign policy activities. Under these circumstances, it is more difficult for the scientist to defend his own research and honestly assure others that he is an independent scholar. Latin Americans obviously find it a problematic and unproductive task to distinguish whether the researcher is actually a bonafide investigator, free from any involvement with intelligence activities, or is "simply" supported by military funds, or "only" committed to sharing his findings with the government, or is in reality an active agent.

Many social scientists accept military funds, maintaining that they can retain total objectivity. Moreover, they claim, they may be able to further knowledge and understanding of other cultures, thus helping to diminish anti-Americanism. This raises the question whether acceptance of such government support does not actually intrude on the independence of scholarly research, affecting subject of study, interpretation and use of findings. By their acceptance of certain types of government funds, furthermore, researchers may be associated with subversive activity by Latin Americans which will result in increased anti-American feelings.

These questions must be seriously considered by all members of the American scientific community if they do not wish to find themselves ultimately excluded from many sources of data and from much meaningful research. The problem is further complicated, of course, by professional ethics and conscience. A strong case has been made for encouraging federal government support for social science research. With the great advantages accruing from such funds comes the responsibility to discriminate between those activities which truly advance scientific knowledge and those which compromise us and breed distrust. The recent catastrophic end of the Camelot Project indicates how dangerously close we have come to closing the door to further research in Latin America.

Most social science research necessitates not only theoretical and methodological sophistication, but also the cooperation of informants and respondents. Respect, good-will, and confidence, the major ingredients of high reputation, are priceless in every field work investigation. I believe that my Chilean experience clearly indicates how easily they may be forfeited. Moreover, *Chilean* social scientists have also found it more difficult to gain acceptance of their research efforts as a result of Camelot. To fail through one's personal blunders is regrettable. To experience near disaster because of the follies of our colleagues is a risk which we all rightfully seek to minimize. In this sense, the Camelot Project was of direct concern to every member of the university and national community, both in Chile and the United States. My own brief experience with the Camelot Project is worth noting as an introduction to the broader issues which now have so clearly arisen.

The Implications of Project Camelot

When a team of Camelot researchers visited Princeton University in October, 1964, seeking evaluation and advice relating to their projected research activities, they were presented with a variety of theoretical suggestions. Near the end of the meeting, which included over a dozen staff members of the Center of International Studies, I cautioned the Camelot scientists about the extreme dangers they faced in attempting to implement their project in Latin America. Having just returned from Chile, I related how close I had come to failure. The burden of military support for a project dealing with the causes of revolution, I stressed, would be unbearable. Neither Chileans nor other Latin Americans would gracefully cooperate with North Americans under contract from the Pentagon, intent on learning about the techniques of counter-insurgency.

The response from one of the Princeton participants clearly implied that sophisticated investigators could well handle such a simple technical problem by disguising the source of support. The Camelot members never responded. The hour was late and perhaps they felt the warning too obvious to necessitate a reply. In any case, I was angered by the implied deception and the cavalier response to what I knew was a major criticism of the project.

Exactly nine months later the research effort was still-born in

Chile. Indeed, the first Camelot representative on the spot had initially attempted to disguise the source of financial support. When he was severely challenged by local social scientists, not only about the source of Camelot's funds, but also its alleged intervention in the internal affairs of other countries, the truth could no longer be denied. As a result of the subsequent furor, exacerbated by the reaction to the Dominican intervention, the project was cancelled by the Defense Department.

The personal agony of the social scientists associated with the Camelot venture can well be imagined. Indeed, my own fate is entangled with it, providing an excellent example of professional interdependence. Project Camelot was destroyed, and in its aftermath my personal credibility seems to have been challenged in two notable episodes. Over a year ago the Chilean Communist party published a pamphlet in connection with the parliamentary hearings on the affair. It emphasized the number of American researchers in Chile and strongly implied that these men were involved with intelligence agents of the United States. These accusations had gained a measure of plausibility as a result of Camelot. My project was cited.

A second incident occurred at a large dinner party in Santiago, where the Camelot affair was the major topic of conversation. A former student at the School of Physics related with apparent satisfaction that he now knew the forerunner of Camelot. It was a project conducted in his school just a year before, by two Americans claiming to be graduate students with no government affiliation. He carefully related the situation, convincing all present of the validity of his observations. When he concluded his lengthy discourse another guest spoke. He realized how logical it appeared that the two studies were inter-related. The facts, however, did not support the interpretation. The project in the School of Physics was well known to him, since he had worked on every aspect of it. The North American students were not guilty.

But as the Queen's messenger rarely arrives to save a condemned MacHeath, so is it unlikely that good friends will often arise in my defense. How many other evenings have occurred such as this one? Future research for me in Chile will be far more difficult because of Camelot. I cannot simply claim my innocence; I will be judged as a representatives of my country and profession. Thus, I am obligated to myself, to my colleagues, to my

Chilean friends, and to my country to debate the issues involved and contribute toward their solution.

Three major components must be isolated if we are to unravel the complex situation with which we are faced: a) the crisis of credibility, b) the undermining of scholarship and basic research, and c) the kinds of national policy with which scholars are identified. The problem of credibility is the most obvious and the one which frightens most of the social scientists who have become aware of Project Camelot in Chile, Operation Sympatico in Columbia, or Michigan State University's projects in Saigon.

Yet a second related question we are now facing is more complicated and subtle. Are we witnessing and participating in a dramatic change in the concept of basic research? Traditional scientific investigation has meant the disinterested accumulation of a body of knowledge, judged by other scholars whose first commitment is to a search for greater understanding of reality. However fallible the various individuals may have been, the international scientific community has insisted upon open and free communication and the exclusion of non-scholarly purposes from determining the course and evaluation of research. Is it possible to call research inaugurated at the request of military and intelligence agencies disinterested accumulation of knowledge? The corruption of this concept is most evident when contract research is involved. In Project Camelot several men, in their role of university professors and claiming a commitment to basic research, accepted the task of designing a research project to answer certain questions, many of which were influenced by the Army. The Army's considerations in selecting these problems are implementation of military policy, a criterion quite different from those traditionally used by scholars.

What is the case with those who design their own research and then apply for government grants? What if the grant is given but requests are made for certain small changes? Don't others have a right to know under exactly what kind of conditions a government grant was applied for and awarded?

Beyond the question of the impact on the individual researcher lies another aspect of this problem and one which is applicable even to those scholars who may be unaware of the military or C.I.A. source of their sponsorship, as is sometimes the case when money is channeled indirectly through university institutes or foundations. The enormous sums supplied by these military and intelligence agencies may have a decided influence on the course and accumulation of knowledge, especially in areas of comparative studies in which policy makers are now especially interested. The selectivity of projects along lines of military or "national" interest may actually lead to distortion of available data. Many findings might be seriously qualified, modified, or in some way validated, by research which is proposed by scholars but for which they are unable to obtain financial support. Here, then, is the crux of the problem—who decided, and on what basis, the course of the development of social science?

The answers to these questions are extremely complex but are at the heart of the dilemma. Certainly there are a variety of serious and scholarly investigations which have received support from the Air Force or the Navy. Indeed, many social scientists attest to the high degree of independence which is granted by these agencies. Important studies might have been delayed or not undertaken had it not been for the willingness and the ability of these institutions to define the research in the "national interest."

The problem remains. Why should any military branch have vast sums at its disposal to support social science? Why should these funds not be distributed by competent social scientists familiar with the progress of research and concerned with an orderly development of the field? We are all familiar with the argument that many congressmen will be loathe to allocate large sums for research. Our task is to support those striving for more enlightened policies, rather than to accept the realities which have been most blatantly exposed by the recent debacles. These are not isolated incidents but part of a total pattern. There is no surer way to guarantee continued explosions of overseas research projects than to ignore the roots of the problem. The development of basic social science research must be controlled by practitioners and not by even the most well-meaning government functionaries concerned with military and intelligence needs.

Contemporary social science research is a highly competitive enterprise. The era of the lone independent scholar working in his laboratory or study is over. Those in possession of computers, assistants, and consultants are now in the strongest position to achieve professional recognition. Precisely because honorable men are susceptible to a variety of temptations and rationalizations, it is essential to channel this competition carefully. The problem of finances is central and here the most extreme caution must be exercised. The universities and professional associations, in conjunction with individual scholars, must more fully assume thier responsibility for preventing the corruption of academic values by supporting legislation which will underwrite basic research.

Finally, the great concern which many social scientists have voiced for the underprivileged masses of Latin America and elsewhere often runs counter to the policies and actions of our military and intelligence agencies. The professional writings of most scholars consistently affirm the importance of social change, and indict as obstacles the great inequalities in wealth, the maldistribution of the good things that any nation may offer its citizens, and the desire of elite groups to maintain their privileged position. While deeply concerned with the importance of disciplined, scientific investigation, many scholars working in the field of comparative studies support programs of land redistribution, increased educational opportunity, tax reform, unionization of workers, and a variety of other actions clearly associated with structural change. Most social scientists have committed themselves, whether implicitly or explicitly, to an international public. Those who are critical of certain aspects of the present military and interventionist posture of the United States should be most wary of being associated with a policy they oppose.

In summary, several challenging issues face the academic community and all Americans who value scholarly endeavors, professional ethics, and the respect of other nations. It is necessary, then, for social scientists and others to strive for a greater degree of public support which will underwrite the independence of research. It is also vital to secure the good will of those who have provided essential assistance in field investigations by making explicit the determination of scholars to prevent the dubious use of academic credentials. Scholars must be concerned with their respondents who have placed faith in them; with their profession which is built on the premise of open research, motivated by scientific questions; and with their commitment to international humanitarian values.

NOTES

1. A UNESCO sponsored organization for the training of Latin American sociologists—Facultad Latino Americana de Ciencias Sociales.
2. Each class elects a representative to handle its relationship with the administration. He is usually well acquainted with the students in his year.
3. It is instructive to indicate the other difficulties we faced. Students usually do not live at the schools which, in turn, are not centrally located, but are spread throughout the city. Since telephones are scarce, and transportation is very inadequate, it required a major effort to make appointments. It was not unusual for respondents to arrive late; others never showed up at all. Follow-up was extraordinarily difficult, but as a last resort we did visit many students in their homes.
4. Although the School of Physics was incorporated into the Institute of Sciences, the titles will be used interchangeably here.
5. The institute had approximately forty students.
6. The Chilean academic year begins in March. The Brazilian Revolution occurred in early April.
7. Movemiento Universitario Izquerdista.
8. The co-author's study of the FECH did not encounter such charges during its execution in 1956 and 1957 although sensitivity on this score was already manifest in Chile. Long after completion it too has come under suspicion. Further comment by Bonilla on the problems raised here can be found in "Research and Development Planning: Some Issues for Americans," *Latin American Research Review,* Fall, 1967.

Appendix B

Interview Schedule for Part I

I. History of Participation in the Student Federation

A. Offices Held

    1. What was the first elective office you held in the FECH?

    2. What university year were you in then?

    3. What were your subsequent elective or appointed posts?

    4. When did you leave the organization?

    5. What do you regard as the most important aspects of your participation in FECH-related activities?

B. Important Events for FECH during Period of Participation

    1. What do you consider the principal victories won by the FECH during your period?

    2. What were its most serious defeats? Failures?

    3. What important pronouncements of principle, manifestoes, speeches, etc., do you recall?

    4. Were there any large-scale demonstrations, strikes, parades?

    5. What part did the FECH play in national elections of the period?

    6. Were any important national or international conventions held?

    7. What links were maintained with students in other countries?

    8. Were there any important curriculum changes or other internal reforms in the university?

    9. Did the FECH carry on any sizeable educational or social welfare work among workers?

    10. What important publications—magazines, pamphlets, etc.—were put out by the FECH during this time?

C. Important Events for School Center of FECH during This Time (Follow check list as in B)

D. Post-University Contacts with the FECH and Self-Evaluation of FECH Experience

1. What contacts have you had with the FECH after leaving the university?
2. Has your association with the FECH helped you professionally in any way?
3. How long lasting were the political associations you established while in the university?
4. What do you think of the FECH as it is today?

II. Organizational Structure: Cultural-Institutional Level

A. Principal Goals: Dominant Value Patterns

1. What were the main goals pursued by the FECH in your period?
2. What relative priority did these several goals have?
3. How did the FECH justify the importance of these goals?
4. Why were they important goals for *university youth* to work toward?
5. Were goals defined as objectively attainable or was "striving" toward an ideal seen as a worthy end in itself?
6. Was there generalized consensus about these over-all goals?
7. Were there important sub-groups presenting contending set of goals?
8. How much freedom did sub-groups (school centers) have about establishing subsidiary or independent goals?

B. Operative Code: The Modes and Co-ordination of Action

1. What kinds of action are seen as appropriate in the pursuit of goals?
2. What were regarded as the main functions of leaders?
3. What personal qualities made for a successful leader?
4. Did people who were best qualified tend to win elections?
5. Who was qualified to vote in an election?
6. How were nominations made at different levels?
7. What were some common campaign slogans or appeals?
8. What was prevailing theory of representation and delegation— were leaders supposed to mirror constituency's views or set the tone themselves?
9. How binding were decisions of council and commands from leaders?
10. How could the rank and file initiate or request policy decisions, make appeals from existing decisions, get rid of poor leaders?

C.   Bases of Participation: Criteria of Membership, Patterns of Tension Management

    1. What was definition of over-all membership? How were obligations of members defined?

    2. How much effort was made to induce more participation by laggards?

    3. What form did these efforts take?

    4. Were there any organized groups resisting participation?

    5. Was there any formal machinery or criteria for evaluating the performance of individuals at different levels?

    6. What disciplinary measures could be applied?

D.   Spheres of Competence: Accepted Limitations in Radius of Action

    1. What kind of role did FECH claim for itself in the matter of:

      a. student activities?

      b. curriculum reforms?

      c. appointment of professors?

      d. university administration generally?

      e. national political and social problems?

      f. international affairs?

    2. What explicit limits were recognized in each sphere?

E.   Command of Resources: Legitimated Claims on Contributions and Services of Members, External Sources

    1. What kinds of contributions were expected from members? In money? Time? Work?

    2. How much personal risk or sacrifice was demanded of members?

    3. What kind of support was sought from without? From university, teachers' groups, parties, unions, etc.?

    4. What were conventional terms of exchange—kinds of deals made with outside groups?

    5. How stable or reliable were resources from outside groups?

    6. What kind of internal machinery existed for allocating resources? Who decided what was to be used for what and by whom?

    7. How much control did leadership exercise over resources received from outside?

F.   Links with Key External Groups: University Administration, Political Parties, Organized Labor, the Government

    1. What kind of relationships with these outside groups did the FECH seek?

2. What formal lines of contact existed for the FECH as a whole with these groups?
3. Was there any attempt to control contacts of sub-groups within the FECH with these outside groups?
4. Did these groups seek to penetrate into councils or decisions of the FECH?
5. What organized groups were regarded as most friendly and useful allies of the FECH?
6. Which groups were regarded as most dangerous for the FECH?

III. Organizational Structure: Collectivity Level

A. Size and Composition of Membership (supplementary to documentary sources):

1. What was approximate total of student population when you were attending university?
2. At what age did students generally enter and leave?
3. What proportion of total students was active in FECH (attended meetings, voted, marched in demonstrations)?
4. What party groups were represented in force? Was any dominant?
5. Which faculties or schools took the lead or set the tone for the organization?
6. Was there any sizeable nucleus of foreign students active in the FECH?
7. Were students from other than central provinces important as a group?
8. What was socio-economic status of majority of students? Of leaders?
9. What proportion of leaders looked to politics or public administration as a career?

B. Informal Organization: Actual Patterns of Co-ordination and Command

1. How much freedom of action did top leaders have, i.e., power to make statements, commitments in name of organization on their own?
2. How frequent were meetings of top councils, by whom called, etc.?
3. What kinds of issues could be decided at this level without consulting schools?
4. Under what notions of representation did school delegates actu-

ally function—were they under instruction by officers in their schools, did they try to represent over-all opinion, or make their own choices of what was best for FECH?

5. What other lines of communication did top leaders have with schools?
6. How much initiative did school centers have—was co-ordination good or poor?
7. How much effort was made to line up voters on different sides before important meetings?
8. Did party groups meet as caucuses within schools? Within top leadership?
9. How much overlap was there between party leaders and FECH leaders?
10. Were important party or former FECH leaders consulted even when they no longer held official jobs?

C. Main Activities: Day-to-Day Activities at Different Levels

1. How often was the normal student called on to take part in some FECH-related activity? What was he supposed to do?
2. What did class delegates do from day to day?
3. What about officers of school centers?
4. What about top leadership—was most of their time consumed in planning sessions, making speeches, writing, representing FECH before other organizations?

D. Mobilization of Resources: Sources of Financing and Services

1. How was the FECH operation financed?
2. What was obtained in money and other contributions from students? The university? Political parties? Other sources?
3. How responsive was rank and file to calls from leadership for different kinds of activity?
4. How often did activities come up that required mobilizing almost the entire student body?
5. Was the FECH often called upon by other groups to provide support?
6. How much support did the FECH receive in return? Press, publicity, tactical advice, manpower, etc.?

E. Conflicting Roles: Leader-Student, Leader-Family Member, Leader-Party Man

1. What year did you enter the university? Complete course work? Receive degree?

2. Was this par for the course? Longer? Shorter?
3. How many hours of class weekly did you usually have? How many additional hours of study were necessary?
4. What was your grade average?
5. Did FECH participation interfere with your academic life? Relations with professors? Other university authorities?
6. How did your family feel about your participation in FECH activities?
7. Were you a regular party member while a FECH leader?
8. When did you join a party? Did you have an official post in it?
9. How much time did party activities take up? What kinds of activities were they?
10. Did you ever feel that party responsibilities made your job in the FECH more difficult? in what ways?

IV. Attitudes and Personal Background

A.   Vocation: Meaning of Job or Profession for Individual, Determinants of Vocational Choice

1. When did you decide to be a   ?
2. What are the main advantages of being a   ?
3. What are the main disadvantages or less attractive aspects of being a   ?
4. What does the future look like in this field?
5. Have you ever seriously considered other vocations? Had other dreams?
6. Do you feel you are "cut out" for this type of work?
7. Under what conditions might you change?
8. What did your parents want you to be?
9. What do your parents think of (your choice of field)?

B.   Religion: Early Religious Training, General Importance of Religion, Strength of In-group Feeling

1. What was the nature of your early religious training?
2. What was the religious atmosphere in your home?
3. In what ways do you differ from your parents regarding religion?
4. What appeals to you most in religion?
5. What is your concept of God?
6. How important should religion be in a person's life?
7. What are the main differences between your religion and others?
8. How important are the differences among the various sects?

C. Politics: Present Affiliation and Extent of Activity, Analysis of Major Current Problems and Solutions Proposed, Image of World of Politics

  1. What are the major problems facing the country today?
  2. What groups have the most influence in political affairs?
  3. How do they work?
  4. What political groups offer the best solution to current problems?
  5. What is the outlook for the future?
  6. What would an ideal society be like?
  7. What political activity are you carrying on?

D. Communications: Main Sources of Political Information and Ideas, Ideological Mentors, Parental Identification *vs.* Rebellion in Political Attitudes

  1. What newspapers and magazines do you read regularly?
  2. Are these enough to keep you sufficiently informed of developments in Chile and abroad?
  3. What other sources of information do you have?
  4. What do you consider were important books or writings that have influenced your political outlook?
  5. What individuals do you feel have especially influenced your political ideas?
  6. Which of your professors or teachers do you think influenced most your political views?
  7. What was your father's political philosophy?
  8. Did you discuss political ideas with him often?

E. Family Background: Socio-economic Status of Parents and Grandparents, Social Mobility

  1. Were both your parents Chilean?
  2. What about your grandparents?
  3. What was your father's (mother's) occupation? How much schooling did they have?
  4. When you were a child, did your family own the house you occupied? Did they own any other property? How long had it been in the family?
  5. What was the most prosperous time for your family?
  6. Did you ever have any important financial difficulties?
  7. How early did you begin to work and contribute to your own and the family's support?

F. Family Figures: Attitudes toward Parents and Siblings, Relations between Father and Mother

1. What things do you admire most in your father (mother)?
2. Assuming most people aren't perfect, what human frailties does your father (mother) have?
3. In what ways are your parents most different from each other?
4. What kinds of things do they disagree about?
5. How did your parents get along together?
6. Which parent are you most like?
7. Who was your favorite brother (sister)?
8. What did you like about him (her)?
9. What things did you sometimes quarrel about?
10. Who usually made family decisions about finances, recreation, discipline, etc.?

G. Childhood: Superego and Reaction to Discipline

1. What things about your childhood do you remember with most pleasure?
2. Which parent did you feel closer to when you were about six? What about when you were 10? 16? 25? Now?
3. Which parent do you think had more to do with your becoming the kind of person you are?
4. Which parent exercised the discipline in your family?
5. Whose discipline did you fear most?
6. What kind of discipline did your parents use?
7. What things did they discipline you for mainly?

H. Social Relationships: Degree and Type of Social Libido, Genuine Feeling and Sociability *vs.* Detached Manipulativeness or Individualism

1. How important are friends in a person's life?
2. What is the main thing friends have to offer a person?
3. Do you have a few close friends or do you tend to have a lot of friends?
4. How do you choose your friends?
5. What things do you find most offensive or irritating in other people?

Appendix C

Interview Schedule for Part II

This study is a scientific investigation being carried out by a student working for his doctorate at Princeton University. Your responses to this questionnaire will remain strictly confidential and your name does not appear anywhere. No one will know your answers and only the answers of the *total* group will be made public. The purpose of this investigation is to help scholars and other interested people to understand better the thinking of Chilean youth.

Thank you very much for your co-operation.

Background (general)

1. Sex

2. Year of Birth

3. University: School or Department:
   Faculty: Year of Study:
   In what month and what year do you expect to get your degree?

4. Marital status: S   M
   If married, how many children do you have?

5. In what country were you born?

                              Chile
                              Other (specify)

   If you were not born in Chile,
   are you a Chilean citizen?   Yes   No

6. Do you have any siblings?
                Age   *Sex*

343

7. Which types of communities have you lived in for as long as 1 year?

	Name and province	*No. of years lived there*
a. rural		
b. small town		
c. small city		
d. large city (more than 100,000)		

8. What is your family's religious background?

   a. Both parents Catholic
   b. Both parents Protestant
   c. Both parents Jewish
   d. No religious affiliation
   e. Mixed: (specify) Father   Mother
   f. Other: (specify) Father   Mother

9. What is your religious preference?

   a. Catholic
   b. Protestant
   c. Jewish
   d. None
   e. Other (specify)

   How strong are your religious beliefs?

   a. Very profound
   b. Sincere but not profound
   c. Member by birth only

10. In what countries were your parents born?

    a. father   alive   deceased
    b. mother   alive   deceased

11. Which was the last course completed by your parents?

    Father   *Mother*

                   elementary incomplete
                   elementary complete
                   humanidades incomplete
                   humanidades complete
                   technical incomplete
                   technical complete
                   normal school
                   university incomplete
                   university complete
                   no schooling (can read and write)
                   no schooling (cannot read or write)

12. What is your father's usual occupation? (If he has more than one or if your father is deceased, describe the one which best typifies his work experience.)

    Position:
    Major duties of that position:
    Type of employer or firm:
    Approximate monthly salary: E^o

13. Has your mother worked regularly at any time during the last five years?

            Yes   No

    (If yes):

          What job?
          For how long did she work?
          Approximate income:

Financial Support

14. During the present academic year, in what manner are you able to support yourself?

Source	*Approximate per cent*
Parents	
Loans	
Job	
Scholarship	
Other	

15. Compared with other students that you know, would you say that your financial situation generally is:

    a. much better
    b. slightly better
    c. about the same
    d. slightly worse
    e. much worse
    f. no idea

16. Do you currently have a job?   Yes   No
    If yes: Describe your job:

    a. type of tasks:
    b. title of position:
    c. institution:
    d. hours per week:
    e. salary: E^o a month

17. Have you interrupted your studies, except for summer, since you first began your studies in the university?

        Yes   No

    If yes: What were you doing "in-between" (e.g., full-time employment, physical illness)?

    Would you have really preferred to stay in school at that time?

    Dates   *Reason for interruption of study*   *Preferred to*
                    Job (specify)   Other (specify)   remain in school

Educational Background

18. Starting with your present faculty, what have been all the university faculties and secondary schools in which you have been enrolled?

    Name of School   Year   Year   Degree   Private   Location
    and Faculty   Entered   Left   Obtained   or Public
    (most recent first)

19. Which of the following best describes the situation in your family when you were in high school?

    a. It was "naturally assumed" that I would go to the university.
    b. If I wanted to go to the university, one or both of my parents encouraged me to do so, but it was not assumed that I would go.
    c. My parents did not want me to go to the university.

20. Please think back to the time that you decided to enroll in the university. To which schools did you apply at that time? To which were you accepted?

            Schools   *Accepted*

21. Here are some of the factors which might have influenced you to enter the school in which you are now studying. What were the *first, second,* and *third* most important factors to you *at the time you made the decision to enter this faculty?*

    a. Influence of parents

    b. Definite aptitude and/or preference for the subject matter

    c. Ease and speed of getting degree

    d. Political character of the student body in this faculty

    e. Prestige of this career in the general society

    f. Friends studying in this faculty

    g. Possibility of obtaining a good job after graduation

    h. Influence of *liceo* teachers

    i. influence of people you knew practicing this profession

    j. Other

22. Was there any particular event which seriously influenced your decision to enter this career? When was it? What happened?

Nature of the School

23. How do you rate the difficulty of the work in this faculty compared to others in the university?

    a. more difficult

    b. equally as difficult

    c. less difficult

24. Would you say that your study habits are:

    a. fairly regular?   Generally put in about   hours per day

    b. quite erratic?   on the average spend about   hours per week

25. At this point in your studies, how would you evaluate the probability of your completing your degree?

    a. excellent

    b. good

    c. fair

    d. poor

26. Do you feel you have had enough opportunities to discuss your career plans and work formally or informally with professors in your faculty?

        Yes   No

27. How many times have you actually done this?

       many   some   few

28. How would you evaluate the teaching ability of the professors with whom you have studied in this faculty?

    Ability   *Number of Professors*
                        Most   *Few*   *None*

    Good
    Fair
    Poor
    (Probe for what seems to comprise good or poor teaching.)

29. In every faculty some professors seem to have high standing with the students and some low standing. Which characteristics give professors in your faculty high prestige with the students? (Indicate two most important.)
    a. having a pleasing personality
    b. demonstrating research or scholarly capacity
    c. teaching ability
    d. being concerned about applications of the discipline to the non-academic world
    e. keeping up on things outside the discipline
    f. dedication to the field
    g. interest in problems of students
    h. not being too critical of students
    i. having contacts which can help students obtain good jobs
    j. being an intellectual critic of the society
    k. other

30. Is there any professor in this school, or any particular person whom you know that is practicing in the profession for which you are training and whom you think of as a model to emulate in your professional career?

    a. Yes, a particular professor
    b. Yes, a particular relative
    c. Yes, a particular good friend
    d. Yes, a particular acquaintance
    e. No particular person, but a composite of 2 or more people
    f. No

    If yes: What are the particular characteristics which you would like to emulate?

31. What characteristic gives a student in your school high prestige with you? Indicate 2 most important.

    a. having a pleasing personality
    b. demonstrating research or scholarly capacity

c. being concerned about applications of the discipline to the non-academic world

d. keeping up on things outside the discipline

e. participating in political and community activities

f. dedication to the field of study

g. participating in student organizations (nonpolitical)

h. lack of participation in political activities

i. has contacts that assure him of getting a good job

j. is an intellectual critic of his society

k. is a good friend

l. other

32. What do you think that professors think of you? How do you think that other students define you? How do you think of yourself?

	Professors	Students	Self-Definition
a. One of the best students			
b. Good student			
c. Average student			
d. Poor student			
e. Not interested in studies			
f. Have no definition of me			

33. University faculties have been criticized and defended on a number of accounts. Here are some of the comments which have been made. What do you think are the two most important in your school? What are the two least important?

a. it encourages over specialization and does not give sufficient general education to prepare for positions of leadership.

b. the training has little or nothing to do with the jobs students will eventually get.

c. it accepts and encourages more students than ultimately can get desirable jobs.

d. many students do not have a genuine interest in political affairs.

e. it does not encourage students to apply their knowledge to the most important problems of society.

f. faculty members are not concerned enough with teaching.

g. the faculty is too politicized.

h. the level of politics is very low.

i. there is too much emphasis on having good contacts.

j. the students are too political but do not have enough interest in being genuinely critical of their society.

k. other.

The two most important   The two least important

34. We are interested in the kinds of activities in which students participate. In which of the following activities did you participate: 1) in the *liceo*, 2) in the university, and 3) which might you possibly join in the future in the university?

	A joined in liceo	*B* joined in university	*C* might join in future
a. sports groups			
b. drama/literary/music/art			
c. religious			
d. political			
e. academic			
f. journalism/publications			
g. other			

35. In regard to those activities in which you participated in *liceo* (fill in activity in boxes to right and check off correct answer for each activity)

Activities

How active were you?
a. leader
b. very active, not leader
c. not very active

(If did not continue membership in university group) Why did you not pursue these activities in the university?

a. too busy with studies
b. other activities more important
c. had to have job
d. did not like university group
e. no comparable group in university
f. other

Which group was most important to you?
How and why did you join this group?

36. In regard to those activities in which you are a member in the university. (Fill in name of each activity in boxes to right)

Activities

In what years did (or do) you belong?

year
year
year

Are you now (or were you)

a. leader
b. active, but not leader
c. not very active

37. a. Which group(s) is (or was) most important to you?
    b. How did you come to join this group?
    c. What do (or did) you do as member?
    d. How much time does (did) it take?   hours a week.
    e. Does (did) it conflict with your studies?
    f. If you are no longer a member, why did you leave?

38. In regard to those activities to which you have never belonged but are considering joining, when do you think you might do so?

Activity	Year of study when you might join
1.	year
2.	year
3.	year

Tasks

39. What do you think are the main types of work you will do as a professional in your field?

40. Has your education provided you with sufficient opportunity to learn and practice these tasks?

    Yes   Which ones?
    No   Which ones?

41. If the primary emphasis has not been on these tasks, what has been the emphasis of your education?

42. What are the main goals you hope to accomplish as a professional in your field?

43. Is there a certain area of your field that you consider your specialty?

         Yes   No

    If yes:

    What is that specialty?

Position

44. Which of the following comes closest to describing your career plans now?

a. definitely committed to the field and a preference for a specific type of job in that field
b. definitely committed to the field, but no preference for a specific type of job in that field
c. trying out the field to see if it might lead to a desirable career
d. not definitely committed to the field, but committed to obtaining a title
e. other

45. Thinking ahead to the time when you obtain your degree, what would be your realistic guess as to what will be your first job as a professional?

> Doing (type of work)
> For (type of institution
> Location
>   or
> Don't expect to be employed (specify)

46. How do you feel about this prospect?

a. very satisfied
b. not satisfied, not dissatisfied
c. dissatisfied

47. If your highest aspirations should be realized, what kind of position would you like to hold at the peak of your career?

> Doing (type of work)
> For (type of institution)
> Location

48. What do you think will be your chances of achieving this?

a. very good
b. good
c. regular
d. poor

49. (If b or c): Which of the following factors might hinder you from obtaining such a position? (Put 1 next to most important reason and 2 next to second most important reason)

a. difficulty of acquiring necessary knowledge and skills
b. social position of my family
c. lack of personal contacts
d. shortage of such jobs
e. political factors
f. racial, religious, and/or nationality factors
g. other

50. Here are a variety of institutions where it may be possible for you to obtain employment after you complete your degree. What is the likelihood of your accepting a position in such an institution?

(for teachers)	Definitely accept	Probably accept	Probably not accept	Definitely not accept
a. government school in rural area				
b. government school in callampa				
c. government school in middle class area in major city				
d. private school				
e. university				
f. private industry (nonteaching)				
g. national government (nonteaching)				
h. international agency (CEPAL, FAO) (nonteaching)				

(for others)*

a. foreign company- rural area				
b. foreign company- urban area				
c. national private company-rural				
d. national private company-urban				
e. national government- rural area				
f. national government- urban area				
g. international agency (CEPAL, FAO)				
h. university				

*Medical students had separate sheet

51. After completing your degree, would you consider taking a position in a foreign country?

        yes   no   don't know

52. Which two of the following job characteristics are *most* important to you, regardless of the specific job you would like to have? Which two are of *least* importance?

   a. social standing and prestige in the community
   b. political freedom
   c. a chance to earn enough money to live very well
   d. a chance to do work through which I can gain recognition from others in the profession
   e. opportunity to increase my professional knowledge
   f. to work directly with people to improve their life situations
   g. other

most important 1)   2)
least important 1)   2)

(for female students only)

53. During the first five years after you finish your degree, which of these would you prefer?

   a. marriage only
   b. marriage with occasional work in your field
   c. combining marriage and career
   d. career only

Social Position

54. What is your evaluation of the income you will probably earn at various points in your career?

Your salary will be	When you first begin work	After five years	At the peak of career
a. sufficient to maintain a high standard of living			
b. sufficient to maintain an adequate standard of living			
c. just barely enough to get by			
d. not enough to support a family			

55. Do you believe that the respect or prestige which society gives to your career is what it deserves to have?

    a. yes
    b. no, it is less
    c. no, it is more

56. Different professional groups have varying degrees of influence in affecting events in their society. How would you rate the influence of the profession for which you are training in the following areas?

	Degree of Influence			
	Great	*Some*	*None*	*Don't know*
a. making educational policy for the training of future professionals				
b. conditions of employment (salary, hours, legal restrictions)				
c. affecting government policy in matters in which the profession is competent to offer advice				
d. other				

57. Here are a group of characteristics which might influence the ability of a student to obtain a desirable position after receiving his degree. How would you rank their importance for students in your school? (Place 1 next to most important. . .6 next to least important, etc.)

	Order of importance	*How order should be*
a. high grades		
b. social position of family		
c. political activity		
d. recommendation of professors		
e. professional ability		
f. personal contacts		
g. other		

Now, what do you believe the order of importance should be?

Pre-University Political Background

58. To the best of your knowledge, what is your parents' present political preference?

	Father	*Mother*
Conservative		
Radical		
Socialist		
Communist		
Liberal		
Christian Democrat		
Frapist		
No political preference		
Other		

59. (If parents have political preference):
    How active are your parents politically?

	Father	Mother
a. very active		
b. members of party but not very active		
c. supporters		

60. To the best of your knowledge, has there been any change in your parents' political identification in recent years, especially from the time you were in *liceo*?

    Father: Yes   No   Mother: Yes   No

    If yes, what was their former preference?

    Father   Mother

61. Was there any particular person(s) who you think influenced your earliest political attitudes?   Yes   No

    (If yes):   Who was that person?   (Probe for relation of person rather than name)

62. What were the most important factors in influencing your earliest political ideas?

63. (If respondent has older siblings):

    Were your older siblings active in politics in *liceo* and/or university?

	Number of siblings	
	Liceo	*University*
a. very active		
b. somewhat active		
c. not active		
d. I have no older siblings		

(If siblings were *very active* or *somewhat active*) In what groups did they participate?

64. What do you think that professors think of you politically? How do you think that other students define you? How do you think of yourself?

                              Professors   Students   Self-Definition

(check as many as apply)

a. person not interested
   in politics
b. leftist
c. centrist
d. rightist
e. political leader
f. have no definition of me
g. other

65. (If not now a member nor has any intention at this point of joining a political group)

Is there any political group at the university with whose ideas you are generally in accord?

          Yes   No

(If yes) which group?
Do you believe there is a need for a new group?

          Yes   No

(If yes) What type of group would you like to see organized? Describe briefly.

66. Did you vote in the last FECH election?

   Yes   No   First year student and could not have
                            voted

67. (If yes above) For which group?
    (If no) Why did you not vote?

a. did not know enough about the candidates
b. was not favorably impressed with any of the candidates
c. did not think it made a difference who won
d. does not think that there should be a FECH organization
e. other

68. Of your three best friends, how many belong to a university political group?

      0   1   2   3

   For those who belong to a university political group, what group is it?

69. Have you personally engaged in the following activities with students who are members of the following groups? (Place an X in each box where student has engaged in such activity)

	Chrst. *Dem.*	*Comm.*	*Soc.*	*Rad.*	*Lib.*	*Conser.*	*Non-affiliate*
in close friendship							
study sessions							
political arguments							
visits to your home							

70. Do you believe that professors in your faculty generally:

   a. encourage students to be politically active
   b. neither encourage nor discourage students to be active
   c. discourage political activities
   d. have no idea

   (If a or c) In what way?

Attitude toward National Politics

71. In your opinion, what three factors (list in order of importance) are most important in currently impeding Chile's development?

   a. It is not an open society with equal opportunity to achieve.
   b. The people do not feel personal responsibility and take initiative.
   c. The country is subject to imperialism.
   d. People are not judged according to what they have achieved, but according to whose friend or relative they are.
   e. People are consuming rather than saving and investing.
   f. People are not sufficiently competitive.
   g. There are no wars or threats of war that have challenged the economic system and rendered it more efficient.
   h. It does not have rich natural resources.
   i. The population does not belong to an intelligent and industrious race.
   j. Political and economic life is monopolized by a small upper class.

    k. Current national political leadership is not interested in taking the necessary measures.

    l. Chile has not yet had its social revolution.

    m. Other

72. How sure do you feel about your response to this question about Chile's problem?

    a. very sure

    b. fairly sure, nor have some doubts

    c. not at all sure

73. Thinking about the major problems which have impeded Chile's development over the past few years, how would you evaluate the attempts of the current national government to solve them?

    a. Their policies have been generally successful and they have accomplished as much as any other government could have.

    b. Their policies have had reasonable success, but another group might have accomplished more.

    c. The policies of the present government have had little or no success, and it is definite that another group could have done much more if it had been in power.

    d. I do not know enough about the situation to answer.

    (If a or d, skip immediately to question 77)

    (If b or c): Which group do you think could have accomplished more?

74. What do you think are the chances of this group coming to power in the next presidential election?

    a. good   b. fair   c. poor   d. none

75. If this group were to come to power, do you think its general policy would be to

    a. make mild reforms

    b. make major reforms but preserve the general structural framework of Chilean society

    c. make major structural changes in the society

76. If it were to become evident that this group could not win an election in the foreseeable future, do you think that this group should then

    a. attempt to form a new coalition with another group

    b. continue to work as a minority opposition and put forth the best election campaign so that their point of view will be known

    c. seek some means outside the electoral process in order to come to power

    d. other

77. Do you think that any group, no matter how detrimental you believe its policies to be, should be allowed to come to office if it wins the next presidential election?

Yes   No   Undecided

78. University students have different ideas about the goals of a university education. Which two are most important to you?

    a. provide training; develop skills, and techniques directly applicable to your career
    b. provide you with a title which makes you an esteemed member of society and assures you of a good job
    c. provide a basic general education and appreciation of ideas to prepare you as intellectual and as critic of your society
    d. develop your knowledge of and interest in community and world problems and provide opportunity for participation in politics
    e. help develop your moral capacities, ethical standards and values
    f. prepare you for a happy marriage and family life

79. Do you think that the student political organizations should be concerned with

    a. nonpolitical university affairs only
    b. university affairs (political and nonpolitical)
    c. university affairs primarily, but some emphasis on national affairs
    d. university and national affairs equally
    e. national affairs primarily, but some emphasis on university affairs
    f. I have not thought of this

Choice Questions

80. Several very bright students in your class have asked you to study with them for an examination. You know that this will be very helpful, but on other occasions you have heard several of them make political statements which are very repulsive to you. You would:

    a. definitely study with them   c. probably not study with them
    b. probably study with them   d. definitely not study with them

81. There is a probability of a student strike in your faculty for what you consider to be a justifiable reason. You are an officer on the *Centro de Alumnos* and can have an important voice in the decision to strike or not. At the same time you are involved in several interesting and important courses in which you are receiving valuable professional training. You would vote:

    a. definitely to strike   c. probably not to strike
    b. probably to strike   d. definitely not to strike

82. A says that students interested in Chile's future should engage in political activities and work with a political group to facilitate the implementation of its program.

    B says that all political groups are compromised in the system and a student should not be tied to a party line, but rather stand off and criticize all groups, or attempt to form a new group.

    Do you

        a. definitely agree with A
        b. agree more with A than with B
        c. definitely agree with B
        d. agree more with B than with A
        e. neither with A nor with B

    Why?

83. A says that the most important factor for the development of Chile is to have well-trained and prepared people. Therefore the major responsibility of the student is to devote the majority of his time to learning the materials in his field and only a minimum of time to other activities.

    B says that Chile needs basic social changes before it can bring about any other changes effectively. He believes that the student has a responsibility to devote a good part of his time to political activities, even if this reduces somewhat the amount of time he can spend on his studies.

    Do you

        a. definitely agree with A
        b. agree more with A than with B
        c. definitely agree with B
        d. agree more with B than with A
        e. neither with A nor with B

    Why?

84. Two professors have asked you to serve as assistant and you can accept only one of these positions.

    Professor A is very highly thought of as an expert in his field and you are certain that you will be able to learn a great deal from him. However, he has very few contacts which would be of help to you in getting a job after graduation.

    Professor B is also a competent professional. Even though you do not have as high regard for his ability, you know that he has many contacts that will be of great help to you when you begin to look for a job.

You would work:

    a. definitely with Professor A
    b. probably with Professor A
    c. probably with Professor B
    d. definitely with Professor B

85. You have just graduated and have been offered two jobs.

Job A is a very desirable position, especially for a person of your age. However, there will be very little opportunity to apply the most modern methods you have learned in your education.

Job B is a job of much less prestige, but you will have the opportunity to use directly your professional knowledge and the opportunity to improve your skills.

You would:

    a. definitely accept job A
    b. probably accept job A
    c. probably accept job B
    d. definitely accept job B

Thank you very much for your co-operation. Is there anything else that you would like to add to help us understand your point of view about the areas covered?

Index